What They S

"A cold case that will intrigue and excite."

"Every now and then a book comes along
of but turns out to be a riveting page–turner. This week I read a marvellous
new work of Irish social and criminal history as Jack Kiernan investigates a
forgotten miscarriage of justice. Mullingar man Joseph Heffernan was hanged
for the murder of Mary Walker. Kiernan has meticulously gone through the
police investigation, witness statements and the court case and has found
major flaws in the investigation. By the end ... the reader is left in no doubt
that beautiful young Mary Walker was the victim of a heinous crime, but that
crime claimed another life the day Joe Heffernan fell to the hangman's rope."
– **Joe Duffy**, writer and broadcaster

"*Is It Me?* would make a brilliant true crime movie. I love reading true crime
stories and I thoroughly enjoyed *Is It Me?* You should approach the *Cold
Case* film makers; this story would make a powerful television documentary.
Well done Jack." – **Brush Shiels**, legendary rock guitarist

To

Kathleen, My
favourite aunt

Lots of Love

Is It Me?

The Joseph Heffernan Story:
Last Man Hanged in Kilmainham Gaol, Dublin
Early 20th Century British Injustice in Ireland

Jack Kiernan

Jack Kiernan

TMP
Publications

First published in 2011 by Saltwater Publishing.

This edition is published by **The Manuscript Publisher**, 2013.
Publishing solutions for the digital age. See our website –
www.TheManuscriptPublisher.com

ISBN: 978–0–9576729–0–1

A CIP Catalogue record for this book is available from the British Library

Typesetting, page layout, cover design by DocumentsandManuscripts.com

Printed and bound in Ireland

Is It Me?

Dedication

To my late parents, Seán and Iris.

Contents

PREFACE

The horrible crime of murder is the most heinous act that one human being can inflict upon another. While I was studying the history of Mullingar and its people, I came across an article published in the *Westmeath Examiner* concerning one such murder and the resulting execution of a local man, Joseph Heffernan, from Mullingar, who was convicted of murdering Miss Mary Walker on 7 July 1909.

I decided to research the case further. I studied the original witness statements, the police statements, the inquest report, the Magistrates' and assizes reports. There were peculiarities in this story, which soon led me to become suspicious of the manner in which the police and the legal authorities had gone about their work. It seemed that the locals co–operated with the authorities. Of course, I now understand why the locals behaved as they did. It was a natural response to an unnatural situation: the unprovoked murder of a decent, lovely young lady.

When I decided to write about this incident, my initial intention was to give the reader a brief synopsis of what had taken place. However, my findings dictated the need to publish a full account of the events that led to the conviction and death of Joseph Heffernan. The following document gives an accurate account of this fateful day in the life of Mary Walker. It also describes the circumstances surrounding the arrest, conviction and execution of Heffernan. I will demonstrate how the evidence changed as time progressed, and how the evidence was moulded to suit the prosecution's case.

With the exception of court transcripts, the remainder of the file, including the actual statements was stowed away at the National Archives, Bishop Street, Dublin. The *Westmeath Examiner* account was held at the Westmeath County Library, Mullingar. The National Archives also facilitated me with a breakdown of Heffernan's previous convictions. Unfortunately, the authorities at Kilmainham Gaol informed me that there was no information whatsoever on Heffernan held on the premises. I handed over everything I had to the archivist and brought him up to date on the outcome of my research at that time. I took numerous photographs of the prison while I was there and was kindly given permission to publish same.

The perception around Mullingar still is that Heffernan was guilty as charged and deserved the ultimate punishment. I know living relatives of the various witnesses will have great difficulty in accepting my findings. However, I can assure them, that everything I have written is backed up by the evidence that

I have uncovered. What I hope might ease their pain is the fact that the police coerced the witnesses, particularly the children, and forced them to give the evidence that they gave.

There is no doubt in my mind that the man responsible for Miss Walker's death was a lunatic and if the evidence is anything to go by, the guilty person killed before and if he had been allowed to roam the streets would have killed again. It was a brutal attack that inflicted sheer terror on this unfortunate young lady and, despite her cries for help, nobody came to the rescue.

I hope the reader, when finished the book, will have a clearer understanding of how the police went about their business, and realise that "damning evidence" might not always be what it seems.

A very interesting thing happened to me while I was researching this story. I travelled to Leighlinbridge at one point, and my wife believes that while I was there, Mary Walker took me by the hand and guided me to her grave. When I arrived in the town, I stopped to enquire about directions to the cemetery. I unknowingly stopped beside a small brown sign pointing towards the "Old Cemetery." I drove out the road as directed by the sign, even though I did not know whether this was the right cemetery. On coming towards a van parked at the side of the road, I asked my wife to pull over. I got out and asked the gentleman sitting in the driver's seat about Mary Walker and where she was buried. The man replied, "There's a cemetery behind the house where we had parked, and it can't be seen from the road." He directed me down the laneway to the cemetery. He did not know where the grave was. I then, unbelievably, walked straight over to Mary's grave.

INTRODUCTION

"Is it me? What do I know about it? I'm not that bad." These were the final words spoken by Joseph Heffernan as a free man. Six months later, Joe Heffernan was executed for the murder of Miss Mary Walker, a Co. Carlow native, who was employed as a telegraphist and sorter at Mullingar post office. While growing up in Mullingar, I had heard my dad talk about the Joseph Heffernan story. My dad, like all Mullingar locals, was convinced that the right person had been arrested and paid for the crime at the hands of Henry Pierrepoint on 4 January1910. However, my granddad, on my mother's side, a Sheffield man and former British soldier, maintained right up to his death that the wrong man had been executed, adding that he was assured of this before he ever set foot in Mullingar. I thought my grandfather was all talk, as I never saw anything in writing. I let it go and carried on with life.

I became more interested in the story in July 2009, exactly one hundred years after the murder. The *Westmeath Examiner* published an account, written by local man Richard Coplan, which was largely the "legal" account of what had taken place on the banks of the Royal Canal on Wednesday 7 July 1909. After reading the article over and over again, I just could not believe the amount of evidence produced by the authorities to ensure the conviction of Joe Heffernan. I walked to the murder scene and took photographs of the area. I ventured down to the tunnel where it was alleged the murder weapon was found. I visited and photographed every area mentioned in the article. Of course, I was very familiar with each and every location associated with the crime. For example, I was born in St. Anthony's Cottages in 1949, just a couple of hundred yards from the murder scene. I first saw the light of day in my granduncles home at 9 St Anthony's Cottages, Mullingar. I later lived in my grandparents' (on my father's side) home in Clown (or Clonmore as it is called today), an area which features prominently in the trial. I was reared in St. Laurence's Terrace, just a five–minute walk to the canal.

The tunnel where the knife was allegedly found was located on the opposite side of town. In the late fifties, my brother Tommy and I, (Tommy was informed, by classmates, about the existence of the tunnel) decided to walk down to the Springfield end of town, just to have a look. Actually, I was disappointed with the tunnel. It was small, dark and, for a couple of kids from the other end of town, it was a little scary. Having said that, we went through the tunnel and discovered a new world on the other side. We could not believe what we came across: hundreds of houses that we never knew existed. I felt like Christopher Columbus. Since then, we have ventured through the tunnel on numerous occasions: right up until the Westmeath County Council replaced it a few years later.

I spoke to Mullingar residents, old and not so old, and by and large, they confirmed what had been written in the recent *Westmeath Examiner* article. I spoke to a number of local Gardaí and while there are no records in the local Garda station, they were fully convinced of Heffernan's guilt. One Sergeant had discussed the case with the grandson of an RIC constable. This man had retired from the RIC before the murder of Mary Walker. However, he assured his grandson that Heffernan was guilty. Of course, he was a civilian at that time and he was told the same story the police told everyone else.

My next port of call was the Westmeath County library in Mullingar. The library really impressed me; within minutes of speaking with the assistant, I was sitting down in front of a computer reading copies of the *Westmeath Examiner* from 1909. Around the same time, I approached the National Archives in Bishop Street, Dublin. I found the staff very helpful and, with the assistance of Gregory O'Connor, I found myself perusing the case file. While the court transcripts were missing, the actual statements, full of dust, were safely tucked away inside the box. I discovered unbelievable evidence – evidence that, if produced by the defence team during the assizes in Dublin, would, in my opinion, have resulted in Heffernan's case being dismissed. I believe, when I opened the box at the National Archives, I truly opened a Pandora's Box.

As an ordinary man in the street, untrained in the science of criminology, I went through the evidence. I studied the crime itself, the inquest; the actual statements, the Magistrates' and assizes reports, and I believe I have blown the prosecution's case out of the water. I look at Heffernan's previous convictions, for which he served three prison sentences in Kilmainham Gaol, Dublin. However, I decided to deal with his previous convictions after the reader has read and studied what took place during the murder trial itself.

You may ask why the prosecution would do such a thing. Why did the locals row in behind them? Why did the media run with evidence released by the police while Heffernan was in custody? Why, during the Magistrates' hearing, did the Church plead with local parishioners to co–operate with the police and "ensure the conviction of the perpetrator?" Why was Heffernan charged with the murder before he was questioned? Why did the police fail to check out his alibi first? Why did they decline to take statements from potential defence witnesses? Why, in 1923, fourteen years after the murder, did the Home Office request one of Heffernan's files from Dublin Castle? This file went missing and was not returned to Dublin Castle. Incidentally, the British had left southern Ireland at this stage.

In order to answer these questions, I want to take the reader to the scene of the crime, to the inquest, to the Magistrates' hearing and finally to the assizes in Dublin. I feel the reader would like to see everything the people of Mullingar were exposed to all those years ago.

I invite you to take this journey with me, to read the evidence and to come to whatever conclusion the facts of the case lead you to. I am confident that most of you will be amazed at the skulduggery the British authorities got up to in order to convict and execute the unfortunate Joe Heffernan.

As you read through the inquest report, statements, Magistrates' and assizes reports you will come across repetitive evidence. However, you will also notice changes in some of this evidence as the case progressed. I believe it is necessary to publish the entire proceedings exactly as they were presented to the people of Ireland at that time. The changes, orchestrated by the prosecution, ensured that the people of Mullingar, and indeed Ireland, sided with their blatantly false account of what had taken place on 7 July 1909, and also ensured that they had a watertight case, making it easier to convict and execute Heffernan.

1.

EARLY TWENTIETH–CENTURY MULLINGAR

In 1909, Mullingar was a busy market town with a population of approximately 5,000 inhabitants. A substantial number of workers were employed by the authorities in various establishments throughout the town. The local military barracks, the police station, the hospital, the railway station, the post office, schools, the county council and so on provided a living for a large number of local families. Of course, private enterprise, such as shops, pubs, building contractors, farmers and local newspapers, played their part as well. Most people seemed to be doing nicely and keeping their heads above water. However, like every other town in the country at that time, Mullingar, had its fair share of unemployment and all the hardship that goes with it.

The relationship with the British occupiers usually depended upon a person's status in the town. Employment, to a large extent, dictated one's perception of the occupying forces. People working for the authorities believed that it was best for their future, and indeed the future of their families, to ensure they maintained a pleasant relationship with their employer at all times. On the other hand, low–paid workers and the unemployed had a different perception of the British authorities and the local British Landowners. One British officer, while writing home in 1909, stated that, "there was no dirtier town in Ireland" than Mullingar, adding, social life consisted of visits to the local gentry."

I wonder why he refused to socialise in town. Maybe his next quote explained the situation, when he stated that there were, "occasional bad words between the soldiers and locals." In a letter in May 1910 he writes, "The new King George V was proclaimed at Mullingar without public enthusiasm, only the military singing the National Anthem." I think, we can safely say that the British did not like the locals and the locals certainly did not like the British. During 1908, a number of local, low–paying, abusive landowners were boycotted by local farm labourers. This was in reaction to the treatment the landowners regularly dished out to these unfortunate people, who found themselves in the employment of what any right–thinking person would call slave drivers.

A local newspaper carried the story, and it was not long before the news of the boycott reached the Houses of Parliament in London. This, of course, brought local Head Constable Crudden into the picture. Crudden was, by all accounts, a very domineering person, and especially so when it came to protecting his masters. It seems he was prepared to do almost anything. He even attempted to dictate to the local media, threatening the editors if they printed certain articles that he felt should not be brought to the public's attention. At the behest of Chief Secretary Birrel, who was said to be very angry at one local newspaper, Crudden called to the newspaper's office in Earl Street, Mullingar. He warned the editor in the following terms, "I am directed to inform you that should you publish in your newspaper, any boycotting or intimidatory reports or notices, naming or pointing out certain individuals, and exposing them to intimidation or attack, immediate proceedings will be taken."

He turned a blind eye to the intimidating tactics deployed by the ruling loyalists on local working–class people and he did not agree with workers' rights. He feared retaliation by means of further boycotting, which would have put justified pressure on his friends, who were, after all, the real offenders in the first place. His bullyboy tactics failed on this occasion. On 5 November 1908, the newspaper in question published his threat in full. He was prepared to threaten a local newspaper, simply because it highlighted the intimidation inflicted on the poor classes of Mullingar and surrounding areas. He just did not care about the people he was actually paid to protect. There is no doubt that he would use his intimidating tactics on anyone who failed to assist him, as he merrily screwed the local unfortunates who he believed Mullingar – and especially his masters – would be far better off without.

The town had its share of alcohol–related crime: instances of drunk and disorderly behaviour, assault and petty theft appeared regularly in the local papers. The defendants were a mixed bunch, and not all locals. Some were army personnel; others were just passing through, or had moved to Mullingar from other parts of the country. Criminals at that time moved from town to town for a fresh start, which mostly meant a clean criminal record. It was a very difficult task for the police to establish if an outsider had previous convictions, especially if they could not ascertain where the suspect came from in the first place. Hardened criminals with long lists of convictions often appeared in court as first–time offenders, and as a result, received much lighter sentences. These criminals, after completing their sentence, simply moved on to another town in order to continue their illegal activities.

On the positive side, the locals had numerous facilities and opportunities to become self–employed. The surrounding lakes, the River Brosna and the Royal Canal produced numerous species of freshwater fish, and local fishermen were regularly seen selling their catch on the market square. Others were involved in hunting. Rabbits were in abundance and sold daily to the local housewives and "hare soup" was often the soup of the day in many households. Some hunters specialised in birds, with pheasant, duck and pigeon providing delicious main courses in some households. Unfortunately, not every family could afford such luxuries on a regular basis, and simply lived from day to day on whatever scraps of food that came their way.

Some local fishermen worked as gillies; they hired their services to visiting anglers. Their fishing knowledge of the lakes, the Brosna and the Royal Canal was very much appreciated and sought after. This was at a time when a local fisherman, while fishing off the Belvedere Shore of Lough Ennell, landed the heaviest brown trout ever recorded in Ireland, and to this day, the record still stands. This received enormous publicity among anglers from all over these islands. All the hype, of course, attracted numerous "gentlemen" anglers to the town, each and every one of them hoping to break the record, but all attempts ended in failure. Of course, the local gillies did a roaring trade for many years to come.

2.

MISS MARY WALKER

During 1901, Miss Mary Walker, a native of Co. Carlow, arrived in Mullingar to take up employment as a telegraphist and sorter at the local post office. She had been transferred from Blackrock, Co. Dublin. Mary also worked in post offices at New Ross, Co. Wexford, and Callan, Co. Kilkenny. Mary, a regular churchgoer, was a very popular and highly regarded young lady among the townspeople of Mullingar. She was a very friendly and obliging person: she was very helpful and aided numerous people when her assistance was called upon. She spoke to everybody and was involved with local church activities. By all accounts, she was a lovely young lady. Her contribution at the post office entailed reading, writing or simply giving advice to people who requested it. Many adults who were illiterate approached Mary for assistance with letters, telegrams, and forms, simply because she was very honest and trustworthy.

Miss Walker's employment entailed working unsocial hours; this seemed to suit her. She often had free afternoons and, if the weather was favourable, she was regularly seen strolling around town and sometimes along the canal line. During bad weather, she would sometimes call on her many friends in various parts of Mullingar, and other times she would stay at home chatting with her landlady, Mrs Anne Daly. It is not known if Mary had a boyfriend in Mullingar, back home in Carlow or indeed Dublin, Wexford or Kilkenny. Mary lived the rest of her short life in Mullingar. She was horrifically murdered on a summer's afternoon in July 1909. She was 32 years of age.

On the morning of Wednesday, 7 July 1909, Mary Walker, got up early as usual, attended Mass in the local Cathedral and afterwards walked to the post office to commence her early shift as telegraphist and sorter. She completed the shift at 1.45pm and left her place of work, heading for her lodgings at 3 Fairview Terrace, in Patrick Street, arriving there at about 1.50pm. Her landlady, Mrs Anne Daly, had Mary's dinner ready for her as usual. Miss Walker sat down and enjoyed her meal, and afterwards she relaxed with a cup of tea and a chat with Mrs Daly. Mary left her lodgings to go for a stroll. She did not tell Mrs Daly where she was going: only that she was going for a walk. Her landlady put the time at about 3.15pm. Mary walked towards the town and arrived at the Green Bridge less than two minutes after leaving Mrs Daly's. She would never return alive to her landlady's home, which had been hers for fifteen months. Miss Walker's dead body was found at 8.35pm that Wednesday evening. Her throat had been cut.

Miss Walker was due to return for tea at her usual time of 6pm. When she failed to turn up, Mrs Daly became a little concerned. Later still, at 7.30pm when Miss Walker was due to return to work, Mrs Daly, who at this stage was very worried, sent her son Michael to the post office to enquire about Mary's whereabouts. Michael was informed that Miss Walker failed to show up for her 7.30pm shift. He then tried the neighbourhood in Patrick Street, in the hopes that Mary called in to see a friend and overlooked the time.

At the time of her murder, Mary's Mother, Ellen, a sixty–three–year–old widow, lived at the family home in Carlow with her twenty–two–year–old son, William and her daughter, Julia, Mary's twenty–year–old sister. Her mother gave birth to five children but only three survived. Her husband died after 17 years of marriage. It is not natural to bury your child, but to bury three children is more than a tragedy. God only knows how Ellen coped for the rest of her life.

3.

JOSEPH HEFFERNAN

Joseph Heffernan, known locally as Joe, was an unfortunate young man, deemed by many to be the town fool. As a result of a serious accident, Heffernan was left with a deformed right hand. He was born in Moneylea (Monilea), near Mullingar. He liked a drink and frequented the local pubs whenever he could afford to. After a couple of pints, he was known to entertain his fellow customers. He would sometimes whistle a tune or he would sing and keep time with his feet. He sometimes laboured on the buildings. However, most of the work he got was from local farmers, and as it was seasonal, he often found himself unemployed. Between jobs, he occasionally delivered telegrams for the post office. A number of unemployed people would, from time to time, queue outside the side door of the post office. If all the telegram boys were out making deliveries and an urgent telegram arrived, a post office employee would get the man at the front of the queue to deliver the telegram. Heffernan would sometimes be lucky enough to be that man.

Joe was a nuisance when he was drunk; he would call to houses and walk straight in when the owner opened the door. Some people encouraged this by feeding him whenever he called. He was very thin and delicate looking and because of his appearance, locals felt sorry for him. He had no family home in Mullingar. His parents were dead. His father was found drowned in a bog hole near Mullingar. His brothers, John and Edward, and his cousins were patients in the local psychiatric hospital. John, when he was well, resided at 18 Patrick Street, Mullingar. Joe also had a sister; she was married to local man Edward Willis. Locals pitied Joe and believed him to be his own worst enemy. He was also well known to the police. While Joe lodged in a number of houses around town, he sometimes lived rough when he was out of work. He slept under hedgerows, in hay barns and any place else where he could put his head down. From time to time, he resided in the local workhouse.

Heffernan had no property or means of transport, so he often walked for miles in search of employment. As social welfare did not exist at that time, it was vitally important, especially for homeless people living on their own, to obtain employment. Without employment, they would simply starve to death – that is if sleeping rough through the winter did not kill them. Heffernan, on numerous occasions, walked to Killucan, about ten miles from Mullingar to get work from local farmers. As a result, he was well known in the area. Of course, when his employers no longer required his services, he was let go and left with no alternative but to walk the ten miles back to Mullingar. I have been told by a number of people that he worked in various remote areas around Co. Westmeath. The 1901 census states that he was employed as a "farm servant", for William Grimes and his family, at Loughagar, Knockdrin, about six miles outside Mullingar. He later worked as a "servant boy" for Ms Jane Garry in the same area. Joe also worked for Mr William Walshe of Dominick Street, Mullingar.

Heffernan tried numerous ways to earn some money; from time to time he bought and sold (and sometimes swapped) penknives. For a short period of time, he worked at the harbour in Mullingar, unloading goods arriving from Dublin by boat. For the price of a drink, he was often seen cleaning out yards, shops and the odd pub. Heffernan was a rogue, but according to locals at the time, a likable rogue. He was simply the town idiot and he was regularly taken advantage of. When Joe worked on farms out in the country, and miles from the nearest pub, he would accumulate up to six or eight weeks' wages. When the work finished he would walk back to Mullingar and once there, he had the habit of doing a pub–crawl. He would buy drink for his friends in every establishment he visited. Unfortunately for Joe, his "kindness" (or as I believe it to be, his foolishness), was not reciprocated by his friends.

On 5 July 1909, Heffernan took up lodgings at Mrs Anne Moran's house, in Austin Friars Street, Mullingar. At this stage, he was unemployed and actively seeking employment at farms in the Mullingar area. On 7 July, Heffernan got up at about 6.45am. He told his landlady he was going out to Callaghan's farm in Robinstown to work. He told her he would be back that night, "if they had not a bed for him," otherwise he would be back the following Saturday night. Heffernan did not go to work. Instead, he decided to spend the morning in a number of pubs. His first port of call was Mrs Sullivan's public house in Greville Street. According to the barman, Charles Quinn, Heffernan arrived on the premises sometime between 10am and 11am and ordered a pint. He stopped about three quarters of an hour. He had a glass of porter before he went out.

His next port of call was Fallon's public house in Mount Street. He arrived at the pub with another man between 11am and 12 noon. John Fallon, the publican, did not know the man who was with him. Heffernan called for two pints of porter, and they drank them. The man he was with then called for two more pints of porter. Heffernan only drank half of his pint. Heffernan's friend left before he did and said he was going towards the lake. Heffernan did not say where he was going. He was next seen in Charles Skelly's house. Skelly lived almost opposite Mrs Anne Daly, Mary Walker's landlady. Skelly said he arrived home about 2.30pm and found Heffernan in his house. He said Heffernan was sober and was quite well aware of what he was doing and saying, as he had a conversation with him. He asked Skelly for the loan of a razor. Skelly said he did not give it to him, but Heffernan asked him for a loan of the razor a second time, saying, "Anything at all that would tear the hair off my face would do." Skelly's wife gave him some food to eat. He said he was going to work for Merlehan the next morning.

At about 3.15pm, Skelly left the house and Heffernan went with him; Skelly was going back to work at this time. They walked as far as the Green Bridge and Skelly did not see Heffernan again that day. Joseph Heffernan decided to walk out the canal line; a walk, which, just like Mary Walker's, would result in his death. Unfortunately for Joe, he would be arrested, charged, convicted and executed for the murder of Miss Mary Walker.

4.

IS IT TRUE?

Did the real killer appear before the courts? I went online and came across "Kilmainham Executions" by one "Buckley" from Dublin, written in 2006. Buckley's version read as follows:

HANGED BY PIERREPOINT (ASSISTED BY THOMAS)
Joseph Heffernan, January 4 1910
For the murder of Mary Walker in Mullingar.
Mary Walker had worked in the post office in Mullingar for eight years, had befriended Heffernan and managed to secure him a job in the post office where she worked. It seems Joseph Heffernan was fired from this job for reasons unknown in a matter of months.
Around this time Heffernan was trying to develop his relationship with Mary Heffernan [should read Mary Walker] into something more intimate than just casual friends and colleagues.
On July 7 1909, Joseph Heffernan left his lodgings early as he said he was going to a nearby farm to seek work. He did not return until very late that night in an advanced state of intoxication, and when his landlady asked him where he had been all day, he told her that he had witnessed the murder of a girl down at the Great Bridge [should read Green Bridge]. The landlady assumed (and presumably hoped) that this entire story was a fabrication inspired by his drunkenness, but became suspicious when the next day she asked Joseph to fix a broom handle and he produced a bloodstained pen–knife to do the job.
As news of the discovery of Mary Walker's body circulated, having been found at 11pm on the night of her death with her throat slit from ear to ear, the landlady reported him to police who found that Heffernan matched the description given by a witness of the man seen arguing with Mary Walker, just prior to her death.
At his trial Heffernan's defence tried to plead insanity.

This version of events is far from being an accurate recording of what took place on that horrible day back in 1909. In an attempt to discover where this information came from, I tried unsuccessfully to locate Buckley.

In July 2009, the *Westmeath Examiner* published the following article, written by fellow Mullingar man Richard Coplan:

One hundred years ago July 7 1909, was a dry blustery summers day. At 1.45pm a telegraphist, Mullingar–based, Mary Walker, 32, a native of Ballinabloey, near Bagenalstown, Co. Carlow, had just finished her early shift at Mullingar's general post office. Mary made her way home to 3 Fairview Terrace where she had been lodging with a Mrs Daly for the past 15 Months. She arrived home at 1.50pm and after a while relaxing, sat down to dinner. At 3.19pm, wearing a dark navy blue dress, and a light green hat, Mary, who was of 'a quiet, retiring disposition,' set off alone for a stroll along the nearby Royal Canal. Mary was due back for tea at six o'clock that evening, but history tells us Mary failed to keep that appointment. Her dead body was carried into Mrs Daly's at about eleven o'clock the same evening. She had been brutally murdered as she strolled along the banks of the Royal Canal.

Her dead body was discovered some five hours later by three work colleagues from the post office. Her remains were partly hidden by long grass and lay between the canal bank and the railway line.

Constable William Holmes was the first police officer to arrive at the scene. He noticed the grass trampled and blood in a number of areas. This led him to believe a violent struggle had taken place and outrage or rape had been attempted. Holmes noticed the victim's throat had been cut and her blouse and upper part of her corset had been torn open. The lower part of her clothing had been slashed into ribbons, exposing her legs and groin. Holmes also discovered a distinct track of footprints in a drain near where the body lay.

The *Examiner* also touched on the Bishops remarks at Mass the following Sunday, 11 of July 1909. Most Rev Dr Goughran referred to the murder as a stain on the parish, a very black cloud and the "Mullingar Horror." He went on to compare the crime to the murders of Jack the Ripper in Whitechapel, some twenty–one years previously. He concluded with prayers for the repose of the soul of Mary Walker and that the perpetrator of this "dreadful crime" be soon brought to justice.

Within nineteen hours of Mary's murder, two men were arrested on suspicion of having committed the gruesome crime. The first, an unidentified young man, was discharged from custody the following morning, having been able to satisfactorily account for his movements at the believed time of the murder. The second was Joseph Heffernan, a twenty–seven–year–old labourer from Mullingar.

The testimony given by postman, Thomas Nooney would prove central to the investigation. Nooney was one of the last to see Miss Walker alive, and also one of the first to discover her body some five hours later. Perhaps it was the shock of having made this gruesome discovery that can explain why he did not recall a vital piece of evidence until the following morning. Just five minutes before Mary passed Nooney and his brother as they fished on the canal, a man whom they knew to be Joseph Heffernan had walked in the same direction. In that time, no other person passed along the towpath. Eight other people came forward with eyewitness accounts that placed Heffernan at or near the murder scene. Together with the fact that Heffernan had already served nine months imprisonment for assaulting a young woman, this was enough to see a warrant issued for his arrest.

Heffernan was arrested at 11.30am on the morning of Thursday 8 July, at the farm of James Callaghan, Robinstown, where he had just started work thinning mangolds. PC Charles Moore charged Heffernan with the murder. After the usual caution was administered, Heffernan responded, "Is it me? What do I know about it? I know nothing about it." Plaster casts taken of four footprints found at the murder scene were also found to match the prisoner's size–nine boots. Joseph Heffernan was then brought before a Magistrate, Owen Wickham, J.P. and he was remanded in custody for a week. The Magistrate enquiries, three in total, took place on Thursday 15, Monday 19 and Monday 26 July. Joseph Heffernan was undefended. Journalists present in court described Heffernan as "a cadaverous, rather unkempt–looking man" of medium height, thin, unshaven with a sallow complexion and a drooping fair moustache.

With the amount of evidence and eyewitness testimony produced over the course of the three enquiries, many came to see it as an open–and–shut case. A sixteen–year–old stable boy named Richard Monaghan was exercising a horse in a field adjoining the Ballymahon Road. At approximately 4.30pm, he saw a woman appear suddenly on the opposite side of the canal some 200 yards distant. She was running, trying to get up the canal bank. She wore a hat and dark clothes. Then he saw a man catching up close behind her. He too was wearing a cap and dark clothes. When the woman reached the top of the bank, she turned, only for the man pursuing her to grab her and shove her back down head first. They then disappeared from view. The spot where Richard Monaghan saw the couple was the exact same spot that Mary Walker's body was found, four hours later. Monaghan knew Heffernan to see, as the latter had previously lodged in his parent's house. Despite the distance, he could tell that the man was the same height as Heffernan and he swung his arms just like him. Monaghan deposed that he did not hear a scream, but put this down to the fact that there was a strong breeze blowing towards the canal at the time.

Other witnesses did hear a scream. One of these was Ellen Woods, a young girl living at Valley Cottages. She was out looking for her brother Patrick when she heard a squeal "like that of a cat." Passing no remarks, she started picking watercress along the canal. When she came up to the bank some ten minutes later, she saw Heffernan on the opposite side. He was sitting with his feet in the water and was in the process of washing his hands and wiping his boots with grass. When he saw her, he pulled his cap down over his eyes.

Five further witnesses, Michael Murray, Richard Merlehan, Bridget Nugent, Elizabeth Feeny and Christopher Downes came forward to depose of having seen Heffernan, skulking through hedges and along the railway line, as he made his way back into Mullingar in the half hour following Mary's murder. Other witnesses deposed having seen Heffernan, loitering around the town and drifting in and out of pubs over the next five hours. Four more witnesses, Christina McCormack, Bridget Creevy, Michael Veldon and Luke Sullivan, came forward to report having witnessed Heffernan behaving suspiciously in the vicinity of Gas Lane and the Mill Road at 10.30am on Thursday 8 July.

In an early example of forensic science being used in a court of law, Dr Edmond J. McWeeney, Professor at the School of Medicine, Dublin, testified that minute human blood spatters had been found on Heffernan's trousers, leggings and shirt, as well as on the recovered penknife.

At Heffernan's trial on 2 and 3 December 1909 at Green Street Courthouse, Dublin, Sergeant Moriarty recalled all the evidence presented at the magisterial inquiries over four months earlier. No fewer than thirty–five people were called to the stand to provide damning evidence against Heffernan. Dr McWeeney once again recalled his forensic medical evidence and the plaster casts matching Heffernan's boots were also displayed. New evidence in the form of an alleged confession was also presented to the court. Heffernan, it was stated, confessed his guilt to Warder John Mansfield, while recovering in the prison hospital at Kilmainham Jail.

A plea of insanity was raised on Heffernan's behalf by his defence lawyer, Mr William J. Gleeson, BL, based on the fact that two of his brothers, John and Edward and two of his cousins, also called John and Edward, had been or were at that time interned at Mullingar District Lunatic Asylum, suffering from melancholia, delusions and dementia. The Lord Chief Justice, Lord O'Brien of Kilfenora, on hearing this charge, said that it was for the jury to say, "whether, having regard to Heffernan's proximity to the scene of the murder, and the other circumstances deposed to, they could have any doubt as to the guilt of the accused." As to the question of insanity or degeneracy, he had found by experience that most criminals were of a degenerate type and he had never seen a man in the dock on the same charge who was not of low order.

The jury, made up of twelve men, retired at 4.25pm and after an absence of twenty–five minutes, returned to court with a guilty verdict. And so it was that Joseph Heffernan ended up in the condemned cell at Kilmainham Gaol.

After his sentence, Heffernan appeared to be very repentant as he awaited his doom. He was attended every day by the Sisters of Charity from Basin

Lane, and they prayed with him as he attended to the ministrations of the Church with great devotion. On the morning of his execution, 4 January 1910, Heffernan attended Mass in the prison chapel and received the last rites of the Church. When these were finished, he had a short time to himself for reflection and, at 7.55am, he was formerly handed over to the executioner, who on this occasion was the notorious English hangman, Henry Pierrepoint. The hangman and his assistant (his brother Thomas Pierrepoint) pinioned Heffernan's arms and led him to the scaffold. The scaffold itself had been specially constructed, as the last criminal executed at Kilmainham Gaol was James Reilly, for the Stepaside murder in 1893.

It was claimed that Heffernan was perfectly calm on the scaffold and he delivered the responses to the Litany with much fervour. The only other persons present at the execution were the Governor of the Gaol, Mr Michael McGann; Mr Hyde, High Sheriff of Westmeath; Mr Featherstonhaugh, Sub-Sheriff; the Chaplain, Fr O'Ryan of Golden Bridge; Fr Flood of James Street; Dr John O'Donnell, the medical officer, and the warders.

Outside the prison, a crowd of about three hundred had gathered. The cold and foggy weather reflected the solemn proceedings within the gaol. A heavy mist continued to shroud the place when, at 8am precisely, the prison bell began to toll solemnly, informing those outside that the law had taken its course. It was reported that when the gallows door opened, Heffernan died instantly. Based on Heffernan's height (5 feet 5 inches) and weight (10 stone), the meticulous Pierrepoint calculated that a seven-foot drop would be sufficient to bring about a swift, clean death.

This official version of events comes from what came out in the courts. In fairness to Richard Coplan and the *Westmeath Examiner*, this version was taken in good faith from the true crime history books.

I have no qualifications or training in this area. Nonetheless, I decided to go through each and every piece of evidence. I spent the last two-and-a-half years researching and studying this case and I now believe, no matter how compelling the presented evidence is, facts are not always what they seem.

After reading the above, I am sure, at this stage, there is no doubt in your mind that Heffernan did indeed murder Mary Walker, and I am also sure most of you believe he deserved his punishment. However, after studying the Inquest report, the witness statements, the magistrates' hearings in Mullingar and finally his trial in Green Street Dublin, I am not so sure.

5.

THE INQUEST

On Saturday 10 July 1909, the *Westmeath Examiner* published the following report on the inquest into the death of Mary Walker:

The inquest was held on the evening of the arrest Thursday 8 July with D.I. Ruttledge examining the witnesses.

Mrs Anne Daly, Fair View, Patrick Street, identified the body of the deceased. She knew her as she lodged for the past 15 months in the witness's house. She remembered the 7 July. On that day witness saw deceased about 15 minutes past 3pm. and that was the last time she saw Miss Walker alive. At that time deceased left the witness's house and went out for a walk. Deceased was then in perfect health. Witness next saw deceased between 10 and 11 that night when she was carried in dead. She did not tell the witness when leaving what way she intended to walk, nor did the witness see what way she went.

Mr Harvey Savage, acting Postmaster at Mullingar post office, deposed he knew the deceased who was employed in the post office where she had worked for about the past eight years. On the 7 July witness saw her in the post office at 1.45pm when she was coming out of the office from duty. She was then in her usual health. She was due back for duty at 7.30pm. The son of deceased's landlady came down to the post office about the time she should have been back for duty and asked if she had been seen at the post office as she had not come in for her tea and witness told him that she had not turned up.

Thomas Nooney, auxiliary postman, Mullingar, deposed he knew the deceased Mary Walker who was also employed in the post office. On the 7 July between half past three and four o'clock pm, witness saw the deceased going along the canal line towards the racecourse. Witness was on the opposite side of the canal about Merlehan's field and was fishing. His younger brother Matt was with witness at the time. Shortly before that, witness saw a man named Joseph Heffernan going along the same side of the canal as the deceased and preceding her. Witness knew that that walk was a favourite walk of the deceased. Heffernan had no one with him; he seemed to not to be in a hurry and had no sign of having drink taken.

Nooney then went home and later on in consequence of a communication from Mr Lundy to whom Mr Daly had spoken, witness went to look for her. That was about 8.20pm, and witness, accompanied by Mr Daly and Jack Lundy, went along the canal line towards the racecourse. About a quarter of a mile from Mullingar witness saw the body in the hollow on the left–hand side of the line. Her body was partly covered with grass.

She appeared to be dead, but witness did not go near her. Lundy went nearest to the body. Afterwards they met Mr Wilson of the Ulster Bank and told him they suspected foul play. They then went into the town and informed the police constable in the town of what they had seen. "I think the deceased knew Heffernan; he often took special messages from the office for her."

Matthew Nooney, fourteen years of age, brother of Thomas, was fishing on the 7th with his brother Thomas on the canal. It was a little after two o'clock. That was the hour at which he began to fish. He knew the deceased. He saw her walking along the canal line that afternoon whilst he was fishing. She was on the side next to the town and was going in the racecourse direction. That would be about 3.30pm. Prior to this, witness had seen Joe Heffernan go along the same way. That was about ten minutes previous to the time the deceased passed.

John Lundy deposed he was employed as auxiliary postman in the Mullingar office. He knew the deceased and saw her on the 7 July about 1.40pm. She was just leaving the post office; he next saw her dead. Witness and his companions left the town about ten or twenty minutes past eight. Mr M. J. Daly and Mr Thomas Nooney accompanied witness. It was about an English mile from the town to where he found her. Witness was looking down towards the canal and his companion along the other side and he let a shout and witness looked down the bank suddenly and saw what appeared a heap or bundle of clothes. On examination this proved to be deceased's body. Witness went near and looked into her features and recognised her. Before he saw the body he saw an umbrella near her. The umbrella was about four yards from the body; he also noticed grass over the body.

He knew Joseph Heffernan who was sometimes employed in the post office as a casual messenger when all the messengers were out. "Heffernan seemed to be a bit of a rake, who did not do much work. However, if I gave him a message to do he could do it properly."

Constable William Holmes deposed that he remembered the 7 July. He was walking along the canal line about 8.30 that evening, on the town side. He met Mr Wilson of the Ulster Bank and, as a result of what Mr Wilson said, he came back with Mr Wilson and Mr Cuppance to a place about 200 yards from where he met Mr Wilson, and then found the body of Miss Walker lying in soft marshy ground. She was dead and her body was covered with grass. She was lying on her back, her head towards the racecourse and her feet towards Mullingar. He noticed her face and throat covered with blood and on examination found that the throat was cut. Her clothes were very much disarranged. It occurred to witness from her appearance that the deceased had been subjected to very great violence. Her hat was still on her head. Her left arm raised up, as if she had been dragged by it, her right arm was down by her side.

About 20 feet back from where she was lying, he noticed a pool of blood in the grass and the grass had the appearance of her body having been dragged from where the pool of blood was to where she was then lying. Above the place where the pool of blood was, about 5 feet, there was on the slope a little bush, and there was the appearance as of someone having sat there, and also the appearance as if the body had been dragged from it. The grass was plainly beaten down as if someone had been sitting down there. He subsequently saw Constable Foskin and another constable find a pocket of her frock, which had been torn out; also her gloves and belt. These were beside the bush also. He also noticed two tracks from where the body lay to the drain, which was soft; it was as if someone had jumped down in the drain. Opposite this place was a gap through which a person could get through to the railway line. He remained in charge of the body till it was removed to Mullingar.

Dr Joseph Dillon–Kelly J P deposed that he was not personally acquainted with the deceased. He remembered the 7 July, and about 8.30pm a messenger arrived to bring him out to where the body was. He got out to the place as quickly as possible – about 9pm. It was a mile from where the body was. The police pointed out the body, and witness made a rough superficial examination. Her face was covered with blood and grass, the latter adhering through the blood to the body. Her neck was all covered with grass, and, as a matter of fact, witness had to pull it off to examine the throat. He then saw a wound about four inches long on front of the throat, and about equal on both sides of the windpipe. It was not very deep, but went clean through the larynx. Her clothes were very much disarranged. She was probably some hours dead when witness saw her.

She was two, three or four hours, but he would not like to bind himself as to the number of hours. There was a little heat under the clothes over the abdomen; she was fat, which would account for that. Witness then deposed to making, with Dr Ballasty, the post–mortem just held. They made a superficial examination of the body, including the clothes and their position on the body.

They discovered that there was no wound whatsoever on the body, except that on the throat. There was a slight abrasion on the forehead. They found that the wound went almost clean through the larynx or Adam's apple, as it is sometimes called. The wound was 4 inches long; it divided a number of blood vessels   the super–thyroid   and a number of other vessels, which, with shock, would account for death, and he believed death was caused by haemorrhage and the shock of the wound. He would say the wound was caused by a sharp instrument – probably a pocket knife. He would think there was a push or stab – and also a draw of the knife – when it was used in making the wound. Dr Kelly also described the torn condition of the deceased's clothes and underclothing. The doctors were of the opinion that an outrage had been attempted, but they could not say whether or not the attempt had succeeded. From the appearance of the clothes, witness would say deceased had been subjected to very great violence; the bodice, stays and frock were badly torn. He said on examination of the internal organs everything appeared to be healthy, but they did not make a very detailed internal examination. They would do so if it was desired. He was quite satisfied that death resulted from the wound received. The jury did not ask for any further post–mortem examinations nor did the district inspector.

Dr Michael Ballasty deposed that he had heard the evidence of Dr Kelly and had assisted him in the post–mortem. He agreed with Dr Kelly's evidence except in regard to the question of how the wound was likely made. He thought it was a draw in which the man leant on the centre portion more than any other, and not a stab at all.

The centre portion was the deepest part of the wound, which pointed to this, and it would be necessary to lean heavily on the knife to do this. The wound caused her death. The deceased was a healthy, well–nourished woman; he also believed there was an attempt at outrage.

The evidence having concluded, the coroner addressing the jury said he was sorry he had to preside at such an inquiry as that. It was one of the saddest affairs, he supposed, that had ever occurred in Mullingar or Westmeath. They had very full evidence as to what happened to that poor girl. They had nothing to say from the evidence except that she had been done to death by someone and they did not know who it was.

There was a certain amount of suspicion running all through the case, but it would remain for another court to see if that suspicion could be established, and if it was established, he was certain that none of them could have any sympathy with the party who committed this deed. He thought they would have done their duty if they found that deceased was done to death by some person unknown on the canal bank on the previous day.

A verdict to this affect was returned and on the suggestion of the foreman a rider was drawn up which expressed their sympathy with her relatives and her colleagues at the post office.

The inquest, held one day after the murder, was reported in the local papers. After you, the reader, digest the statements, the reports from Magistrates' hearings and the assizes, we will revisit part of the inquest report.

6.

ACTUAL STATEMENTS TAKEN

CONSTABLE CHARLES MOORE

FIRST STATEMENT TAKEN 8 July 1909

I am stationed at Mullingar. From information received I arrested Joseph Heffernan the prisoner now present on this date on the charge of murdering Miss Walker on the canal bank on yesterday evening. I cautioned him. He said, "Is it me? What do I know about it? I know nothing about it." He repeated this a few times on the way to the Barracks. I believe I will be able to produce further evidence against him and I ask for a remand for that purpose.

Prisoner declines to cross–examine and states, "I know nothing about the girl, I heard she was murdered yesterday evening, I am not that bad."

Dr DILLON–KELLY

STATEMENT TAKEN 15 July 1909

I am the Dispensary Doctor of Mullingar. On the night of Wednesday the 7 of July 1909 I was sent for by the police. I went out along the Royal Canal towards the Racecourse. I was pointed out the dead body of a woman by the police; it was then about half past nine o'clock. I made a superficial examination of the body. I found her face covered with blood and grass; her neck was covered with grass. I removed the grass. I found a wound four inches long in front of her throat, equal on both sides of the windpipe. I looked at her clothes; they were very much torn and disarranged. She was dead; she had been so for some hours. On the 8 of July 1909 I held a post mortem examination on the body in conjunction with Dr Ballasty. I found the body well fed and nourished and that of a healthy young woman. I carefully examined her head. I noticed no injury, depression or abnormal state of her head that would be caused by violence. I found a small abrasion on her forehead; it appeared to have been there for some time. There was no wound or injury on the body except on the throat. This wound was four inches long; it penetrated clean through the Larynx, dividing it almost. The carotid arteries were not injured; the superior thyroid arteries were severed. The haemorrhage from these arteries and shock were the cause of death. I believe a pocket knife would cause this wound. The blouse was torn open, and also the upper part of the corset; the centre of the corset was caught by a metal catch which we had difficulty in opening; the lower part was torn open and torn into ribbons, particularly on the right side. The deceased was wearing bloomers and underneath, knickers. The bloomers were torn from the waistband down to the knee and the knickers were similarly torn. I formed the opinion that the deceased had been subjected to great violence. I have no doubt that outrage was attempted.

Dr MICHAEL JOSEPH BALLESTY
STATEMENT TAKEN 15 July 1909

I knew deceased Miss Mary Walker. I am the Medical Attendant at the post office, Mullingar. I think the deceased was a healthy young woman. On 8 July 1909 I held a post mortem examination on her body with Dr Kelly. I have heard the evidence he has given with respect to that post–mortem and I agree with it; I have nothing to add to it.

Mrs ANNE DALY
STATEMENT TAKEN 15 July 1909

I live at Patrick Street, Mullingar. The deceased Mary Walker lodged with me for the last fifteen months and during that time she was always in good health and spirits. I remember Wednesday 7 July 1909; the deceased returned from the post office on that day at about ten minutes to two o'clock pm; I knew she was employed in the post office. She had her dinner and then left for a walk, this was about fifteen minutes past three o'clock. She was dressed in a navy costume and green hat. I expected her back about six o'clock for her tea. She did not come back. In consequence of her not coming back I sent my son Michael to the post office. He is employed there as a clerk. When he came back, in consequence of what he told me, I sent him to Mrs Kearney who lives in Patrick Street and who used to sew for the deceased. I did not see Mary Walker alive again. Her dead body was brought back to my house about eleven o'clock pm on the same day.

THOMAS NOONEY
STATEMENT TAKEN 15 July 1909

I am an Auxiliary Postman at the Mullingar post office. I live in Trinity Cottages in Patrick Street, Mullingar. The canal bank is about a hundred yards from where I live. I knew the deceased Mary Walker who was also employed in the post office. I know the prisoner Joseph Heffernan well; he was employed occasionally as a casual messenger. I remember Wednesday 7 July 1909. I went to fish in the canal at about two o'clock pm on that day. My brother Matthew went with me. I commenced to fish in the canal directly in front of my own house; this would be about half way between the Green Bridge and where the murder was committed. I fished slowly back towards the town. I know the iron gate of the Galway cattle bank; I remember fishing opposite it, I was on my own side of the canal; the towing path is on the other side.

While I was fishing opposite this gate I saw the prisoner Joseph Heffernan coming along the towing path and going towards the racecourse. He stopped and spoke to me; there was just the width of the canal between us. He asked me if I was catching anything, I told him no, that I did not think there was anything in it to catch. He asked me what I was fishing with and I told him minnow. He was about a minute talking to me. I am not sure how he was dressed. He then walked towards the racecourse. He was walking slowly and did not seem to be in a hurry. He was sober as far as I could see. Beyond where I was speaking to him, at some distance, the canal winds to the right. After he left me I fished towards the Green Bridge. I came to what is called Merlehan's field. When I was fishing opposite this place I saw the deceased, Miss Walker; this was about five minutes after Heffernan, the prisoner, had passed on. Where I saw Miss Walker was twenty yards nearer the town than where I saw Heffernan. Miss Walker bid me "good evening" and passed on out towards the racecourse. She was on the same side of the canal as the prisoner Heffernan. I know that she was in the habit of taking this walk; she often took it. I did not pay much attention to her or to Heffernan. I fished on back to the Green Bridge and then put up the rods; it was about four o'clock pm at this time. I know Head Constable Crudden; I showed him where I was fishing when I spoke to Heffernan and also where I was fishing when I spoke to Miss Walker. On the evening of 7 July 1909 I went out along this canal bank to look for the deceased; a boy named John Lundy and Michael J. Daly, both of whom are employed in the post office were with me. We went towards the racecourse on the same side as I had seen her walking. We went about three quarters of a mile ["three quarters of a mile" is crossed out and replaced with "half a mile." This change is initialled but not by Nooney] from the Green Bridge. I noticed a white thing in the hollow below the canal bank. I gave an exclamation and the three of us then went down the bank to see what this was. Lundy went first, Daly next and then myself. When I got down I found the white thing was a bare knee. I then saw a body covered with grass. I afterwards saw it was Miss Walker. Her face was covered with blood; this was about twenty–five minutes to nine o'clock pm. I saw Lundy pick up an umbrella. The deceased appeared to be lying on her back and the hollow where she was lying is between the bank of the canal and the Galway railway line. I then returned to Mullingar and informed the police. No person passed between the time I saw Heffernan and the time I saw Miss Walker.

MATTHEW NOONEY
STATEMENT TAKEN 15 July 1909

I am the brother of Thomas Nooney and I am fourteen years old. I know the prisoner Joseph Heffernan well; he used to be working down about our cottages. I knew Miss Mary Walker. On 7 July 1909, I went fishing with my brother in the canal; it was about two o'clock pm. I have heard how my brother described the fishing; it was quite correct. I was with my brother when Heffernan came along the towpath on the opposite side to me. I had been fishing about an hour and a half when I saw him coming. He spoke to my brother across the canal. I noticed how he was dressed; he was dressed in a navy suit and a pair of brown leggings. I didn't notice his cap. This conversation took place opposite the Galway cattle pen. He passed on, he was going quite easy. He did not come back again. I fished on towards the Green Bridge back to the town. I know Merlehan's field. When I got there I noticed Mary Walker coming along the towing path. About five minutes passed between the time I saw Heffernan and the time I saw Miss Walker. Miss Walker spoke to my brother across the canal. At the time she spoke to my brother I could see Heffernan on a good distance before her walking slowly on. After Mary Walker spoke to us we fished on towards the Green Bridge. We got there about four o'clock. From the time that Mary Walker passed us when we were fishing until we reached the Green Bridge at four o'clock, no one passed along the tow path except one man who came up and spoke to us. He then turned and went back to the town and out on the road.

PATRICK LYONS

STATEMENT TAKEN 15 July 1909

I am a Labourer and live at Kilpatrick near Mullingar. I remember 7 July 1909. On that day I was carting material at the Valley Cottages; these are new cottages that are being built. Where I was carting was in view of the canal and quite close to it. I know the prisoner Joseph Heffernan. I have known him for the last four or five years. I saw him that day while I was carting, coming along the canal line. He was on the towpath on the opposite side of the canal from me. He was coming from Mullingar and going towards the racecourse. He was walking slowly. This was in or about twenty minutes to four o'clock pm. I remarked him walking slowly along the line and looking and viewing all directions of him.

He looked towards me in particular. He was dressed in all dark clothes, cap and all. He had leggings on but I could not say what colour they were. I never remarked leggings before on him. I looked closely at him on that account and saw it was Joseph Heffernan. He was something over a hundred yards from me where I first saw him; he was about ten minutes in my view. This part of the canal was straight in front of the Valley Cottages. I walked along this canal often. I would say he was close on half a mile from the Green Bridge when I saw him. I was loading a horse and cart and during the ten minutes I was there he was moving slowly on looking about him. I then took my load into Mullingar. When I last saw the prisoner he was something over two hundred yards away. I showed Head Constable Crudden where I was standing when I saw Heffernan first and last.

MICHAEL DALY

STATEMENT TAKEN 15 July 1909

I am a son of Mrs Anne Daly and a clerk at the Mullingar post office. I knew the deceased Mary Walker. She lodged in my mother's house. I did not know the prisoner. On 7 July 1909, in the evening, in consequence of what my mother told me I went down to the post office to enquire about Mary Walker. She was not at the post office. This would be about ten minutes to eight o'clock pm. I then came home and went to Mrs Kearney's house. I then went out along the towing path of the canal towards the racecourse along with John Lundy and Thomas Nooney. I heard Thomas Nooney's evidence as regards the finding of Mary Walker's dead body, and it is quite true; I have nothing to add to it. It was twenty–five minutes to nine when we found the body. I fix the time this way: about forty yards this side of where the body lay, two girls asked me the time and I looked at my watch – it was then twenty–seven minutes to nine.

ELLEN WOODS

STATEMENT TAKEN 15 July 1909

I am a daughter of James Woods and live at the New Cottages, near the Valley, Mullingar. The canal is not far from these cottages where I live. I remember Wednesday 7 July 1909. On that evening I went out to look for my brother Paddy. I went in the direction of the canal bank on the side opposite the towpath. I came straight down from the cottages and walked along it, going in the direction of Ballinea and the racecourse. This would be about ten minutes to five or five o'clock. I know where the dead body of Mary Walker was found. I walked out to look at the place. When I was walking along the canal on the evening of the 7th last, I was nearly opposite the place. While I was walking there I saw no one on the towpath. The bank of the canal slopes down on both sides at this place and if there had been anyone on the opposite side below the towpath I could not see them. I know where a tunnel goes under the canal; it is almost opposite a signal post on the railway line. I went down the bank on my side of the canal to pick watercress. While I was picking the watercress I heard a scream. The scream was like the squeal of a cat. There was no person or cat where I was picking the watercress to give the scream. When I heard the scream I saw Father Magee going along the road from Ballinea to Mullingar. He was riding a horse. The road comes near the canal at this place. I did not pay much attention to the scream. I did not see my brother Paddy and I then turned and went towards my house picking cress below the level of the bank.

I then came up on the bank and I looked across and saw the prisoner Joseph Heffernan, whom I fully identify, on the bank on the other side. He was sitting on the side of the canal with his feet down in the water washing his hands and wiping his boots. When he saw me he pulled his cap down over his eyes. I knew the prisoner before this. He spoke across the canal and said to me "have you aira match?" I said "No." I said if I had one how would I give it? He said, "I thought you'd carry two." I couldn't describe his clothes, except I saw his sleeve was blue. I did not remark leggings on him. I know where the dead body of Mary Walker was found. Where I saw Heffernan sitting on the side of the canal was about ["about" is crossed out and initialled but not by Woods] not very far from it. I showed Head Constable Crudden where I was standing when I saw the prisoner sitting on the bank. I also showed him where I was when I heard the scream. At the time I saw Heffernan sitting there I heard a train coming into Mullingar.

RICHARD MONAGHAN

STATEMENT TAKEN 15 July 1909

I am sixteen years of age. I am employed as a stable boy by Mr Thomas Dibbs of the Valley, Mullingar. I remember Wednesday 7 July 1909. On that afternoon I was exercising a horse for Mr Dibbs in the fields adjoining the Ballinea Road. I was exercising from three to half past five o'clock. The horse I was riding was 16.1 hands high. In the course of the exercising, at one time, I would be facing the Ballinea Road, at another I would have my back to it, and sometimes I would go up the fields. These fields slightly slope up from the road. When I was on this horse I had a clear view of the canal bank across the road. While exercising the horse at about half past four o'clock I saw a man and a woman come up the bank. The woman was first and the man behind her; they were almost close together. She was partly running, trying to get up the bank of the canal. She had dark clothes on and a hat. I saw the man the moment she got to the top of the bank shove her head down first. He had dark clothes on and was wearing a cap. I could see on his legs something white like the tops of leggings but the rushes hid his feet. I noticed his coat was blowing open. There was wind at the time blowing across the canal from me to where he was. It was a hard breeze. I did not hear a cry or scream. I did not recognise who the woman was that I saw come up. I knew Mary Walker. I did not know who the man was that I saw throwing the woman down the bank. I know the prisoner Joseph Heffernan. I know him well. He used to lodge in my mother's house some time ago. He is like the man that I saw on the canal bank. He is the same height. When the man came up after the woman I saw him swing his arms. Heffernan swings his arms in the same way; I saw him do so. Before I left the fields that evening I formed the opinion that the man I saw was Heffernan. I was over two hundred yards off when I saw the occurrence. I showed where I was to Head Constable Crudden. I know where the dead body of Mary Walker was found. Where I saw the man and woman come up the bank was just at this very spot, two yards this side of the signal post. About ten minutes after I saw the man shove the woman down the bank I saw a girl come along the towpath. When she came to the place I saw her stand and look down into the hollow of the far bank. She looked for about a minute. She walked on about two yards towards the racecourse and then came back and looked down again. She then went on towards the racecourse again out of my view. She was dressed in dark clothes. I think she wore a white hat with dark ribbon; she was middling tall and thin. She was fairly ["fairly" was inserted afterwards and not initialled] young. I do not know who she was. At this time ["At this time" is crossed out and initialled but not by Monaghan] I saw Father Magee riding a horse along the road from Ballinea to Mullingar. The time I saw him was before I saw the man push the woman down the bank.

CONSTABLE WILLIAM HOLMES

STATEMENT TAKEN 15 July 1909

I am stationed at Mullingar. I remember 7 July 1909. I went out for a walk along the canal towards the Newbrook Racecourse. I left Mullingar at about twenty minutes past seven o'clock pm. I walked along beyond the racecourse. I noticed nothing wrong going out. I was not looking for anything. I then turned back. On the way back I met Mr Wilson of the Ulster Bank and in consequence of what he told me I hurried along the canal bank to a spot about half a mile from the Green Bridge. I got to this place between half past eight and twenty–five minutes to nine o'clock. At this place the canal bank slopes down a considerable distance; at the foot of the slope there is some marshy ground with long grass. I saw the body of Miss Mary Walker lying there; it was covered and concealed with grass. Her knee was bare. She was lying on her back. Her hat was on.

I saw her face was covered with blood. I saw that her throat was cut. She was dead. Her head was lying towards the racecourse and her feet towards Mullingar. Her right arm was close to her side and her left arm was raised up over her head. From the position in which she was lying, I believe, she had been dragged there by this hand.

Her dress had been very much disarranged. I saw a pool of blood a few yards from her body, towards Mullingar. From the appearance of the grass I think that her body was dragged from this place to where I found it lying by the left hand. The marshy ground is banked on the one side by the canal bank and on the other by the railway line.

The railway line is on a higher level than this marshy ground. Separating the railway from this marshy ground is a water ditch, a fence with a hedge growing and a wire paling. A few yards from where the body was lying there is a gate in the hedge. On the far side of this water ditch I found, under the fence, two boot tracks, as if someone had jumped across the water ditch. I took charge of these tracks and allowed no one to interfere with them. Above where the pool of blood was, half way up the bank of the canal, there is a little bush, and the grass beside the bush bore the appearance as if someone had been sitting on it – it was flattened down. From the bush down to the pool of blood the grass was also flattened as if a body had been pulled over it. From the appearance of the ground there must have been a great struggle. I took charge of the body until it was removed. I saw Constables Foskin and Harrington picking up gloves, a belt and the pocket of a skirt from the ground close to where the body was lying.

RICHARD MERLEHAN

STATEMENT TAKEN 19 July 1909

I live at Clownmore and am a farmer. On Wednesday 7 July 1909 I was working at Clown Bridge from two o'clock until half past three, as well as I can remember. I then went home to my dinner; my house is on the racecourse road. After I had my dinner and spent some time about my yard, I went along the racecourse road and came to an iron gate that leads into one of my fields. This gate is over 200 yards from my house.

This field runs down towards the railway line and the canal. I went through the gate and down the mearing ditch to the foot of the field. At the foot of the field there is a hedge between it and the railway line. There is a cartway through this hedge at the end of it. I went through this cartway and went along the hedge on the railway side until I came to a field where there were turnips planted. At that time I was walking towards the racecourse with the railway line and the canal on my right.

I know where the dead body of Miss Walker was found. When I was halfway between the gate and the turnip field I was about 100 yards from where her body was found. This was the nearest point I was to the place where the murder was committed. I did not see anyone at this time on the canal bank, railway line or anywhere about. There was no one in my view. I did not hear any scream or cry. This would be about twenty–five to five o'clock pm to the best of my opinion.

I know a little bush on the slope of the canal bank just above where the body was found. This bush was in my view when I was there. Going along between the gap and the turnip field I could not see the slope of the canal below this bush. I could not see the hollow between the bank and the railway line – it would be impossible to do so. Anyone could be in the bottom of that hollow without my knowing it. When I came to the turnip field I crossed a fence into it and went up the field looking at the turnips. I had my back to the railway line then.

At the top of the field where the turnips are there is a sandpit and I passed by it and went out through ["out through" is crossed out, initialled, but not by Merlehan] on towards a gate that leads on to the racecourse road. This is a different gate from the gate I went in at. When I was within some four or five yards of the gate coming up to it, I saw some bones lying about. I stopped to pick up these bones. I gave a man permission to throw old bones into the sandpit in my field. When I was picking up the bones I turned round and looked in the direction of the railway line and the canal.

I then saw a girl standing on the canal bank. She was standing right over the place where the dead body was found. She was standing apparently looking over at me as if she wanted to speak to me. She was staring, I thought, at me; she was about 300 yards away from me. When I saw her facing me I moved a couple of paces to the right on to higher ground to give her a better view of me. She still stood looking and I then went back to where the bones were. I had some bones in my hand. I then looked again at the canal and I saw her *walking on towards the racecourse. She then walked back to where I first saw her; she walked seven or eight steps before she turned back.*

Facing her, I then moved five or six paces to higher ground near the road and I then had a still better view of her. She looked for about a minute this second time – this would be about a quarter to five o'clock pm, to the best of my opinion. She then turned and went on towards the racecourse. I lost sight of her at the bushes at Mr Downes' field.

From the time I saw her first till I last saw her she was almost ten minutes in my view. She was dressed in a long dark jacket; she was wearing a hat. I could not say exactly what colour her hat was. She was apparently a young woman and medium sized. There was a strong wind blowing from the canal to me at the time. The girl kept her hands in her pockets or down by her sides, I did not see her hat blow off and I did not see her try to keep it on. I did not know who she was.

When she turned and went on towards the racecourse for the second time, I saw a boy ["boy" crossed out and replaced by "man" – initialled, but not by Merlehan] *coming up on to the railway line. He came up a little to the left of where the dead body was found, and right opposite where the girl was looking down. This was between a signal pole and a telegraph pole. When he got on to the line he started to walk along it in the direction of Mullingar. I saw him go five or six perches and then he was hid from my view by some bushes – they are midway between where I saw him first and the red cabin on the line. I did not see him again. He was dressed as follows: a short round dark coat and a small dark cap or ne'er a one at all; it was a close–fitting cap if he wore one. He was a low sized man.*

I know the prisoner Joseph Heffernan; I know him well. I could not tell if the man I saw walking on the railway was like him. Heffernan was working with me off and on for the last two years. He was not working with me since last November. He smoked sometimes when he had a toothache but he was not a constant smoker.

I often saw him with a penknife and I saw two with him sometimes. He had a habit of trucking with knives, and was constantly changing them. He carried a razor. After seeing the man going along the line I went home. I got home about a quarter past five o'clock; I looked at my watch.

All the time I was present, as I have described, I saw no one but the girl and the man I have mentioned. I heard no screams at any time. When I was coming up from home to the fields after dinner I thought I heard the voice of children and that is what brought me down in the way I went. I thought they were at crabs, which are growing in the ditch, and I went down to put them off to prevent them tramping the meadow.

Prisoner: "Had you a meadow cut?"

Merlehan: "No."

Prisoner: "That is what drove me out in that direction."

BRIDGET NUGENT

STATEMENT TAKEN 19 July 1909

I live at Mary Street, Mullingar and am the wife of John Nugent. I remember 7 of July 1909. I left Mary Street, Mullingar on that date to go out to my father's house on the racecourse. I can't say what time I left, but I thought it should be a quarter to five pm when I got out to the Valley. I went out along the canal bank and I passed Trinity Cottages on my right.

I know a little red signal cabin on the railway line. When I got to that cabin I saw a man on the railway line coming towards me. I do not know where the body of Miss Walker was found. When I passed the red signal cabin I saw a man coming towards me. He was walking slowly along the railway line; he had his head down; he had dark clothes on and a cap. He was a low sized man. I know a signal pole on the railway line just a short way beyond the red cabin. When I saw the man first he was on down the line towards Galway, a good way beyond this signal pole. I know two stone filtering beds that cross the hollow between the canal and the railway line – they are beyond the signal pole. It was a little beyond these stones that I and the man passed each other, I going out and he coming in. He did not look at me when he passed me.

I see the prisoner Joseph Heffernan. He is not unlike the man I saw on the railway line; I did not know Joseph Heffernan. As I was coming up to him I did not see anything down in the hollow; I did not stop at the signal pole and look. My hat blew back before I came to the man, somewhere, it should be, about the signal pole. I turned round slightly and eased my left arm to my hat. I stopped about a minute. I did not move on a few paces and then stop and come back; I just went straight to my father's house. Except the man I have mentioned at this part, I saw no person on the railway line or canal. I did not hear any cry or scream. When I passed the man he was walking on the middle of the railway line; I can't say what distance it was but I saw him distinctly.

ELIZABETH FEENEY

STATEMENT TAKEN 19 July 1909

I am the wife of John Feeney, a signal man on the railway. We live at the Railway Terrace, Mullingar. These houses look out on the racecourse road. I live in an upper room with the window looking on to the racecourse road. I remember Wednesday 7 July 1909. My children came home from school that day at about half past three o'clock pm. About an hour and a half after the children came home I was looking through my window on towards the racecourse road. Somewhat to the right of my window on the opposite side of the road at a laneway there is a gate leading out of Mr Dibbs' field – it is an iron gate. The gate comes out at the top of the lane where it opens onto the road; this gate has barbed wire along the top bar of it. I saw a man squeezing out under the gate. There is a very narrow space between the bottom of the gate and the ground and he nearly stuck in it. He was dressed in dark clothes, a cap and brown leggings. I see the prisoner Joseph Heffernan. He is not unlike the man I saw go under the gate. I cannot swear to his face; I was about 20 yards from him when he squeezed out. He is about the same height as the man I saw. The prisoner is very like him. When he squeezed out under the gate he did not come out on the main road; he went down the lane a couple of yards and went through a gap in the hedge. When he got through the gap he turned to the left and sat down under the hedge. This field is just across the road from the window where I was; the hedge is pretty tall there. I had some fowl running in that field. Sometime ago some fowl were stolen from me. When I saw this man acting in the way I described, I ran downstairs and came out to look after my fowl. I got through a gap in the hedge directly opposite my house – this was a different gap from the gap that the man got through. My children were playing in the field also. When I got through the gap in the hedge I saw the man still sitting where I first noticed him. He was holding his head down and I could not see his face very well. When I saw him sitting there I circled round him in the field and got out in the lane through a gap below where he got in. I came up the lane to the main road. When I came to where he was sitting I heard him moving. I looked through the hedge and I saw him going down along the hedge on the field side towards Mullingar. At the end of the hedge along by which he was walking, there is a gap by which one can get down on to the main road near Clown Bridge.

ELIZABETH FLANAGAN'S FIRST STATEMENT

STATEMENT TAKEN 19 July 1909

I am a daughter of Joseph Flanagan. I live in Barrack Street, Mullingar and am aged fourteen. I remember Wednesday 7 July 1909. On that evening I was left at home to mind my three little brothers and a sister. On that evening before my father came home, a man came into my house; he asked for Molly Roddy. He said he was working out in the country and that Molly Roddy invited him in to have a great day of it. He was dressed in a black cap, black clothes, brown leggings and nailed boots; I noticed these boots were newish. There is a bed in the kitchen. He came into the kitchen; he went over to the bed and sat down on it. He said it was a grand bed. He then lay down on it; he put one hand on the back of his head and one on the front of his throat. He then sat up, put his hand in his pocket and took out some tobacco. It was not in a pouch. He then took out a knife and cut the tobacco. He filled his pipe. It was a new wooden pipe with a tin lid and a white mouthpiece. I saw the knife he had. It had a lead handle. It was a knife you open like a penknife. It had a thin blade, narrow, and it wasn't too bright. It had a stain like blood on the handle. He then asked for a readier to ready his pipe; he then lit it and smoked. At this time he took a handkerchief out of his pocket and wiped his nose with it, it was stained with what appeared to me to be like blood. I asked him what happened to the handkerchief and he said I was looking for news;

he was cross when he said this. He said, "I was skinning a goat and that the meat of it tipped against the handkerchief."

He was getting up off the bed and walking up and down and sitting down again. I told him my mother was sick in the next room and the priest was coming to see her. He then said he would go up to the room and see her. My mother was not in the house at all; I wanted to get rid of him and that is why I told him that. When he went to the hall he asked me was I ever married and would I like to be married. I said, "What do you want to know that for?" He then took out some money and asked me to go down and get a quart of porter and that we would drink it together. I told him I had to get my father's dinner and that I would not go.

I was getting frightened at ["of"] him; he was getting wicked looking. I then ran out of the house to my cousin Susan Giff. She came back with me and ordered this man out of the house. I had never seen him before. The prisoner is the man. I saw him ["I saw him" crossed out] ... when I and my cousin Susan Giff came back, I saw him shove the knife down in his pocket. I noticed that his face was clean and looked as if it was after been washed; his ears were red. I noticed little bits of grass on his boots. He was in the house about half an hour. I cannot fix the time but it was in the evening before my father came home. I see the pipe produced; it is the pipe he had.

Prisoner: "Did I ask you was Mary Roddy at home?"

Flanagan: "You asked for Molly Roddy."

Prisoner: "Was I two minutes in the house?"

Flanagan: "You were half an hour."

SUSAN GIFF

STATEMENT TAKEN 19 July 1909

I am the wife of Bernard Giff and I live in Barrack Street, Mullingar. I know Lizzie Flanagan; she is my cousin and she lives in the same street. I remember her coming to me in my house on the evening of 7 July 1909. In consequence of what she told me I went out with her to her house. When I went into the kitchen of Lizzie Flanagan's house I saw the prisoner Joseph Heffernan sitting on the bed; I knew him before to see him. He had his two hands together and just as I went in he put one in his pocket – he done this quickly. To look at him quickly you would take him to have drink in. I said to him "get out, out of this you blackguard." He said, "Excuse me ma'am, I am looking for Mary Roddy." Mary Roddy lives in this street a good ways above where I live. She is never in Flanagan's house to my knowledge. She was living in Flanagan's house at one time. I can't give the exact time. He was dressed in dark clothes, a cap, brown leggings and boots. I was not feeling well on this day and I was keeping to the house. The time the prisoner was in Flanagan's house was about three hours before it got dark or a little more. It was before the Flanagan's came to the house that Molly Roddy lived in it.

Mrs ANNE MORAN

STATEMENT TAKEN 19 July 1909

I keep lodgings in Austin Friars Street, Mullingar. I know the prisoner Joseph Heffernan; he came to my house on 5 July 1909. He was lodging with me on 7 July 1909; he was with me that morning. He got up about a quarter to seven o'clock on the morning of 7 July and left my house about a quarter to eight. He told me he was going out to Callaghan's in Robinstown to work. He said he would be back that night if they had not a bed for him; and if not he would be back the following Saturday night. He was dressed in dark blue clothes and a cap with brown soft leggings. The cap was dark and I think a blue colour. He did not come back until nearly ten o'clock that night. He was dressed in good boots in the morning; they had nails in them. He was dressed in the same way when he came back. When he came in I asked him what kept him. He told me that he was up at the Green Bridge, that a girl was killed and that he was looking on. I asked him where he was working and he said that it was in Callaghan's he was working and that he would not stop unless he got seven shillings instead of six as he had worked for him. He was under the influence of drink but he knew what he was doing and saying very well. He then went to bed. He got up on Thursday morning, 8 July 1909, at about a quarter to seven. His face was clean – he did not wash his face in my house. When he got up he sat in the kitchen and while he was there a boy asked me if I wanted a besom and I said I did and bought one. This besom is long pieces of heather tied together and the handle is the roots of the heather. The handle was badly made and I asked him would he trim it for me. He put his hand in his pocket and I went to the front door; when I came back he was nicking off parts of the besom. I said, "That's not a sharp knife." I am quite positive that he had a knife. I could not see the handle but I saw the blade.

He did not finish the besom; he put it to one side. He went for milk and brought some back. He then took his breakfast. I then asked him after breakfast which of the men he worked with yesterday. He said neither of them; that he was knocking about the town looking for a few pints of porter. I advised him to go to work today and he seemed willing and went. The besom produced is the one the prisoner cut.

Prisoner: "Had I a knife?"

Moran: "Yes, I saw the blade when you were cutting the besom."

CHARLES QUINN

STATEMENT TAKEN 19 July 1909

I am a shop assistant in Mrs Bridget Sullivan's Public House in Greville Street, Mullingar. Our shop is beside Whitty's, the bicycle shop. I know the prisoner Joseph Heffernan. On 7 July 1909, he came into our shop between ten and eleven o'clock in the morning. He bought a pipe from me and paid a shilling for it. The pipe produced is the pipe. He sat down and cut tobacco with a knife. I only saw the blade of the knife. He then smoked in the shop.

He called for a pint and got it. He stopped about three quarters of an hour. He had a glass of porter before he went out. He was dressed in a dark suit, a cap, brown leggings and boots. He came back that night about eight o'clock. He had a glass of porter then. He had a little drink taken but he was not drunk. He was dressed then in the same way as he was in the morning. He stopped until about a quarter to nine and during that time he smoked with the pipe he bought from me. A man named Francis Judge was in the shop in the evening. Somebody said there was a girl drowned in the canal. The prisoner was present and passed no remark.

Prisoner: "Do you remember me giving Jack Doyle a glass of porter?"
Quinn: "Yes."
Prisoner: "Did you hear me ask Jack Doyle was there any work about?"
Quinn: "Yes."
Prisoner: "Did Jack Doyle say that Merlehan had four acres of meadow cut?"
Quinn: "I did not hear him say that."
Re–examined, Quinn confirmed this conversation was in the morning.

FRANCIS JUDGE

STATEMENT TAKEN 19 July 1909

I am a shoemaker and live in Mount Street, Mullingar. I remember being in Mrs Sullivan's Public House, in Greville Street on the evening of 7 July 1909. Charlie Quinn is the assistant there. I went there about a quarter to eight o'clock. When I was there about twenty minutes the prisoner Joseph Heffernan came in: this would be about five or ten minutes past eight. About half past eight I went out on to the street. I heard some news in the street; I came into the shop again. The prisoner was there. I said I was after hearing a girl was after been taken out of the canal drowned. The prisoner said nothing. The prisoner was dressed in dark clothes, cap, leggings and boots. His face appeared recently washed and also his hands.

Prisoner: "Do you remember me whistling, and keeping time with my hands in the shop?"
Judge: "I do."

JOHN FALLON

STATEMENT TAKEN 19 July 1909

I am a publican and reside in Mount Street, Mullingar. I remember 7 July 1909. The prisoner Heffernan, with another man, came into my shop between eleven and twelve o'clock on that day. I do not know the man who was with him. The prisoner called for two pints of porter and they both drank them. The man who was with Heffernan called for two pints of porter. Heffernan only drank half of his pint. The prisoner went away; the other man went before the prisoner and said he was going towards the lake. Heffernan did not say where he was going. Heffernan was sober. He was dressed in blue clothes with a blue cap. I could not see whether he had leggings as I was inside the counter.

CHARLES SKELLY

STATEMENT TAKEN 19 July 1909

I am a wash–out Man at Mullingar railway station. I live in Patrick Street, Mullingar. I know the prisoner Joseph Heffernan. I have known him for two years. On 7 July 1909, I went home about 2.30pm. I found Heffernan in my house. He was sitting at the fire smoking a brown pipe with a white mouthpiece. The pipe produced is it. He had drink taken. He was sober and was quite well aware of what he was doing and saying. I had a conversation with him. He asked me could I give him a loan of a razor. I did not give it to him. He asked me to get him one a second time. He said, "Anything at all that would tear the hair off my face would do." My wife gave him some food to eat. He said he was going to work for Merlehan next morning.

After some time, I would say about a quarter past three o'clock, I left the house and he came with me. I was going back to my work at this time. He accompanied me as far as the Green Bridge. I could not say whether he stopped there; I turned and went down to the railway station. I did not see him anymore. I knew where the deceased, Miss Mary Walker lived. The house she lived in is one door further up Patrick Street than mine on the opposite side. I often seen Heffernan with knives; I saw him show them for sale. At the time I left him on the Green Bridge he was dressed in dark clothes, brown leggings, good, new boots with nails in them and a cap.

Prisoner: "Wasn't I often in your house?"

Skelly: "You were."

Prisoner: "Wasn't I often in your house when you lived near Ned Tuite's gate?"

Skelly: "Yes."

Prisoner: "Don't I know you well?"

Skelly: "Yes."

JOHN RAINEY

STATEMENT TAKEN 19 July 1909

I am a Publican and reside in Earl Street, Mullingar. I know the prisoner Joseph Heffernan. He came into my shop on Wednesday 7 July 1909 at about 8.40 or 8.45pm. He asked for a drink. I refused to supply him; I did not consider him drunk and it was not on that account I refused him. I thought him excited; he seemed as if he had been in a row and was running away from some parties. He was keeping his head down. He stopped about a minute and then went out. I was at the door and when going out he said he would get the drink. He used some oath and said something about that he would have revenge. He was dressed in dark suit, cap, brown leggings and boots.

PROFESSOR EDMOND McWEENEY

STATEMENT TAKEN 26 July 1909

I am a professor of medicine in Cecelia Street, Dublin. On 15 July 1909 I received from Constable Charles Moore a parcel containing two sealed packets. In one packet there were articles of clothing stated to have been found on Joseph Heffernan when arrested on 8 July 1909 and a list of the same. In the other packet there were articles of clothing stated to have been taken from the body of the deceased, Mary Walker on 7 July 1909, with a list of same. I examined these articles on 21 July 1909.

As regards the trousers of Joseph Heffernan, I found stains of blood on the left leg. About the left knee and situated 12 inches above the lower end was a diffused dark–coloured stain to which mud was adhering. I found this stain to be due to blood; it is marked Number 1. Higher up the leg on the trousers produced and more to the inside I found a dark superficial indistinct stain about 2 inches long situated 16½ inches above the lower end of the garment; it was also due to blood; it is that marked Number 2 on the same leg of the said trousers. About 13 inches above the lower end of the same leg I found a third stain due to blood, this is marked Number 3. Much higher up the same leg, 22 inches from the lower end and 7 inches from the fork situated towards the back and inside of the leg, I detected another bloodstain; it is that marked Number 8. All the bloodstains which I discovered on this garment were on the left leg. They were all of the nature of superficial ill–defined smears. They responded to all the usual tests, and by means of the new Precipitin Re–action Test I was enabled to determine the stain marked Number 1; the only one to which I applied this particular test, was due to human blood. The lower part of the body of the trousers in front and the adjoining portion of both legs looked and felt damp. The original colour of the stuff was fresher in this place and there was an absence of stains. This moisture and freshness of tinge may have been caused by an attempt to wash the garment.

As regards the leggings produced, on the outside of these were many dark stains not due to blood. I also found a smaller number of minute stains, which were due to blood. Some of the places where I found blood are marked with the labels 1. 2. 3. 4. At the place I marked 1; I found the largest quantity of blood. It was a small, encrusted stain partly hidden in the seam. From this stain I succeeded in obtaining sufficient coloured extract with which to carry out the Precipitin Test, which at once yielded the reaction characteristic of human blood. In addition to the marked stains, close scrutiny with the hand lens revealed many minute splatters or droplets, which at once yielded the reactions characteristic of blood. Near some of these small droplets were little cup–shaped depressions where the surface of the leather was of a brighter colour than elsewhere and seemed to have been scooped out. This may have been done with the object of removing the more obvious spots of blood. I have indicated some of these places with a square in yellow pencil.

As regards the shirt produced, this presented a great number (dozens) of minute bloodstains, none bigger than a pins head. They were scattered over the garment and not confined to any special part. They were mostly on the outside but some were on the inside. I have marked with black ink a few of those, which I tested. As regards the mode of origin of these minute stains, many of them resemble those often seen on the undergarments of verminous individuals. But the wearer of these articles does not seem to have been affected by vermin to the extent necessary to produce so many blood marks on his undergarment. Moreover some of the stains appear to me rather too large to be produced in this way. I have marked with a circle in black ink a group of stains, which I consider too large to have been produced by the bites of vermin. Again, the majority of the stains are on the outside of the shirt. I have not tested these stains as regards the origin human or otherwise. The lower part of the shirt presents a good deal of diffused greyish discolouration. The discoloured places have not the stiffness which is characteristic of seminal stains and even on careful microscopic examinations I have failed to detect Spermatozoon.

As regards the penknife produced, this has a metal handle; it originally carried two blades, the smaller of which now only remains, the larger having been broken off. The fracture has a dull rusty surface and does not look very recent. The instrument also contains a tin opener and a corkscrew. There was some brownish matter resembling a mixture of soil or earth with rust adhering to the knife and especially to the screw but this crumbled away and is now scarcely visible. At first sight no marks resembling bloodstains were to be seen on the knife or outside of the handle. Closer inspection with a powerful lens, however, revealed suspicious reddish or brownish incrustations in the following places: inside the handle, hinges of the blades, the sides and grooves of the tin opener and most of all on the down–turned side of the broken– off blade. On microscopic examination I was enabled to see the individual red blood corpuscles in these incrustations and I noticed that in size, shape and appearance they corresponded with those of human blood. With some trouble I was able to obtain enough solution to apply the Precipitin Test and I then found that the blood was of human origin. On the small blade I found starch grains such as would be contained in bread. They were adhering to minute traces of blood. As regards the clothing of the deceased, I examined them, especially the under garments and they bear the aspects of having been violently rent asunder. Beyond the obvious evidence of violence having been applied to the under garments my examination did not yield any additional evidence of outrage.

CONSTABLE CHARLES MOORE

SECOND STATEMENT, TAKEN 26 July 1909
I am stationed at Mullingar. I arrested the prisoner Joseph Heffernan on 8 July 1909 at about a quarter past eleven am. He was working with Mr Callaghan of Robinstown at the time. I charged him with the murder of Mary Walker on 7 July 1909. I cautioned him. He said, "Is it me? What do I know about it? I know nothing about it." I brought him to the Police Barracks of

Mullingar and his clothes and boots were removed from him in my presence. He had no knife on him. I saw a list made out of his clothes and I then had them made up in a parcel and sealed. I did not in any way interfere with them. I noticed that the left knee of the trousers was damp. I conveyed those clothes to Dublin myself and handed them over to Dr McWeeney myself on 15 July 1909. I also handed him a parcel of the clothes of the deceased, which I received from Sgt Brennan on the 11th last. On Saturday the 24 ["Saturday 24" crossed out and replaced by "Friday 23"] *last I went up to Dublin and received the clothes from Dr McWeeney. They were in a parcel. I also received a parcel of the deceased's clothing. I brought both parcels back to Mullingar on that evening the 24th* ["that evening the 24th "crossed out and replaced by – believe it or not – "the 24th last"]. *I did not allow anyone to interfere with them in any way. The clothes that are produced in court here today are the clothes the prisoner was wearing when I arrested him. He was wearing a dark cap, dark clothes and gaiters when I arrested him. In the parcel of clothes I took to Dr McWeeney, I enclosed the knife produced in court. I see the boots produced; they were worn by the prisoner when I arrested him. I removed them off his feet and have since kept them in my custody.*

ELIZABETH FLANAGAN

SECOND STATEMENT, TAKEN 26 July 1909

I refer to my deposition of 19 July 1909. I see the penknife produced; it is like the knife I saw in Joseph Heffernan's hand in our house. It has the same metal handle.

MICHAEL MURRAY

STATEMENT TAKEN 26 July 1909

I am the son of Patrick Murray and I live in Patrick Street, Mullingar. I will be twelve years old on 15 August next. I have been confirmed. I remember on Wednesday 7 July 1909 going out to milk a goat. The goat was in a field on the racecourse road on the left–hand side going out to the racecourse. This field belongs to my father. The gate leading into it is close to the gate leading into Richard Merlehan's sandpit about nine ["twenty" is added to this figure and initialled – not by Murray] *paces from it on the opposite side of the road. As I was going out to this field at the Green Bridge; I looked at the Chapel clock, it was then about* ["about" crossed out and initialled – not by Murray] *a quarter past four o'clock. It would take me about a quarter of an hour to walk from the Green Bridge to the field. I delayed about five minutes on the Green Bridge and I then walked out along the racecourse road to this field to milk the goat. When I got to the gate of the field, as it was locked, I went in over the paling. The field slopes upwards; the goat was in the middle of the field. I began to milk the goat. Just after I began to milk I heard a scream. It was a middling loud scream; it came from the direction of the canal line. There was a pretty strong wind blowing from the direction of the canal to me at the* time. It was the scream of a woman. I stopped milking and got up and looked about me; I couldn't see anything to account for this scream. From where I was milking, my view of the canal was hidden by some bushes. I then began to milk again. I then heard two or three more screams; they were loud screams and were the screams of a woman. They came from the same direction as the first scream. The last scream was very short. The screams frightened me. I finished milking the goat (it takes me about ten minutes to milk her) and I then came down to the gate of the field which opens on the racecourse road. I got over the paling again. As I was getting over the paling Richard Merlehan passed by. He was coming apparently from the sandpit gate of his own field, which was then in my view about nine ["twenty" added to this figure] paces off. He nodded to me. I did not speak to him; I am not in the habit of speaking to him. I got over the paling and stopped to mend it a bit. I saw Merlehan pass on towards his own house. There is a bend in the road and he got out of my view. I then started to go home along the racecourse road. As I went along the road I came to a gate called Reilly's Gate that leads into one of Merlehan's fields. The gate of our field is about 220 yards from this gate; that is to walk along the road. As I passed Reilly's Gate I looked down towards the canal. I saw a man crossing Scollan's field (that is a field running along beside the railway line). He was near the centre of the field when I saw him and he was going towards the back of the Railway Cottages. These Cottages are on the racecourse road. He was about a quarter of a mile off when I saw him. I could not see how he was dressed; I only saw from his waist upwards. He appeared to be a small man; his legs were hidden by the meadow. He was dressed in dark clothes; he was wearing a dark cap. He was going fast; he was carrying his head stooped. This would be about ten past five or a quarter past. I then hastened on home.

Fr MAGEE

STATEMENT TAKEN 26 July 1909

I remember Wednesday 7 July 1909. On that afternoon I went out to see a sick person beyond Brotenstown. I left the palace about ten or twelve minutes to two o'clock pm. Where I went to, is about five–and–a–half Irish miles. I was riding my horse; he is not fast on the road. The road to Brotenstown is out through Patrick Street and on out by the Valley.

When I was returning along the road in the evening, in the Valley I heard a peculiar shrill piercing sound from the direction of the canal. The wind was blowing from where I was in the direction of the canal; it was a stiff wind. From where I was when I heard this sound to the near side of the canal bank it would be about eighty yards; to the far side it would be about 100 or more yards. At the time I heard the cry I saw Mr Dibbs' boy exercising a tall chestnut horse in the field. I didn't see any girl picking watercress, I was not looking in that [the word "that" crossed out and replaced by "the" and initialled – not by Fr Magee] direction [the following added and initialled – not by Fr Magee – "of the marsh between the road and the canal"].

I did not see anyone on the top of the far side of the canal bank when I heard the sound. I listened but did not hear the sound repeated. I did not pay much attention to it. I then [crossed out], I was [crossed out] … I rode the horse on down Patrick Street and the main street as far as Mary Street. I then rode up Mary Street and on to the Palace Gate. It would be then about a quarter to five o'clock pm. It is about an English mile from the Valley to the Palace Gate. From the Valley Cottages to the Palace Gate I trotted the horse most of the way.

JOSEPH O'CONNELL
STATEMENT TAKEN 26 July 1909

I was in charge of the Ballast Train coming to Mullingar on 7 July 1909. I was coming up the Galway line. My train arrived in Mullingar at twenty–five minutes past four o'clock pm. I produce the record of that. I know the place where Miss Walker was murdered. It would take my train about three minutes to go from that place to the station. I would pass the place of the murder at about 4.22 o'clock pm. I noticed nobody on the canal bank at that time.

CHRISTOPHER DOWNES
STATEMENT TAKEN 26 July 1909

I live in Greville Street, Mullingar. On Wednesday afternoon, 7th last, I cycled out from Mullingar to the racecourse. When I passed the post office on my way out I noticed it was twelve minutes to 5 o'clock pm. I did not see Father Magee. On the Green Bridge I turned down towards the railway station and then out on the racecourse road. There are two gates at the railway at the beginning of the road and between these gates and Clown Bridge I met the prisoner.

I know the well just before you come to Clown Bridge. Where I met the prisoner was about 50 yards the Mullingar side of this well. From this place to the field opposite the Railway Cottages would be about 300 yards. The prisoner did not speak to me when I met him; on former occasions when I met him he would invariably speak to me, that is to say "good morning" or "good evening." I have known him for a long time. When he did not speak to me it struck me. He was dressed in dark clothes and a dark cap. He was walking as usual at his usual pace.

PATRICK GROGAN
STATEMENT TAKEN 26 July 1909

I reside off Dominick Street, Mullingar. I know the iron bridge over the railway called Scout Tail Bridge. On Wednesday 7 July 1909 I saw the prisoner Heffernan coming from the direction of this Scout Tail Bridge. I saw him going down Grove Street; this would be between ["between" crossed out and

replaced by "in or about"] *in or about a quarter to five o'clock pm. Scout Tail Bridge is nearly opposite to where the racecourse road comes in.*
I know the prisoner off and on for the last 20 years. He was dressed on that evening in dark clothes and brown leggings; to the best of my opinion he wore a dark cap. He had his two hands in his trousers pocket and his head stooped as he walked along. He did not speak to me.

JOHN DUIGNAM

STATEMENT TAKEN 26 July 1909

I live in Blackhall Street, Mullingar, which is a continuation of Grove Street. Where I live is close to where Blackhall comes into Mount Street. I know the prisoner Joseph Heffernan well. On the evening of 7 July 1909 I saw him come down Blackhall Street and go on to Mount Street. He passed by the door; this was about five minutes past five o'clock pm. He spoke to me. He said, "Hello, God bless your work." I cannot say how he was dressed.

CHRISTINA McCORMACK

STATEMENT TAKEN 26 July 1909

I am the wife of Thomas McCormack and I live in Gas Lane, Mullingar. It leads across from Earl Street to the Mill Road. I know the prisoner Joseph Heffernan. On Thursday morning 8 July 1909, I was standing at my door; I saw the prisoner Joseph Heffernan pass from the direction of Earl Street on to the Mill Road. This was about half past ten am. When he reached the Mill Road he turned towards the canal. He was dressed in a dark cap, dark clothes and leggings.
Prisoner: "Do you remember that morning at about seven o'clock I went out through that Gas Lane to go to work at Callaghan's?"
McCormack: "I only saw you at half past 10 o'clock."

BRIDGET CREEVY

STATEMENT TAKEN 26 July 1909

I am the wife of Michael Creevy and live in Gas Lane, Mullingar. I know the prisoner Heffernan. On Thursday morning, 8 July 1909, I was coming down the Mill Road from Harbour Street. I saw the prisoner in front of me; he turned out of Gas Lane. He was walking slowly towards the canal. This road ends at the Engine House where the water is pumped up. There is a tunnel there, going under the canal where the water pipe runs. It was about half past ten o'clock in the morning when I saw him. He was dressed in dark clothes and leggings.

MICHAEL VELDON

STATEMENT TAKEN 26 July 1909

I work at Mr Bannon's. I know the prisoner. I remember 8 July 1909. I was working on that morning at Mr Bannon's Store on the canal. I saw the prisoner coming along the canal. He came along a small bit of the bank as I got to the bridge. I know where the Mill Road and Tunnel are; he came from that direction. This was about half past ten o'clock. He came out on the road at Harbour Street and crossed the Harbour Bridge and went out on in the direction of the Workhouse. He was walking at just a nice pace and did not seem in a hurry.

JAMES CALLAGHAN

STATEMENT TAKEN 26 July 1909

I am a farmer; I have a farm at Robinstown. I live there with my brother Patrick who has another farm. I know the prisoner Joseph Heffernan. I have known him for a short time. On Thursday 8 July 1909 he came out to me in a field where I was thinning mangles. It was about a quarter to eleven am when he came to me. If he went by the direct road he should go by the workhouse over the Harbour Bridge. I had not hired him to come out and work for me this Thursday morning. He was not working with me on Wednesday 7 July 1909. When he came out he bid me "Good Morning." I said, "Good Morning."

I asked him did he see my brother and he said he did not. I asked him that because I thought my brother might have hired him. I told him to go and work. There was a man named Gill working with me at this time. Gill asked Heffernan did he hear was there was a girl killed or murdered. He said he heard there was, either killed or drowned. Soon after this the police came and arrested him. I often walked from the Harbour Bridge to my house in a quarter of an hour.

CONSTABLE ROWLETTE

STATEMENT TAKEN 26 July 1909

I am stationed at Mullingar. I know the tunnel that runs under the canal where the water pipe passes to the engine house. A person could get through this tunnel and it is a place that is constantly used as a short cut. I remember 10 July 1909. I went to this tunnel on that day at about 4pm. I went to it through Gas Lane and down The Mill Road. Constable Moore was with me. Sergeant Brennan met us at the tunnel. I searched the tunnel. I found a knife in it. I see the knife produced; it is the one I found. It was seven paces into the tunnel from the Mullingar side where I found it. There are fifty–eight paces in the whole tunnel; the knife was covered with mud under the water pipe. The pipe is close to the floor of the tunnel. It did not appear to be there long. The mud around it seemed to have been recently moved. There was no rust on it. The knife has a metal handle. The large blade was broken, the small blade was intact. It is pretty sharp. It has also got a corkscrew and a picker. I kept it in my possession until the evening of 11 July 1909. I then handed it over in the exact state I found it to Constable Moore. I was present when he put it in the parcel of the prisoner's clothes and sealed it up. It is quite possible to get up from the tunnel on to the canal bank and then on to the Harbour Bridge. I did it myself. I remember 15 July 1909. I was in charge of the prisoner down in the cell in this Court House on that day. He asked to go out to the closet; I took him out. While there he said, "I am afraid they will swear my life away. Do you think if I admitted it, and said I was mad from drink, would I get off with a couple of years? I am sorry I did not run out and down the town when I got the petticoat of a trousers on me. They would say I was mad and send me to the asylum." This statement was absolutely voluntary. I did not use any inducement to make the prisoner say what he did; I did not speak to him at all at the time. When he was arrested and his own trousers taken off him, a trousers was given to him which was much too large for him. This was given until a suit was got for him. I believe that he meant this trousers when he spoke of the petticoat of a trousers.

SERGEANT COOKE

STATEMENT TAKEN 26 July 1909

I was in charge of the escort that conveyed the prisoner Heffernan from Mullingar to Kilmainham Prison on 8 July 1909. In the train between Mullingar and Broadstone he made a voluntary statement. He said, "This is a terrible thing to be charged with. I know nothing about it. I was not even out in that direction yesterday or had no business out that way either. I never left the town on yesterday. I did not take any drink for the past three months until yesterday and I should never take it, because I am not accountable for what I do when I do take it." On 15 July 1909, I was in charge of the escort that brought the prisoner from Kilmainham to Mullingar. When we brought him out of the prison and were conveying him to Broadstone Station he made a voluntary statement.

He said, "I suppose you have plenty of evidence against me now, you have got the knife and everything, but Tom Cole will prove I had no knife. Mrs Moran said I had a knife and that I pared a besom for her ["with it" was entered later and initialled] but I pared it with my fingers. If she got plenty of porter that is all she wants. I suppose her evidence will hang me. She should not tell lies anyhow, many a man was taken in the wrong. They can hang me and if they do they will hang me in the wrong. I don't know the girl at all. I wasn't out on the canal bank that day or had no business out there." Afterwards he said, "They might as well shut me up someplace because if I am left knocking about I will do the same thing again and be taken again. I want to be put someplace where I would be brought up and minded." On 19 July last I was in charge of the escort that brought the prisoner from Kilmainham Prison to

Mullingar. Between the prison and the Broadstone Station he made another voluntary statement.

He said, "I met Jack Doyle in Sullivan's Public House that day; I gave him a glass of porter, I asked him was there any work to be got. He said "Yes, plenty of work, Dick Merlehan of Clown has three or four acres of meadow down. I rambled out the canal bank that day and crossed up the fields; I did not see Merlehan and I did not like to go into the house as I was not great with the woman since I left them last. I slept in Dibbs' field that day. I think it was in the meadow. If I was asked about Clown ["about Clown" is crossed out] was I out about Clown I would have told I was out there but I was not asked. Many a time I went out the canal bank and crossed up to Merlehan's when I was working with him." I did not hold out any inducement at any time to the prisoner to make these statements. I did not speak to him at the time he made the statements or before it.

HEAD CONSTABLE CRUDDEN

STATEMENT TAKEN 26 July 1909

I am the Head Constable at Mullingar. I know the house where the deceased Mary Walker lodged. I took the distance from her house to the Green Bridge (it is 110 Yards) and from the Green Bridge out along the canal line to where the dead body was found (1,188 yards). Thomas Nooney showed me where he was fishing when the prisoner Heffernan passed him going out on the canal bank on 7 July 1909; this place is 484 yards from the Green Bridge and from that place to the scene of the murder is 704 yards. Nooney showed me the spot on the canal where he was fishing when Miss Mary Walker passed out. That place is 384 yards from the Green Bridge, and to the scene of the murder 804 yards. There was exactly 100 yards between the places where Heffernan passed and where Miss Walker passed. Patrick Lyons showed me where he was loading a horse and cart when he looked over and saw Heffernan; that place is at the back of the Valley Cottages. The distance across is 122 yards. I looked across myself. I would recognise any man I knew well at that distance. The place where Lyons pointed out that he saw the prisoner last is 1,100 yards from the Green Bridge and 88 yards from the scene of the murder.

Nellie Woods showed me where she was when she was gathering watercress and heard the cry, this is 49 yards from the scene of the murder. She showed me where she was when she saw Heffernan sitting on the canal bank washing his boots and gaiters. The distance between the two [of] them would be 41 yards. This place where he was sitting, washing his boots and gaiters, is 52 yards from where the dead body was found. Richard Monaghan showed me where he was sitting on the horse when he saw a girl followed by a man come up the canal bank and then saw the man throw her down again; the distance between the two places is 217 yards. The place where the girl was thrown down is 13 yards from where the dead body was found. I know what is called Reilly's Gate that leads into Merlehan's meadow. It is 176 yards from that gate to where a cartway goes through the fence at the foot of the field. From the cartway through the hedge to where he got into the turnip field is 110 yards. As Merlehan walked along across from the cartway to where he got into the turnip field, at half the distance he would be almost opposite where the dead body was found and 126 yards from the spot. Merlehan pointed out all these places to me. From where he pointed out to me that he was picking bones to where he saw a girl stand on the canal bank and look down in the hollow is 314 yards. The distance from there to where he saw the man get through the gap on to the railway is 289 yards. The distance from the sandpit gate to Reilly's Gate is 176 yards and from Reilly's Gate to Merlehan's house is 220 yards.

The boy Michael Murray showed me where he was milking the goat. If you took a direct line from that place to the scene of the murder he would be almost directly behind where Merlehan was standing. He was 154 yards further away from the scene of the murder than where Merlehan was. He was 468 yards from the scene of the murder when he heard the screams. The gate he got out at is 29 yards from the gate of the sandpit field. From the gate of Murray's field to the Reilly Gate is 147 yards. From Reilly's Gate to Merlehan's house is 220 yards. From Reilly's Gate to where the boy saw the man in Scollan's field ["in Scollan's field" is crossed out – replaced by "first"] is 176 yards; the boy pointed out the place. Where Mrs Nugent passed the man who was on the railway, she would be 25 yards from him. The filtering beds are between 50 and 70 yards beyond the scene of the murder. Mrs Feeney showed me where she saw from her window a man squeeze out under a gate in Mr Dibbs' land. From her window to this gate is 41 yards; from that gate to next field where she saw him sit under a tree is 19 yards. I walked from scene of murder to Clown Bridge by the way the man was seen by the witnesses on the 24th last. From the scene of the murder to 50 yards this side of the well near Clown Bridge I walked it in between eleven and twelve minutes. On the same day I walked with the boy Murray from the Green Bridge to the gate in his father's field, it took about fifteen minutes. I walked these distances at an ordinary pace. The average width of the canal is 15 yards.

D.I. RUTTLEDGE

STATEMENT TAKEN 26 July 1909

I am District Inspector at Mullingar. On 7 July 1909 I went out the Royal Canal to where the dead body of Miss Walker was lying and got there at 9.30pm. Her body was lying in the manner described in Constable Holme's deposition. At this place the canal bank slopes down for 30 feet to some marshy ground where there is long grass and rushes. It was in this marshy ground that the dead body was lying. The breadth of this marshy ground to the water ditch is 22 feet; the water ditch is 5 feet across and on the far side of it there is a bank 3 feet high. On the top of the bank is a hedge and wire paling; where the hedge and wire paling are crossed there is a slope up to the railway line of 10 feet.

On examining the scene I saw a bush 18 feet from the top of the canal bank: it is a small hawthorn bush. From the appearance of the grass at that time it was evident that somebody had been sitting there. In my opinion it was the deceased who had been sitting there. From this bush the grass was all dragged down to the foot of the sloping bank for 12 feet as if someone had been dragged down it. At the end of the 12 feet there was a large pool of blood; the grass was greatly trampled about. I believe this was where the murder took place. From that, over to where the dead body was lying, the grass was dragged and where I saw the body lying was 20 feet from the pool of blood. The deceased had evidently been dragged by her left hand and it was still up over her head. From where the body was found to the water ditch is 15 feet. At a place across the water ditch Constable Holmes pointed out two tracks; it was evident that a man had stepped across heavily on the right foot and brought the left one after him. The tracks were sloping up against the bank. At this place there is a gap in the hedge; it is quite easy to get up on the bank across the paling and out on the railway line. By this time it was dark. After the body was removed I left police in charge of the scene with instructions to watch the tracks and allow no one near them. I went out again at 6 o'clock am, on 8 July 1909. I could see the tracks better then; it was only possible to take a cast of the right foot, the left track was too faint.

The ground in which the right track was, was a difficult place to get at: the tracks sloped upwards, the ground was boggy and moist, and there was a good deal of grass and sticks. I thought I would have difficulty in getting an impression at all, and I measured the tracks most carefully. I thought that the hot composition owing to the wet moist ground might contract it.

The length of the track was exactly ten–and–a–half inches; the breadth of the sole was 4 inches, length of the heel 2¾ inches and the length of the instep nearly 3 inches. The track showed that the sole was ribbed with a double row of nails, and there were 3 rows of nails running down the centre of the sole. There appeared to be nails slanting across the toe of the sole, two of which were visible. I produce the boot of the prisoner [the item was then shown]. The measurements I took of the track are identical with this boot. I then took the cast and I produce it. On a later date I got Constable Moore to put on the prisoner's boots and I prepared a place for him to step across at the scene of the murder, just where the first track had been taken. I took a cast of the track he then made and I now produce it. The sole of the original track is slightly shorter than the boot itself, I attribute that to the fact that the footprints sloped upwards and the hot solution shortened it a little. I took a third track of the prisoner's boot in prepared clay at the Barracks and I produce it. The original track was taken before the prisoner was arrested.

INFORMANTS' STATEMENTS

Two other individuals gave statements, but these gentlemen waited until 18 October 1909 to come forward – three months and eleven days after the murder. Luke Sullivan, recently released from prison, and Thomas Rattigan, an ex–convict, gave statements to the police, not as witnesses but as paid informers. With the exception of Sullivan and Rattigan, all of the above witnesses' evidence was written on Form (A. B.) Deposition of a Witness, taken in the presence of Heffernan. Their evidence was written on Form (A.A.) Information and signed at the bottom as Informant. Heffernan was not in attendance while these gentlemen gave their written statements. Sullivan's statement was used at the assizes in Dublin; Rattigan's evidence was not used.

LUKE SULLIVAN

STATEMENT TAKEN 18 October 1909
The information of Luke Sullivan of Barrack Street, Mullingar, Labourer, who saith on his oath that:
I remember Thursday 8 July 1909. I was going from Mullingar to Irishtown by the canal bank on that date. At 8.55 o'clock am I was walking in the direction of the Harbour Bridge when, at the tunnel which runs under the canal near the Pumping Station, I saw Joseph Heffernan on the opposite side of the canal from me, in Mr Christopher Cahill's field. He was about 25 yards out from the tunnel. He was stooped as if tying his boot and looking about him. I said, "Hello Joe." He replied, "Hello my brown son, did you feed him yet." I went on and did not see him after that day. I know the time because I saw the Chapel clock. He wore a blue ["blue" is crossed out and initialled but not by Sullivan] *dark coat and cap. He was looking round him the same as if he was watching someone. To get to the place where I saw him, if going from the town, he should pass through the tunnel, or go round by the Dublin Bridge, or the Harbour Bridge. When I heard of the murder of Mary Walker on quitting work that evening, I thought of Heffernan and where I saw him in Cahill's field. I know Heffernan well I worked with him for a length of time.*

THOMAS RATTIGAN

STATEMENT TAKEN 18 October 1909
The information of Thomas Rattigan of Barrack Street, Mullingar, chimney sweep, who saith on his oath that:
I remember Thursday 8 July 1909. On that morning I was at the Dispensary Corner in Austin Friars Street, Mullingar. There were several other people at the corner at the time. It was about half past eight or a quarter to nine o'clock am. I recollect Joseph Heffernan coming down Austin Friars Street from the direction of the Dublin Bridge. He was walking on the footpath next the Dispensary (that is on the same side of the street). When he reached the Dispensary corner someone spoke to him and said," are you not taken yet Joe?" He said, "For what?" He then ran away towards Gas Lane and turned

into it. I did not see him again that day. I know Joseph Heffernan well. He was then wearing brown leggings and a cap.

This is compelling stuff. At first glance it would be easy to deem Heffernan guilty. There is more than enough "damning evidence" to convict. But is it true? We next move to the Magistrates' hearing in Mullingar where the discrepancies in the evidence begin to emerge.

7.

MAGISTRATES' HEARING, THURSDAY 15 JULY 1909

District Inspector Rutledge opened the case by saying that the prisoner was charged with the murder of Miss Mary Walker between the hours of 4 and 5pm on 7 July. At about 3.15pm, Mary Walker had gone for a walk along the canal line. She did not return. A search was mounted and at 8.30pm, on the canal line, her dead body was found less than a mile from the town. The body was covered with grass and her throat had been cut. From the appearance of the place where the body was found, and from the condition of her clothes, it was evident there was a terrible attack made on her, and that she had put up a hard fight for her life. He would not refer further to the details of the sad business, but would produce the evidence.

Dr Joseph Dillon–Kelly JP stated that he was dispensary doctor in Mullingar and that on the night of the murder he was sent for by the police. He followed the Royal Canal towards the racecourse, to where the dead body of a woman was pointed out to him by the police. That was about 9.30pm. He made a superficial examination of the body, and found her face covered with blood and grass. Her neck was covered with grass and he found a wound four inches long in front of her throat. It was two inches on one side and two inches on the other side of the windpipe. At the same time he examined the deceased's clothes, which were very much torn and disarranged. She had been dead for some hours.

On 8 July, Dr Dillon–Kelly carried out a post–mortem investigation. He found the body well fed and nourished. He made a careful examination of the deceased's head. He noticed no injury, depression or abnormal state of the head or skull, which could be caused by violence. There was a small abrasion on the forehead, which appeared to have been there for some time. There was no other wound or injury on the body except that on the throat. The wound penetrated clean through the larynx and severed it all but a small portion behind. The carotid arteries were not injured. The superior thyroid arteries on both sides were divided. The haemorrhage from these arteries and shock from the injuries was the cause of death. He believed a pocket knife would have caused the wound. The blouse was not torn but was open and also the upper part of the corset. The centre was caught by a little metal catch, which he had some difficulty in opening. The lower part was torn into ribbons, particularly on the right side. Deceased was wearing bloomers composed of dark serge and under that, knickers. There was a large wrench of the bloomers from the centre of the waistband down to the knee. The knickers were similarly torn. The witness formed the opinion the deceased must have been subjected to great violence. Outrage was attempted without doubt.

Dr Michael Ballesty of Mullingar, stated that he knew the deceased. He was the medical officer to the post office in Mullingar. The deceased was, the witness thought, a quite healthy young woman.

Anne Daly of 3 Fairview Terrace, Patrick Street, Mullingar, said that the deceased lodged with her for about fifteen months. She was always in good health and spirits during that time. The witness recalled the day of the murder when Miss Walker returned from the post office about 1.50pm. She had her dinner and then went out for a walk at about 3.15pm. She was dressed in a navy costume with green hat. The witness expected her back for her tea about 6pm. She did not come back, so the witness sent her son Michael to the post office. Michael was employed as a clerk there. On his return, in consequence to what he told her, the witness sent her son to Mrs Kearney in Patrick Street; she used to sew for the deceased. The witness never saw Mary Walker alive again; her dead body was brought to her house about 11pm.

Thomas Nooney, auxiliary postman at Mullingar post office, stated that he lived in Trinity Cottages, Patrick Street. The canal bank was nearly 100 yards from the cottages. He knew the deceased and knew the prisoner also, as he was sometimes employed as a casual messenger in the post office. He remembered that on the day of the murder, at about 2pm, he went fishing in the canal with his brother Matthew. They commenced fishing at a point directly in front of his house. That point was halfway between the Green Bridge and the scene of the murder. They fished slowly back towards the town. He knew the iron gate of the Galway cattle pen and remembered fishing opposite this gate. The witness was on his own side of the canal, (the towing path is on the other side). Whilst fishing at this point, he saw the prisoner coming along the towing path on the opposite side. It was about 3.30pm and Heffernan was going out towards the racecourse. Heffernan stopped and spoke to the witness. There was just about the width of the canal between them. Heffernan asked him if he was catching anything, and he replied that no, he did not think there was anything in the canal there to catch. Heffernan also asked what he was fishing with and witness told him minnow. He had a one–minute conversation with the witness. Nooney could not say how Heffernan was dressed, but he thought he wore leggings.

The witness stated a number of times that Heffernan was walking in the direction of the racecourse. He walked slowly and did not seem to be in a hurry and, as far as witness could see, he was sober. Beyond where the witness was speaking to the prisoner, the canal winds to the right. The Nooney's continued to fish on towards the Green Bridge and came to what they called Merlehan's field. When fishing at that point, Nooney saw Miss Walker coming out on the opposite side of the canal, walking in the direction of the racecourse. That would have been five minutes after the witness had been speaking to Heffernan.

The witness was about twenty yards nearer to the town at the time he saw Miss Walker than when he saw Heffernan. Miss Walker bid him good evening as she passed and continued to walk in the direction of the racecourse. The witness knew that the deceased often walked that way. He did not pay much attention to Heffernan, and fished on to the Green Bridge. He put up his rods about 4pm. The witness knew Head Constable Crudden and had shown him where he was fishing when he spoke to Heffernan; also where he was fishing when he spoke to Miss Walker. When asked if he had any questions to put to the witness, Heffernan replied, "I don't remember talking to you."

In reply to Mr T. J. Shaw JP, the witness stated no person passed between the time he saw Heffernan and Miss Walker.

Matthew Nooney, brother of last witness, deposed that he was fourteen years old. He knew the prisoner well. He used to work around the place where the witness lived. He also knew Miss Walker. On the day of the murder he went to fish with his brother. Matthew had heard how his brother described the fishing, and was with him when Heffernan came along the towpath on the opposite side to the witness. Matthew said they had been fishing for about an hour and a half when he saw Heffernan coming. Heffernan spoke to witness's brother across the canal. The witness said that Heffernan wore a navy suit and wore a pair of brown leggings. Matthew could not say what sort of cap Heffernan was wearing. It was opposite the Galway cattle pen that the conversation took place. Heffernan passed on after the conversation. He did not come back again. Matthew fished on towards the town. He saw Miss Walker coming along the towpath on the opposite side. It was about five minutes after he had seen Heffernan. She spoke across to his brother. At that time, the witness could see Heffernan away in front of Miss Walker on the canal bank. He was walking slowly the same way. After Miss Walker spoke, the witness fished on back to the Green Bridge and got there about 4pm. From the time that Mary Walker passed, until they reached the Green Bridge, no one passed along the bank except one man, who came up and spoke to them, then turned back and went out on the railway road in the direction of the town.

Patrick Lyons, a labourer from Kilpatrick, Mullingar, deposed that he remembered that on 7 July he was carting material at the Valley Cottages, which were being constructed. The place was in view and quite close to the canal. He had known the prisoner for the past four or five years.

On the day in question, he saw Heffernan going along the canal on the towpath on the opposite side from him at about 3.40pm. He was going in the direction of the racecourse and walking slowly. He remarked that Heffernan looked around him and at himself in particular. He was dressed in all dark clothes, including his cap, and he had leggings on him, but the witness could not say what colour they were. The prisoner was over 100 yards from the witness when he first saw him, and remained for about ten minutes in Lyons' view. Heffernan was close on a half mile from the Green Bridge. Lyons was loading the horse and cart at the time and during the ten minutes he was there, the prisoner was moving slowly along, looking about him. Lyons then took his load into Mullingar. When the witness last saw Heffernan he was about 200 yards from him. Lyons had shown the police where he first and last saw Heffernan that day.

Michael J. Daly, son of Mrs Anne Daly, and clerk in the Mullingar post office, deposed that he knew Mary Walker, who lodged in his mother's house. He did not know Heffernan. On the day of the murder, he went to the post office to enquire for Mary Walker. She was not at the post office at the time he called – about 7.50pm. The witness then went home and from there, to Mrs Kearney's home. Miss Walker was not there.

John Lundy, auxiliary postman in Mullingar Office, deposed that he knew deceased. He also knew the prisoner who was sometimes employed as a casual messenger at the post office. To his knowledge, Mary Walker did not come in contact with Heffernan in sending out messages. She used come to the gate at times and hand out messages to the first who was there. Heffernan might have been there on those occasions, and she might have met him in that way.

Ellen Woods, a girl of about 16 years and a daughter of James Woods, of the new cottages near the Valley Cottages, deposed that the canal was not far from where she resided. On the day of the murder, the witness went out about 4.50pm or 5pm to look for her brother Paddy. She went in the direction of the canal bank on her own side. She came straight from the cottages towards the canal bank and walked on it in the direction of the Ballinea road, or towards the racecourse. She knew the place where the dead body of Mary Walker was found. Where Woods was walking on the evening of 7 July was nearly opposite the place where the body was found. When coming out of her house she saw no one on the towpath. The bank slopes down pretty deep on both sides of the canal at this place, and if there had been anyone on the opposite side below the towpath the witness could not have seen the person.

Woods knew there was a tunnel running under the canal. It was opposite the signal pole on the railway line. She went down the bank on her side at this point to pick watercress and whilst so engaged she heard a scream. She said the scream was like the squeal of a cat. There was no person or cat near her. She also noticed Father Magee going along the Ballinea Road towards Mullingar. He was on horseback.

The witness looked across the canal and saw the prisoner on the towpath on the other side. He was washing his hands and wiping his boots. He was sitting on the edge of the canal with his feet down at the water. When he saw the witness, he pulled the cap down over his eyes. The witness knew the prisoner before that time and she identified him as the man she saw. He spoke across the canal to her and said, "Have you aira match?" The witness replied, "No," and added, "If I had one, how would I give it?" He replied, "I thought you'd carry two."

The witness could not describe his clothes except that his sleeve was blue; she did not remark any leggings on him. There was long grass where he was sitting and his feet were only tipping the water, not in it. Where she saw Heffernan sitting was not very far from where the body was found, and was above it. In reply to the Chairman, Woods said it would be about the length from where the chairman was sitting, to where the prisoner now sat in court. She also said she had shown the Head Constable where she was standing when she saw the prisoner sitting on the bank; and also where she was when she heard the scream. At the time she saw Heffernan, she heard a train coming into Mullingar.

The prisoner, in reply to the usual question, then addressed the witness and accused her of making an entirely false statement. The witness denied this but the prisoner then said, "Yes, every word of it. You never saw me that evening, it's all lies."

Richard Monaghan, aged 16 years, deposed that he was employed as a stable boy by Thomas Dibbs. On the afternoon of the murder he was exercising a horse for Mr Dibbs in the fields adjoining the Ballinea road. From 3pm to 5.30pm he was exercising the horse, which was 16.1 hands in height. While exercising the horse, the witness would sometimes have his back to the Ballinea road, sometimes have been facing it, and sometimes he would have gone up the field. The fields slope slightly upwards from the road. When on the horse, he had a clear view of the canal bank across the road.

About 4.30pm he saw a man and a woman run up the bank from the direction of the railway. The woman popped up first and the man came after her. They were almost close together. The woman was partly running, trying to get up the bank. The woman wore dark clothes and hat. He could not say what colour. He saw the man shove the woman down again the moment she came to the top. She went to look around her when she got to the top, but he shoved her down, head first. The man wore dark clothes and cap.

Monaghan could see something on the man's legs – something white, like tops of leggings – but the rushes hid his feet. His coat was blowing open. There was a hard breeze; he heard no cry, nor scream. He did not recognise the woman but he knew Mary Walker. At the time, he did not know whom the man was who threw her down the bank. He knew the prisoner well, as he used lodge in witness's mother's house some time before. Heffernan was similar in height to the man he saw come up the bank after the woman. The witness saw the man swinging his arms in a way that reminded him of Heffernan. Before witness took in the horse, and before he ever heard a word of the murder, Monaghan formed the opinion that the man he had seen was Heffernan. He had shown the place where he was at the time to Head Constable Crudden. The place where the body was found was just at the very spot where he had seen the occurrence described, two yards this side of the signal.

About ten minutes after he saw the man shove the woman down the bank, he saw a girl coming along from Mullingar on the towpath. When she came to the place where the occurrence took place, she stood and looked down the bank. She looked down for about one minute and then walked on about two yards towards the racecourse. Then came back and looked down again. She then continued on towards the racecourse out of the witness's view. She wore dark clothes, and he thought a white hat with a black or dark ribbon. This was a young, thin and reasonably tall girl. He could not say who she was. The witness had seen Fr Magee riding along the Ballinea road towards Mullingar. That was before witness saw the man push the woman down the bank.

Constable Wm Holmes deposed that on 7 July, he was out for a walk along the canal line at about 7.20pm. He walked along past the racecourse and back again. On his way back, he met Mr Wilson of the Ulster Bank and, as a result of what he said, the witness hurried to the spot on the canal about half a mile from the Green Bridge. It was between 8.30 and 8.35pm when he got to the spot. At the foot of the slope there was some long marshy grass. He saw the body of Miss Mary Walker lying there. It was covered with grass; and a knee was bare. She was lying on her back and her hat was on. Her face was covered with blood and her throat was cut. Her head was towards the racecourse and her feet were pointed in the direction of Mullingar. Her right arm was close to her side and her left up over her head.

There was a quantity of blood a few yards on the Mullingar side of where the body was found. The appearance of the long grass gave the witness the impression that the body was dragged from the pool of blood, to where it was found by the left hand. A few yards from where the body was lying there was a gap in the hedge. On the far side of the water ditch, below this gap, the witness noticed two distinct boot prints under the fence, as if someone had jumped across the water ditch.

Holmes took charge of the tracks and allowed no one to interfere with them. Above where the pool of blood was, half way above the bank, there was a little bush and at this bush the grass looked as though someone had been sitting there. It was beaten down and the grass from that to the pool of blood was also flattened, as if a body had been pulled over it. From the appearance of the ground there must have been a great struggle. The witness took charge of the body until it was removed. He saw constables Foskin and Harrington pick up gloves, a belt, and the pocket of a skirt at the place where the body was lying.

D.I. Ruttledge, addressing the bench, said he did not propose to go any further on the present occasion, and applied for a remand, which was granted till Monday at 11am.

While the Chairman was speaking at the end of the hearing, Heffernan broke down and cried.

8.

MAGISTRATES' HEARING,
MONDAY 19 JULY 1909

Richard Merlehan, Clownmore, farmer, deposed that on Wednesday, 7 July he was working at Clown Bridge from 2pm to about 3.30pm or 4pm. He then went home for dinner. His house was on the Racecourse Road. He spent some time at his dinner and, after that, went along the Racecourse Road coming to an iron gate about 200 yards from his house. The field to which this gate led was down towards the railway line and the canal and, having passed through the gate, the witness went down by the mearing ditch, to the foot of the field where there is a hedge between the field and the railway line. There is a cartway through this hedge. Merlehan went through this cartway and then went along the hedge on the railway side, until he came to a field where there were turnips planted. At the time, he was walking in the direction of the racecourse and had left the railway line and the canal to his right. He knew where the dead body of Miss Walker was found. When halfway between the cartway and the turnip field, the witness was about 100 yards from the place where the body was found. He stated that he thought that was the nearest point he was to it.

It was about 4.35pm when he reached that point and at that time he saw no one on the railway line or canal bank. He did not hear any screams or cries. He knew the little bush on the canal bank, a little above where Miss Walker's body was found. It would be in his view from where he was at that time, but he could not see the slope of the canal bank below the bush. He could not see into the bottom of the hollow between the canal bank and the railway line. It would be impossible from where he was to see into it. Anyone could be in that hollow without the witness knowing it. When the witness arrived at the turnip field he opened the fence gate and went up the field looking at the turnips. His back been then towards the railway line. At the top of the turnip field there is a sandpit, by which the witness passed. He then went on towards a gate, which leads out to the racecourse road, but this was a different gate from the iron gate through which he came. When four or five yards from the gate, Merlehan stopped to pick up some bones. He had given permission to a man to throw old bones into the sandpit in his field. When doing this, the witness turned and looked in the direction of the railway line and canal. He saw a girl standing on the canal bank, right over the place where the dead body was found.

She was apparently looking over at the witness, as if she wanted to speak to him. She was about 300 yards from the witness at the time. The witness moved a few paces to the right, onto higher ground to get a better view of her, and to give her a chance of seeing him better. Merlehan then went over to the pit where he deposited the bones, from which they had probably been taken by dogs. The girl still stood looking. The witness again looked towards the canal and saw the girl walking on towards the racecourse, and this gave the witness a still better view of her. The second time she came back she might have been looking for about a minute or two. That would be about 4.45pm. She then turned and went on towards the racecourse, and the witness's last sight of her was at the bushes at Mr Downes' field. From the time the witness first saw her, till he last saw her, she was about ten minutes in his view. She wore a long dark cloak or jacket, dress length, which was blowing open. She was wearing a hat, which was either dark brown or black in colour. He could not say exactly. She was a young woman of medium size.

There was a strong wind blowing from the canal at the time. The girl appeared to keep her hands in her pockets. He did not see her hat blow off, and he did not see her trying to keep her hat on. She kept her arms down by her side. Merlehan did not know who this girl was. When she turned and went on towards the racecourse for the second time, the witness saw a boy come up to the railway line. He believed that he had come up from the left of the place where the dead body was found, and right opposite to the place where the girl had been looking down.

This place was between a signal pole and a telegraph pole. When he came up on the railway line, this boy started to walk away along the line in the direction of Mullingar. The witness saw him go about five or six perch, at which point he was hidden from Merlehan's view by some bushes, midway between where he saw him first and the red cabin on the railway line. The witness did not see the boy again. He had on a short round dark coat, with a small cap or black hair, or ne'er a cap at all. It was a close fitting cap if he wore one. He seemed to the witness to be a low sized man. The witness knew the prisoner well. He could not say if the man he had seen walking on the line was like the prisoner. Heffernan worked with the witness on and off for the previous two years up to the previous November. Since that time, he had not been working with the witness. Heffernan was not a constant smoker, but when he had a toothache the witness had seen him smoking. Merlehan had seen Heffernan with a penknife sometimes. One time he saw him with two penknives. He had a habit of trucking with other fellows. The knife he would have one week might be swapped for another the following week. Heffernan carried a razor.

After seeing the man on the railway line, the witness went home and arrived there about 5.15pm. He looked at his watch. All the time he was out, the witness had only seen the one woman and the one man. He heard no screams at any time. When he was coming up from the house the first time, as he reached the iron gate, he thought he heard the voices of children, and that was what took him down the way he went. He thought the children might be at the crabs, or tramping the meadow and he went down to put them off.

In reply to a subsequent question from the D.I. as to what the meaning of the word "boy" was, the witness said he meant man, he did not mean a little boy. The deposition was corrected accordingly.

The prisoner, when asked if he had any question to put, said,

> *"Yes, I was in Sullivan's that day. Jack Doyle told me that you had four acres of a meadow cut. I crossed over the railway line and could not see you at the house. I was looking for a job, but did not like to go near the house as I had a row with the woman."*

The bench stopped the prisoner, and asked him to put a question if he wished.

> *Prisoner to witness: "Had you a meadow?"*
> *Witness: "No, I was thinking of cutting it today."*
> *Prisoner to witness: "Jack Doyle told me you had. That's what drove me out in that direction."*

Bridget Nugent, wife of John Nugent, who resided in Mary Street, Mullingar, deposed that on 7 July she left Mary Street to go out to her father's house on the racecourse. She could not give a definite time that she left Mullingar, but thought it was about 4.45pm when she reached the Valley. She walked out along the canal bank and passed the Trinity Cottages, which were on her right. She knew a little red signal cabin on the railway line. When she got there, she saw a man on the railway line. He was coming towards her. The witness did not know the place where the dead body of Miss Walker was found. After she passed the red signal cabin, she saw the man on the railway line coming on towards her. He was walking slowly with his head down. He had on dark clothes and a cap and was low–sized. When she saw the man first, he was a good bit below the signal pole in the Galway direction. Mrs Nugent knew two stone filtering beds that cross the hollow between the canal bank and the railway line. These were beyond the signal pole. It was a little past these stones that Mrs Nugent and the man passed each other. The man did not look at the witness as he passed.

At this stage in the proceedings, the police put a navy blue cap on the prisoner and he was ordered to stand up in the dock. The D.I. addressed the witness:

> D.I.: *"Do you see the prisoner in the dock?"*
> Witness: *"Yes."*
> D.I.: *"Is this the man you saw?"*
> Witness (after a look and a pause): *"He is not unlike the man."*
> D.I. to prisoner: *"Sit down."*
> D.I.: *"Did you know Heffernan?"*
> Witness: *"No."*
> D.I.: *"As you came up to him, did you see anything in the hollow?"*
> Witness: *"No."*
> D.I.: *"You pledge your oath to that?"*
> Witness: *"Yes."*
> D.I.: *"Did you stop opposite the signal pole?"*

The D.I. asked Mrs Nugent if she stopped opposite the signal pole. She said her hat blew back and she stopped; that would have been about the signal pole. She turned around slightly and raised her left arm to the hat. The delay was about one minute. The witness then walked straight on after that to her father's house. Apart from the man she had mentioned, she saw no other man on the railway line or the canal. She did not hear any cry or scream. She could not give any idea of the distance the man was from her when she saw him, but she saw him distinctly; he was walking in the middle of the railway line.

Elizabeth Feeney, wife of John Feeney of Railway Terrace, Mullingar, deposed that her husband was then a signalman. The cottages look out on the racecourse road and her room had a window looking out onto same. At about 3.30pm on the day of the murder, her children came home from school. About an hour and a half later, the witness happened to be looking out of the window towards the racecourse road.

Somewhat to the right of her window, on the road a little down a lane, there was a gate leading out of Mr Dibbs' field. The gate came out almost where the lane opened onto the road and had barbed wire on the top rung. The witness saw a man squeezing out under the gate. There was a very narrow space between the bottom of the gate and the ground, and the man nearly got stuck there. He wore dark clothes, a cap and brown leggings. According to the witness, the prisoner was not unlike the man she saw, but she could not swear to his face, as she had not seen it. The witness was about 20 yards from the man when she saw him, but he was the same height as the prisoner.

At this point DI Ruttledge said, "Put the cap on the prisoner." The same cap was again put on the prisoner, and he was asked to stand up. The witness was requested to look at him.

D.I.: "Is that the man?"
Witness: "I did not see his face; it was his back I saw."
D.I.: "Is he like the man you saw?"
Witness: It is very like him. The cap more to his face. I think, it is very like him."

She said that when he squeezed out under the gate, the man did not go along the main road, but went down the lane and got through a gap in the hedge. He then turned to the left and sat down in the hedge. The field was just across the road from her house, and the hedge is pretty tall there. The witness had some fowl running in the field and sometime before, some of her fowl had been stolen. The witness ran down the stairs and went out to look after her fowl when she observed the movements of the man. She got to the gap directly opposite her house – a different one than the man got through. Her children were playing in the field at the time. When she got through the gap, she saw the man still sitting where she first saw him sit down. He was holding down his head and the witness could not see his face very well. She made a circle round him by going out into the field. She got out at the little lane in a gap, below where the man had got in, and came up the lane to the main road. When she was passing the place where he was sitting, she heard him moving. She looked through the hedge and saw him skirting on by the hedge on the field side, towards Mullingar. At the end of this hedge there was a gap, through which a person could get down from the hedge, to the Clown road just near the bridge.

The prisoner, when asked if he wished to ask any questions, said he had taken a sleep in one of Dibbs' fields and that he did not remember seeing the witness.

Elizabeth Flanagan, a girl of about fourteen years and daughter of Joseph Flanagan of Barrack Street, deposed that, on the evening of the murder, she was left at home to mind her three little brothers and a sister. Before her father came home, a man came to the house. He asked for Molly Roddy. He said he was working out in the country and that Molly Roddy invited him in to have a great day of it. The man wore a black cap, black clothes and had on a pair of brown leggings and nailed boots. The witness noticed that the boots were newish. There is a bed in the kitchen of the witness's house. The man went over to it; he said it was a grand bed and sat down on it. He then lay down on the bed and put one hand on the back of his neck and the other at the front of his throat. He then sat up in the bed, shoved his hand down into his pocket and took out some tobacco, which was loose – not in a pouch. He then took out a knife, cut the tobacco and filled his pipe, which was a new wooden pipe with tin lid and white mouthpiece.

The witness saw the knife. It had a lead handle and it opened like a penknife. It had a thin blade, narrow and was not too bright in colour. The witness noticed a stain like blood on the handle of the knife. The man asked witness for a "readier" to clean his pipe. Miss Flanagan did not have one. He then lit the pipe and smoked it. He blew his nose about this time with what appeared to the witness to be a handkerchief. He took it from his pocket and it was stained with what appeared to be blood. The witness asked what happened to the handkerchief and the man accused her of looking for news. He was cross. He gave no explanation except that he was skinning a goat and the meat of it tipped against the handkerchief. He was restless, getting up off the bed and walking about and then sitting down again. Flanagan told him to leave – that her mother was sick in the next room and that the priest was coming to see her. He said he would like to go and see her mother. Her mother was not, as a matter of fact, in the house at the time. The man, when he went into the hall, asked the witness whether she would like to be married. There was laughter in court at this comment. The witness replied, "What do you want to know that for?" The man then pulled out some money and asked her to go down for a quart of porter and that they could drink it together. She told him she had to get her father's dinner ready and would not go for it. She was getting frightened of the man, who was getting wicked looking. The knife was not in his hand at the time.

Flanagan then ran out of the house to her cousin Susan Giff, who came back with her and ordered the man out of the house. Flanagan had never seen the man before. She identified the prisoner in the dock as the man who was in her house. When Susan Giff came in, the witness saw the man shove the knife into his pocket. The man's face looked as if it had been washed, and his ears were red. His boots had a little bit of grass on them, as if he had gone through a field. He was in the house for about a half an hour. This was in the evening, sometime before Miss Flanagan's father came home. The witness identified the produced pipe as that which the man had.

The prisoner said there were two little children in the house. He then addressed the witness:

> Prisoner: "Did I ask you if Mary Roddy was at home?"
> Witness: "No, you asked me if Molly Roddy was at home."
> D.I.: "It is the same – Mary and Molly."

The prisoner then made a statement to the effect that Elizabeth Flanagan said she would go outside and look for Roddy.

Prisoner: "I was only two minutes in the house."
Witness: "No, you were half an hour."
Prisoner: "Tell out the truth. I was only two minutes in the house. Tell the truth and you need care about no one. There may be people who seen me go in and out and they can prove I was only there two minutes, so tell the truth. Before God, I was not more than two minutes; she went out and brought in this woman."

Mrs Susan Giff, wife of Bernard Giff of Barrack Street, deposed that she knew Lizzie Flanagan, who lived in the same street, and remembered her coming to her home on the evening in question. In consequence of what Lizzie had told her, she accompanied her cousin to her house and when she went into the kitchen, she saw the prisoner sitting on the bed. The witness knew him to see. He apparently had his two hands together when the witness came in and he put one in his pocket quickly. He appeared as if he had drink in him.

The witness said, "Get out, out of this you blackguard."

He said, "Excuse me, ma'am, I'm looking for Mary Roddy."

Mary Roddy lived a bit away and, to Mrs Giff's knowledge, was never in Flanagan's house any more. She had lived in that house one time. The man was dressed in dark clothes, a cap, brown leggings and boots. The witness did not feel well that day and was keeping to the house. She said it was not anything like 9pm when this happened. It was about three hours or more before daylight was gone. It was about 9pm when the witness heard of the murder, and it was some hours before this that the events above occurred.

The prisoner asked no question but said he had a misfortune that, through a drop of drink, he might go into any house and not know well which it was, but it was with no bad intention he went in.

Anne Moran deposed that she kept lodgings in Austin Friars Street. She knew the prisoner, who came to her house on the 5 July. She had him three days there: Monday, Tuesday and Wednesday. He was lodging with her on 7 July and was in the house that morning. He got up at about 6.45am and left the house about 7.45am. He said he was going out to Callaghan's in Robinstown to work and that he would be back that night if they had no bed for him. If he was not back he would be back on the following Saturday night.

He was dressed in dark blue clothes, a dark navy blue cap and yellow or brown soft legging, not of leather. He did not come back till very nearly 10pm that Wednesday night. He was then dressed the same way. The witness noticed in the morning that the prisoner was wearing good boots with nails in them. When he came in that night Moran asked him what kept him. He said he had "been up at the Green Bridge and that a girl was killed and he had been looking on." He told her that he had been working in Callaghan's but that he would not stop with him unless he gave him seven shillings a week. He only gave him six shillings a week and no bed.

The witness did not notice him much that night, except that he was under the influence of drink, but he was still aware of what he was saying and doing. The following morning, he got up about 6.45am and did not wash his face in her house. His face was clean. He sat on the form in the kitchen. A boy called at the time selling besoms and the witness bought one. The besom was pieces of heather tied together. The witness gave Heffernan the besom to trim as the handle was badly made. He seemingly put his hand in his pocket for a knife apparently.

Anne Moran went to the front door and when she came back, Heffernan was apparently smigging the tops of the besom off. She noticed his knife and said, "That's not a sharp knife Joe." She could not see the handle but saw the blade of the knife. He did not finish the broom; he put it to one side. He then went for milk and brought some back and he then took his breakfast. After that, the witness asked him whether he had worked with Callaghan or Merlehan the previous day. He said he had worked with neither of them, that he was knocking around the town looking for a few pints of porter. The witness advised him to go to work that day and he replied, saying that he was just going. He seemed quite willing to go out to work and went at about 7.45am. Anne Moran did not see him further.

> Prisoner to witness: "I had no knife. I broke off the top of the besom with my fingers."
> Witness: I was under the impression you had a knife."
> Prisoner: "The besom can be examined if it can be got. There was a tramp there in your house."
> Witness: "He was no tramp."
> Prisoner: "Well, he was a walkabout tramp."
> Chairman: "You must ask a question. Do you wish to ask about what you said, that you had no knife?"
> Prisoner: "Yes, had I a knife?"
> Witness: "I was fully under the impression that you had a knife."

The prisoner said he was working for five weeks at Tom Coloe's, beyond Killucan and no one could see a knife with him there.

Subsequently the besom was produced in court and identified by Mrs Moran, who repeated that she saw the knife and called prisoner's attention to it.

Charles Quinn, shop assistant to Mrs Bridget Sullivan of Greville Street, Mullingar, which is situated beside Whitty's bicycle shop, said he knew the

prisoner. On 7 July, between 10am and 11am, the prisoner came into the shop and bought and paid for a one–shilling pipe, which witness identified as that produced in court. He sat down and cut some tobacco with a knife. The witness saw the blade only. Heffernan smoked in the shop, called for a pint, and stayed there about three quarters of an hour. He had a pint of porter and also a glass of porter just before he went out. He was wearing dark clothes, a cap and brown leggings and boots.

He came back to the shop that night about 8pm and got a glass of porter. He was not drunk but had a little drink taken. He was dressed the same way as in the morning.

He left the shop about 8.40pm. When he entered the shop that evening he was smoking the pipe he had bought earlier in the day. A man named Francis Judge was there in the evening, and someone in the shop said at the time the prisoner was there, that there was a girl drowned in the canal. The prisoner passed no remarks on that.

The prisoner could only put questions and, having stated he wished to ask a question on the matter of this statement, the Chairman put the question as follows for the prisoner:

> *Chairman: "Do you remember hearing me ask Jack Doyle if there was any work about?"*
> *Witness: "Yes."*
> *Chairman: "Did Jack Doyle say that Merlehan had four acres cut?"*
> *Witness: "No, I don't remember that, I did not hear that."*
> *To the D.I.: The witness stated this conversation was in the morning.*

Francis Judge, a shoemaker from Mount Street, deposed that he was in Sullivan's Public House about 7.45pm on the evening in question. Between 8.05pm and 8.10pm, the prisoner came into the shop. The witness went out of the shop at about 8.30pm and heard some news in the street. He went back into Sullivan's again. The prisoner was still there and the witness said to Charles Quinn that he had heard that a girl had being taken out of the canal. The prisoner said nothing.

The prisoner asked the witness if he remembered him playing a trick, whistling and keeping time with his hands, in the shop. The witness replied in the affirmative.

John Fallon, a publican from Mount Street, deposed that on the forenoon of the day of the murder the prisoner came into his shop. It was between 11am and 12 noon. There was another man with him that the witness did not know. The prisoner called for two pints of porter and the men drank them. The other man then called for two pints, but Heffernan only drank half of his second pint. The other man left before the prisoner and said he was

going towards the lake. Heffernan did not say where he was going. Heffernan was sober and was dressed in blue clothes and cap as described, but the witness could not say about the leggings, as he was inside the counter and could not see if he had on leggings or not.

The prisoner asked no questions of this witness.

Charles Skelly, a wash–out man at Mullingar station who resided in Patrick Street, said he had known the prisoner for two years. On 7 July, at about 2.30pm, the witness came home for his dinner and found Heffernan in his house. He was sitting at the fire smoking the pipe produced by the police. He had some drink taken, but was well aware of what he was doing and saying. Heffernan asked the witness whether he could give him a loan of a razor, but the witness did not give it to him, as he did not have one. The prisoner pressed him to get him one, saying, "Anything at all that would tear the hair off my face would do." The witness said his wife gave the prisoner some food. He said he was going to work for Merlehan the next morning. After some time, the witness left the house. It was then about 3.15pm. The prisoner left the house with him. The witness was going back to his work at the time and the prisoner accompanied him as far as the Green Bridge. The witness turned down to the railway station and did not know what way the prisoner went. He saw him no more. Skelly knew the late Mary Walker, as she lodged in the same street as he did. His house was on the opposite side to where Mary stopped, but was nearer to the Green Bridge. The witness often saw Heffernan with knives; he used to be showing them for sale. When the witness last saw Heffernan at the Green Bridge he was wearing dark clothes, a cap, brown leggings and good boots, which were almost new and had nails in them.

> Prisoner: "Wasn't I often in your house?"
> Witness: "Yes."
> Prisoner: "Was I not often in your house when you lived in Ned Tuite's?"
> Witness: "Yes."
> Prisoner: "Yes, I know you well, that is the reason I used to go in, and we often had a drink together, and will again with the help of God."

The witness stated that, to his knowledge, the prisoner had no drink in his house.

John Rainey a publican on Earl Street, deposed that he knew the prisoner. He came into the witness's shop on the day in question at about 8.40pm or 8.45pm. He asked the witness for a drink, but the witness refused to serve him. Rainey did not consider him drunk, but it was not on account of his condition in regard of drink that the witness refused to supply him. He seemed very excited. He thought he had been in a row and was running away

from some parties. He was holding his head down. He stopped in the shop for about a minute and then left, stating that he would get a drink and cursed with some oath, making a remark that he would have revenge. He wore a dark suit and cap, some sort of leggings and boots. The prisoner said he did not remember being in Mr Rainey's shop at all. He might have been in it, but he did not remember.

D.I. Ruttledge addressed the bench and said that he would go no further that day and asked for a remand for a week. The Chairman asked whether he expected to finish then. D.I. Ruttledge replied saying that it depended on the analysis. The Chairman asked whether he had any intimation as to when the analysis was likely to be ready. D.I. Ruttledge said he had not, but that he had been informed that it would take a fortnight. The prisoner was then remanded until the following Monday at 11am.

9.

MAGISTRATES' HEARING, MONDAY 26 JULY 1909

Dr Edmond McWeeney, MA, MD, M Ph., of 84 St. Stephen's Green, Dublin, deposed that he was professor at the School of Medicine in Cecilia Street, Dublin. On 15 July the witness received a parcel containing two sealed packets from Constable Charles Moore. In one of these packets were articles stated to have been found on Joseph Heffernan, when he was arrested on 8th of July and there was a list of the same. In the other packet were articles of apparel taken from the body of the late Miss Mary Walker on 7 July. On 21 July, the witness examined the articles. He stated:

> *I detected stains of blood on the left leg of the trousers. About the left knee, and situated about 12 inches above the lower end was a diffused–dark coloured stain to which mud was adhering. I found this stain to be due to blood. It is marked "No. 1." Higher up the leg and more to the inside on the trousers produced, I found a dark superficial indistinct stain, about two inches long, situated 16½ inches above the lower end of the garment. It was also due to blood. It is the place marked "No. 2" on the same leg of the trousers produced. About 13 inches above the lower end of the same leg, I found a third stain due to blood. This is marked "No. 3." Much higher up the same leg, 22 inches from the lower end and seven inches from the fork, situated towards the back and inside leg, I detected another bloodstain. It is that marked "No. 8." All the bloodstains which I discovered on this garment were on the left leg. They were all of the nature of superficial, ill–defined smears. They responded to all the usual tests and by means of the new Precipitin Re–action Test, I was enabled to determine that the stain marked "No. 1" – the only one that I applied this particular test to – was due to human blood. The lower part of the body of the trousers in front and the adjoining portion of both legs looked and felt damp. The original colour of the stuff was fresher in this place, and there was an absence of stains. This moisture and freshness of tinge may have been caused by an attempt to wash the garment.*

Leggings were now handed to the witness and he said:

> *On the outside of these were very dark stains not due to blood. I also found a small number of minute stains which were due to blood. Some of the places where I found blood are marked with labels "1. 2. 3. 4." At the place marked*

"1," I found the largest quantity of blood. It was a small, encrusted stain, partly hidden in the seam. From this stain I succeeded in obtaining sufficient coloured extract with which to try out the Precipitin Test, which at once yielded the re–action characteristic of human blood. More examination is sought. In addition to the marked stains, close scrutiny with a hand lamp revealed minute splatters or droplets, which at once yielded the re–action characteristic of blood. Near some of these small droplets were little cup–shaped depressions where the surface of the leather was of a brighter colour than elsewhere and seemed to have been scooped out. This may have been done with the object of removing the more obvious spots of blood. I have indicated some of these places with a square and yellow pencil.

A shirt was then handed to the witness, and his evidence in regard to it was as follows:

This presented a great number – dozens – of minute bloodstains, none bigger than a pin's head. They were scattered over the garment, and not confined to any special part. They were mostly on the outside, but some were on the inside. I have marked a few of those which I tested. I have marked these with black ink. As regards the mode of origin of these minute stains, many of them resemble those often seen on the under–garments of verminous individuals, but the wearer of these articles does not seem to be affected by vermin to the extent necessary to produce so many blood marks on his undergarments. Moreover, some of the stains appear to me rather too large to be produced in this way. I have marked with a circle in black ink a group of stains, which I consider too large to have been produced by a bite of vermin. Again the majority of stains are on the outside of the shirt. I have not tested these stains as regards their origin, human or otherwise. The lower part of the shirt presents a good deal of diffuse greyish discolouration.

A pocket knife was then handed to the witness and he said:

This has a metal handle. It originally carried two blades, the smaller of which now only remains, the larger having been broken off. The fracture has a dull rusty surface, and does not look very recent. The instrument also contains a tin opener, and a corkscrew. There was some brownish matter resembling a mixture of soil or earth with rust adhering to the knife, and especially to the screw, but this crumbled away and is now scarcely visible. At first sight no marks resembling bloodstains were to be seen on the knife or outside of the handle. Closer inspection with a powerful lens, however, revealed suspicious reddish or brownish incrustation in the following places: inside of the handle, hinges of the blades, the sides and grooves of the tin opener, and most of all on the down–turned side of the broken–off blade. On microscopic examination I was enabled to see the individual red blood corpuscles in these incrustations and I noted that in size, shape and appearance they correspond

with those of human blood. With some trouble I was enabled to obtain
enough solution to apply the Precipitin Test, and I then found that the blood
was of human origin. On the small blade I found starch grains such as would
be contained in bread. They were adhering to minute traces of blood.

Regarding the clothing of the deceased, which were handed to the witness, he stated he had examined them, especially the undergarments. They bore the aspect of having been violently rent asunder. Beyond the obvious evidence of violence having been applied to the undergarments, his examination of them did not yield any additional evidence of outrage.

Constable Charles Moore, Mullingar, deposed that he arrested Joseph Heffernan at about 11.15am on 8 July. The prisoner was then working at Callaghan's, Robinstown. The witness charged the prisoner with the murder of Mary Walker on the 7 July and cautioned him. The prisoner said, "Is it me? What do I know about it? I know nothing about it." The witness brought the prisoner to the police barracks in Mullingar and his clothes and boots were removed from him in the witness's presence. He had no knife upon him. The witness had a list of the clothes taken off the prisoner drawn up and the clothes were then parcelled and sealed. He did not interfere with the clothes in any way. He noticed that the left knee of the trousers was damp. On 15 July, he conveyed the clothes to Dublin himself and handed them over to Dr McWeeney. He also handed Dr McWeeney a parcel of clothes of the deceased, which he had received from Sgt Brennan on the 11 July. On 24 July, he received the clothes back from Dr McWeeney in Dublin. They were in a parcel and sealed. He also received a sealed parcel containing the deceased's clothing, and brought both parcels back to Mullingar on the same evening. He allowed no one to interfere with them in any way. The clothes produced in court were those that the prisoner was wearing when arrested. He wore a black cap, dark clothes and gaiters when the witness arrested him. The metal knife was included in the parcel of clothing sent to Dr McWeeney.

Elizabeth Flanagan stated that the knife produced by the police was like the knife that she saw in the prisoner's hand when he was in her house on 7 July. It had the same metal handle.

Michael Murray, son of Patrick Murray, Patrick Street, deposed that he would be twelve years on the following 15 August. He had been confirmed. He remembered that on the day of the murder he went out to milk a goat, which was in a field on the left–hand side of the road as one went out to the racecourse. The field belonged to the witness's father and the gate leading into it was close to the gate leading into Richard Merlehan's sandpit, about twenty paces from it on the opposite side of the road. When on the Green Bridge, the witness looked at the chapel clock and saw it was 4.15pm. It would take him about a quarter of an hour to walk from the Green Bridge to his field. He delayed about 5 minutes at the Green Bridge and then walked out the racecourse road to his father's field to milk the goat. The witness went into the field, over the paling as the gate was locked. The witness began to milk the goat. Just after he began to milk the goat, the witness heard a reasonably loud scream. It was a woman's scream. It came from the direction of the canal line. There was a pretty strong wind blowing from the canal line towards the witness at the time. The witness stopped his milking when he heard it, and got up and looked about him. He couldn't see anything to account for the scream. His view of the canal was hidden by some bushes.

The witness began to milk again and heard two or three more screams coming from the same direction. The last scream he heard was very short. The screams frightened the witness. He finished milking the goat. It took about ten minutes to milk the goat. He then came down to the gate that opens on the racecourse road. As he was getting over the paling, he saw Richard Merlehan pass him. He was apparently coming from the sandpit gate of his own field. Merlehan nodded to the witness. The witness did not speak to him. He was not in the habit of speaking to him. The witness got over the paling and stopped to mend it a bit. He saw Merlehan pass on down towards his own house. There was a bend on the road and at this bend Merlehan went out of Murray's view.

He then started for home by way of the racecourse road. As he went along he came to Reilly's Gate (which leads into Merlehan's field). It was about 220 yards from the gate of Murray's field to Reilly's Gate, walking towards Mullingar. As he passed Reilly's Gate he looked down towards the canal and saw a man crossing Scollin's field, which is alongside the railway line. He was near the centre of the field when the witness saw him and was going towards the rear of the Railway Cottages, which are on the racecourse road. The man was about a quarter of a mile off when the witness saw him. He was a small man. He only saw the man from the waist upwards. His legs were hidden by the meadow. He was dressed in dark clothes and wore a dark cap. He was going fast. His head was stooped. The witness was about ten minutes mending the gate. It was 5.10pm or 5.15pm when the witness saw the man. Witness then hastened home.

After further examination by the D.I., the witness said it was no more than 5pm or 5.15pm when he saw the man in the field.

Revd J.L. Magee CC, Mullingar, deposed that on the 7 July he went out in the afternoon beyond Brotenstown to visit a sick person. He left the palace just before 2pm. The place he went to was about five or five–and–a–half Irish miles off. The witness was riding a horse. It was not a fast horse on the road. The road to Brotenstown runs through Patrick Street and on by the valley. When returning in the evening he heard a peculiar shrill, piercing sound from the direction of the canal. A stiff wind was blowing across the canal from where he was at the time. From where the witness was on the road to the near canal bank, he would calculate the distance to be about 80 or 90 yards and to the far side of the canal about 100 or more yards.

At the time he heard this sound, he saw Mr Dibbs' boy exercising a tall chestnut horse in a field. He did not see any girl picking watercress. He was not looking in the direction of the marsh between the road and the canal. He saw no one on the path of the canal at the far side. He heard the sound only once. He concluded, on reflection, that it might be the cry of children playing on the opposite side of the canal.

He was walking his horse at the time through the Valley, and when he reached the first of the cottages, he trotted the horse and rode it through Patrick Street, down Dominick Street, and up Mary Street and home. When he reached the Palace Gate it was probably about 4.45pm. The Palace Gate was about one English mile from the place where he heard the sound on the Valley road. He trotted the horse most of the way from Patrick Street home.

Joseph Connell, 5 Temple Buildings, Dominick Street, Dublin, guard on Midland Great Western Railway (MGWR), deposed that he was in charge of a ballast train coming to Mullingar on 7 July. He was coming up the Galway line and his train arrived at 4.25pm in Mullingar. He produced the record of the hour of arrival. He knew the place where Miss Walker was murdered, and it took him about three minutes to go from that point to the station. He would pass the place of the murder about 4.22pm. He noticed nobody on the bank of the canal at that time.

Christopher Downes, Greville Street, Mullingar, deposed that he cycled out to the Mullingar racecourse on the day in question. He noticed that it was 4.48pm as he passed the post office. Between the post office and the Green Bridge, he did not see Father Magee. At the Green Bridge, the witness turned down to the left and out on the racecourse road. Between the railway entrance gates at the beginning of the road and Clown Bridge the witness met the prisoner. He knew the well just before Clown Bridge; it was about 50 yards on the Mullingar side of the well that he met the prisoner. From that point to the field in front of the Railway Cottages would have been about 300 yards. The prisoner did not speak to witness. The prisoner invariably spoke to the witness when he met him – that is to say "good morning" or "good evening." He had known prisoner for a long time. It struck the witness that the prisoner had not spoken to him on this occasion. He said that the prisoner was wearing dark clothes and a dark cap and was walking in his usual way.

Patrick Grogan, Grove Street, deposed that he knew the iron bridge over the railway called Scoutail Bridge. On the day of the murder, he saw the prisoner coming from the direction of Scoutail Bridge and going down Grove Street. It was about 4.45pm. The Scoutail Bridge is nearly opposite the place where the racecourse road comes in on the railway road. The witness had known the prisoner for twenty years. Heffernan was walking with his hands in his pockets and had a kind of a crith or stoop on him. He did not speak to the witness.

John Duignan of Blackhall Street, a continuation of Grove Street, deposed that his house was close to the point where Blackhall opened into Mount Street. He knew the prisoner well. He remembered that on the evening in question he saw Heffernan come down Blackhall and go on towards Mount Street at 5.05pm. He spoke to the witness as he passed his door, saying "Hello! God bless your work."

Christina McCormack, wife of Thomas McCormack, lived in Gas Lane, which leads from Earl Street to Friars Mill Road. She knew Joseph Heffernan. On the morning of 8 July she saw Heffernan pass through Gas Lane out in the direction of the Mill Road at 10.30am. When the prisoner reached the Mill Road he turned down towards the canal.

> Prisoner: "About seven o'clock in the morning, do you remember, I went out along Gas Lane to work in Callaghan's?"
> Witness: "You passed at 10.30am and Sgt Brennan came up just after you."
> Clerk: "Answer his question."
> Witness: "I saw him at 10.30am."

Bridget Creevy, wife of Michael Creevy, Gas Lane, deposed that she knew the prisoner, and on Thursday 8 of July she was coming down the Mill Road from Harbour Street. She saw the prisoner in front of her. He turned out of Gas Lane. He was walking slowly in the direction of the canal. The road ended at the engine house where the water was pumped up. There is a tunnel going under the canal where the water pipe ran. It was about 10.30am when she saw Heffernan, who was darkly dressed and wore leggings.

Michael Veldon stated on entering the witness box that he was a bit deaf. He deposed that he was a labourer and works at Mr Bannon's. He knew the prisoner. On the morning of 8 of July he was working at Mr Bannon's stall on the canal. He saw Heffernan come along the canal. He came up just a little bit off the bank as the witness was going to the bridge. The witness knew where the Mill Road was and where the tunnel was.

At 10.30am, Heffernan came from that direction. The prisoner came out at the road at the head of Harbour Street, crossed the Harbour Bridge and went on in the direction of the workhouse. He was walking at just a nice pace, not very hard, and did not seem to be in a bit of a hurry.

James Callaghan, a farmer, deposed that he had land at Robinstown and lived there with his brother, Patrick, who had another farm. He knew the prisoner for a short time. About 10.45am on 8 of July, Heffernan approached Callaghan, who at the time was working in a field of mangolds. The witness had not hired the prisoner to come out to Robinstown and work on that Thursday morning. Heffernan said, "Good Morning," to which the witness replied, "Good Morning." Callaghan then asked him if he had seen his brother. The witness thought it might have been his brother who had hired the prisoner.

The witness told the prisoner to go and work. There was a man named Gill working with the witness on that day and Gill asked Heffernan whether he had heard that a girl had been murdered. Heffernan said he had heard that there was a girl who had been either killed or drowned. Soon after that, the police came and arrested Heffernan. Heffernan addressed the witness saying that his brother had asked him to go out to the farm.

Constable Thomas Rowlette, Mullingar, deposed that he knew the tunnel referred to, which brought the water pipe to the engine house. He stated that a person could get through the tunnel but must stoop down and nearly go on hands and feet. It was constantly used as a shortcut. On 10 July, the witness went to the tunnel about 4pm. He went to it through Gas Lane and down the Mill Road. Constable Moore was with the witness and at the tunnel Sgt Brennan met the witness.

They searched the tunnel and the witness found a knife, which was then produced. The knife was lying about seven paces into tunnel from the Mullingar side. There were fifty–eight paces in the whole tunnel. The knife was under the pipe and covered with mud. The pipe was close to the floor of the tunnel. The knife did not appear to have been there for a long time; the mud around it seemed to have been recently moved. There was no rust on the knife. It had a metal handle and the large blade was broken. There was also a corkscrew and a picker on the knife. The witness kept the knife in his possession till the evening of the 11 July, when he handed it over in the exact state in which he had found it to Constable Moore. The witness was present when Constable Moore put the knife in the parcel of the prisoner's clothes and sealed it up. It was quite possible to get up from the tunnel and walk along the canal bank towards the Harbour Bridge. The witness had done it himself; it was often done.

The witness recalled that on 15 July he was in charge of the prisoner in the courthouse, guarding the cell that day. The prisoner asked to go out to the closet and the witness took him out. Whilst there, the prisoner said to the witness:

I'm afraid they will swear my life away. Do you think if I admitted it and say I was mad from drink, would I get off with a couple of years? I am sorry I did not run out and down the town when I got the petticoat of a trousers on me. They would say then I was mad and send me to the asylum.

The witness gave the prisoner no inducement to make the statement. He did not care whether he made it or not. The statement was a voluntary one. The trousers, which had been put on Heffernan when arrested, belonged to another man and were much too large for him. That was what the prisoner meant when he used the words "petticoat of a trousers."

Sgt Cooke deposed that he was in charge of the escort that conveyed Heffernan from Mullingar to Kilmainham on 8 July. In the train between Mullingar and Broadstone, the prisoner made a voluntary statement. He said:

This is a terrible thing to be charged with. I know nothing about it. I was not even out in that direction yesterday or had no business out that way either. I never left the town yesterday. I did not take any drink for the past three months until yesterday and I should never take it, because I am not accountable for what I do when I take it.

On 15 July, the witness was in charge of the escort that brought the prisoner to Mullingar from Kilmainham. When on the way from the prison to Broadstone in a cab, the prisoner made a further voluntary statement to the witness. He said:

I suppose you have plenty of evidence against me now. You have got the knife and everything, but Tom Coloe will prove I had no knife. Mrs Moran said I had a knife, and that I paired a besom with it for her, but I paired it with my fingers. If she got plenty of porter that is all she wants. I suppose her evidence will hang me. She should not tell lies anyhow, many a man was taken in the wrong. They can hang me, and if they do they will hang me in the wrong. I don't know the girl at all. I was not out on the canal bank that day or had any business out there.

Afterwards the prisoner said:

…they might as well shut me up some place, because if I am left knocking about I will do the same thing again, and be taken again. I want to be put someplace where I would be brought up and minded.

On 19 July, the witness was again in charge of the escort from Kilmainham, and between that place and Broadstone the prisoner made another statement, as follows:

I met Jack Doyle in Sullivan's public house that day. I gave him a glass of porter, I asked him was there any work to be got. He said yes, plenty of work. Dick Merlehan of Clown has three acres of meadow down. I rambled out the canal bank that day and crossed up the fields. I did not see Merlehan, and I did not like to go into the house, as I was not great with the woman since I left them last. I slept in Dibbs' field that day. I think it was in meadow. If I was asked was I out about Clown I would have told I was out there, but I was not asked. Many a time I went up the canal bank and crossed over to Merlehan's when I was working with him."

The witness told the Chairman that he offered no inducement to make a statement at any time.

Head Constable Crudden deposed that he knew the house where the deceased lodged. It was 110 yards from her residence to the Green Bridge. From the Green Bridge to where the dead body was found it was 1,188 yards. Thomas Nooney showed the witness where he was fishing on the day of the murder when Heffernan passed. That was 484 yards from the Green Bridge, and on to the scene of the murder, 704 yards. Nooney showed the witness the spot where he was fishing when the deceased girl passed out, that was 384 yards from the Green Bridge, and to the scene of the murder, 804 yards. There were 100 yards exactly between where the Nooney's saw the prisoner and where they saw Miss Walker.

Patrick Lyons showed the witness where he was loading a horse and cart when he saw Heffernan on the canal line. That was the back of the Valley Cottages. The distance across was 122 yards. The witness looked across and he stated that if he knew a man he would recognise him at that distance. The place where Lyons said he last saw the prisoner was 1,110 yards from the Green Bridge and 88 from the scene of the murder. Nellie Woods showed witness where she was when she was gathering watercress and heard the cry. It was 49 yards from the scene of the murder. She also showed the witness where she was when she saw the prisoner sitting on the bank, washing his boots and gaiters. The distance between Woods and Heffernan at the time was 41 yards. The place she stated she saw Heffernan washing his boots was 52 yards from where the dead body was found.

Richard Monaghan showed the witness where he was sitting on a chestnut horse when he saw a woman come up the bank of the opposite side of the canal, and a man throw her down again. The distance from the place Monaghan showed the witness, to where he stated he had seen this was 217 yards. That was about 13 yards from where the dead body was found. He knew Reilly's Gate leading into Merlehan's meadow. From that gate, through the fields, to where there was a cartway going through the hedge, it was 176 yards. From the bottom of the field to the turnip field where Merlehan stated he got in is 110 yards.

From where Merlehan stood when he saw the girl come along the canal and look down to where that person was standing, it was 314 yards. From the same place (Merlehan's) to the gap where he stated he saw a man get up on the line was 289 yards. From the sandpit gate to Reilly's Gate was 176 yards and from Reilly's Gate to Merlehan's house it was 220 yards. Michael Murray showed the witness where he was milking the goat. The boy must have been pretty much, almost behind Merlehan when milking the goat. The boy was 154 yards further from the scene of the murder than Merlehan was. He must have been 468 yards from the place of the murder when he heard the screams.

The field where the boy got out was 29 yards from the sandpit gate, and to Reilly's Gate from that gate it was 196 yards, and from Reilly's Gate on to Merlehan's house it was 220 yards. From Reilly's Gate to Murray's gate it was 147 yards. From where the boy stood at Reilly's Gate to where he saw the man going through Scollin's field was 176 yards. The distance between Mrs Nugent on the canal line and the man walking on the railway, who she passed when at the filter beds, would have been 25 yards. The filtering beds were between 50 and 70 yards from the scene of the murder. The distance from Mrs Feeney's window to where she stated she saw a man squeeze out and under the gate was 41 yards.

From that gate to where she said a man sat under a tree in the field nearby was 19 yards. On 24 July, the witness had walked from the scene of the murder to Clown Bridge by the route taken by the man. From the scene of the murder to 50 yards this side of Clown Well it took him between 11 and 12 minutes. On the same day, he walked out with Michael Murray to his gate. It took about 15 minutes from the gate to the Green Bridge. The witness walked these distances at an ordinary pace. The average width of the canal is 15 yards.

D.I. Rutledge stated that he went to where the dead body of Miss Walker lay at 9.30pm on the day of the murder. The body was lying in the manner described by Constable Holmes. At this place, the canal bank slopes down for thirty feet to some soft marshy ground, long grass and rushes. In the ground where the dead body lay, the breadth of the marshy ground from the canal bank to the water ditch was 22 feet. The water ditch was 5 feet across and on the far side of it there was a bank 3 feet high. On the top of the bank was a hedge and wire paling. Where these were crossed, there was a slope up to the railway line of 10 feet. On examining the scene, the witness saw a small hawthorn bush 18 feet from the top of the canal bank. From the appearance of the grass, it was quite evident that someone had been sitting there, and D.I. Ruttledge believed this person to have been the deceased.

From the bush, the grass was displaced for 12 feet down to the foot of the sloping bank, as if someone had been dragged down it. At the foot of the bank there was a large pool of blood and the grass was greatly trampled. This must have been the spot where the murder had taken place. From here to where the body lay, the grass was also dragged, and the place where the body was found was 20 feet from the pool of blood. The deceased had evidently been dragged by her left hand, which was still up over her head.

From where the body was found, to the water ditch was just 15 feet. At a point across the water, and directly opposite the body, Constable Holmes pointed out two tracks to the witness. It was evident that a man had stepped across on the right foot heavily and brought the left after him. The tracks were sloping up against the bank. At this place there was a gap in the hedge, and it was only necessary to climb up the hedge and through the gap to get onto railway line. It was comparatively easy to get up this way. At this time, it was dark and after the body was removed, the witness left police in charge of the scene until the following morning, with instructions to watch the tracks and allow no one near them.

On 8 July, he went to the same place and could see the tracks better then. It was only possible to take a cast of the right foot – the left track was too faint. The ground in which the right was placed was difficult to get at to take a cast, as it was very boggy and moist and there was a good deal of grass and sticks. Because the witness thought it would be difficult to get a good cast, he measured the track carefully before taking it.

He thought the hot composition might affect the track as it was going into wet ground and therefore might contract it. The length of the track was exactly 10½ inches. The breadth of the sole was 4 inches, length of heel 2¾ inches, and the length of instep nearly 3 inches. The track showed that the sole was rimmed with a double row of nails. There were three rows of nails running down the centre of the sole. There appeared to be nails slanting across the toe of the sole, two of which were visible. The witness produced the boot of the prisoner.

The measurements that the witness took of the tracks, before taking the cast, were identical to those of the boot produced. He produced the cast, which the Magistrate then inspected. The witness stated:

> On a later date, I got Constable Moore to put on the prisoner's boots, and I prepared a place for him to step across at the scene just where the first track had been taken. I got him to step across and took a cast of the impression. I produce that cast.

The Magistrate inspected this cast also. The witness explained that he could not get the ground exactly as it was before. The sole of the original track was slightly shorter than the cast or the boot itself, and this he attributed it to the footprints slanting upwards. He then produced a third track of the prisoner's boots, made in the barracks in prepared clay. The original cast was taken before the prisoner was arrested.

Constable Moore deposed that he had seen the boots. They were the boots worn by the prisoner when arrested. The witness removed them and kept them in his custody. Constable Moore was at that time holding the boots in his hands in the witness chair.

The Clerk asked the prisoner if he wished to ask any questions, to which the prisoner replied, "I have nothing to say, only keep them safe for me – that's all."

The Clerk, Mr R.B. Lee, took the greatest care throughout the lengthy depositions that all details in the evidence should be faithfully and exactly recorded, whether arising out of the direct replies of witnesses or as a result of the prisoner's questions. He read the charge of wilful murder of Miss Walker to the accused and addressed him, asking, "Have you any questions to ask?"

> Prisoner: "No."
> Clerk: "You are not bound to make any statement now, but if you do, I am to tell you that it will be taken down in writing and may be used against you."
> Prisoner (standing in front of dock and with considerable animation): "No: only I did not kill her; that is all; I did not kill her."
> Clerk – Do you wish to examine any of the witnesses now before their worships?"
> Prisoner: "No."

The Chairman said it was unnecessary for him to say anything with regard to the evidence. He wished, however, to congratulate Mr Power and his staff on the very exhaustive manner in which they had examined this very important case. With regard to Mr Rutledge, he had presented the evidence in Court in a manner worthy of the best traditions of his profession. He had been very fair and had asked very direct questions indeed. The prisoner would, of course, be returned to take his trial at the next Winter Assizes for County Westmeath.

The prisoner addressed the Magistrate, saying, "I hope you won't go hard against me anyway."

The accused was taken from the dock by the police, five of whom stood around him, and the court rose, having sat from 11am until 3.45pm, with the exception of a forty–five–minute adjournment.

On the journey to the railway station, which took place some minutes after the close of the court, the prisoner was once more the object of execrations. Desperate attempts were made by a crowd, numbering many hundreds, to seize him. However, the people were kept back by a strong force of constabulary. At the station, there was another manifestation of wild hostility, but the constables, aided by a couple of the priests, succeeded in placing Heffernan unscathed in a compartment of the Limited Mail (Sligo portion).

Joe Heffernan being escorted from Mullingar railway station to local courthouse in Mount Street. Photo taken on Monday, 26 July 1909 at Grove Street as he left the station through the side gate. (Courtesy Irish Newspaper Archives and the *Westmeath Examiner*, Mullingar)

Sgt Thomas Cooke and Head Constable John Crudden pictured at Crudden's wedding in June 1909, exactly one month before the murder of Mary Walker. Both men were involved in Heffernan's trial and conviction. (Courtesy Éamonn MacRodain)

Joseph Heffernan was visiting Charlie Skelly at this house and walked out through the door for the last time at approximately 3.15pm on 7 July 1909. (Copyright © Jack Kiernan)

The Red Cabin (Copyright © Jack Kiernan)

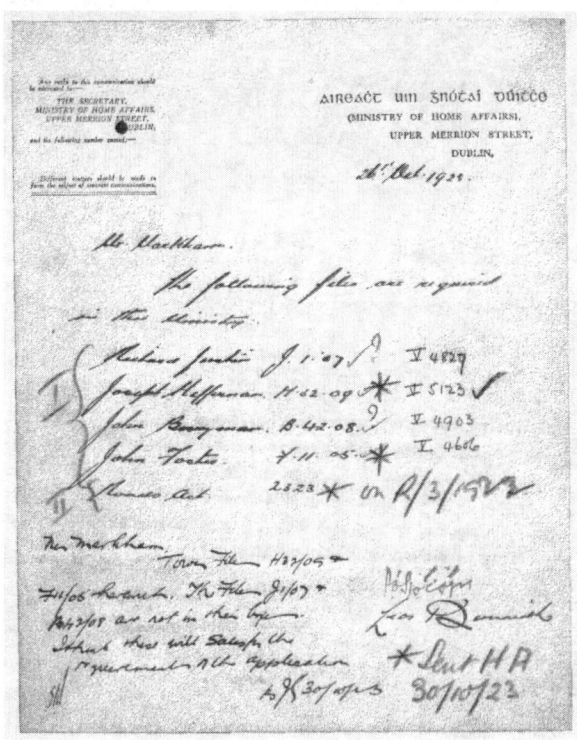

Letter from Ministry for Home Affairs dated 26 October 1923 requesting Heffernan's file. (Courtesy of National Archives, Dublin)

Mary Walker's lodgings. She walked out through the door of this house for the last time at approximately 3.15pm on 7 July 1909. (Copyright © Jack Kiernan)

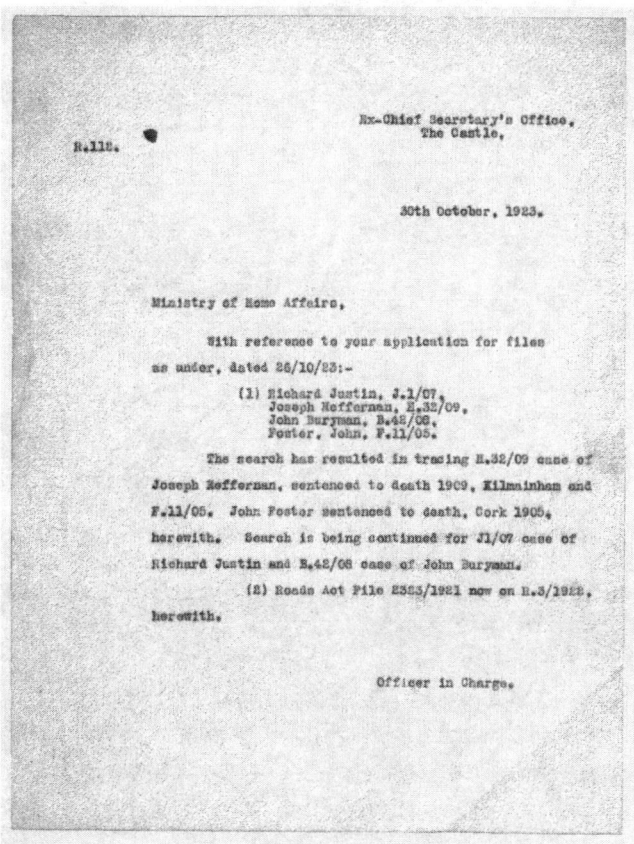

Letter dated 30 October 1923 from Dublin Castle to Ministry of Home Affairs, confirming the fact that Heffernan's case file was traced. (Courtesy of National Archives, Dublin)

The gallows, Kilmainham Gaol, where Joe Heffernan was executed on 4 January 1910. (Copyright © Jack Kiernan)

Picture taken at 4.30pm on 7 July 2009 on the hundred anniversary of the murder of Mary Walker. (Copyright © Jack Kiernan)

Mary Walker's headstone in Ballyknockan Cemetery, Leighlinbridge, Co. Carlow. (Copyright © Jack Kiernan)

The inscription on Mary Walker's headstone reads, "In Memory of Mary Walker, Ballinaboley, who died at Mullingar, July 7th 1909 aged 32 years having nobly won a martyr's crown. He that shall lose his life for me shall find it. Math X." (Copyright © Jack Kiernan)

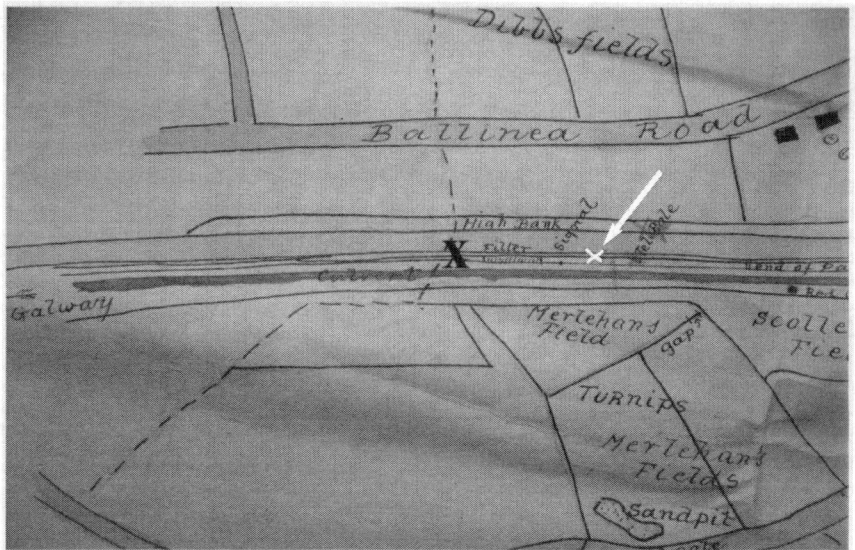

The white X marks the spot where Joyce's map indicates Miss Walker's body was discovered. This is on the Mullingar side of the filter beds. However, Mr Joyce's measurements, together with police measurements, indicate that the body was found on the Athlone side of the filter beds, marked with the black X. The memorial cross erected by locals is situated at the black X. The evidence of Monaghan and Merlehan puts the murder scene on the Mullingar side of the filter beds. How and why did this happen? (Courtesy of National Archives, Dublin)

Fr. Magee (right of photo), who was a witness at the trial of Joseph Heffernan. (Courtesy of Ruth Illingworth, Davy Hynes and Mullingar Showcase)

The arrow points to where Joyce's map indicates the body was found from the railway side. The signal pole is still in place. (Copyright © Jack Kiernan)

Kilmainham Chapel, where Heffernan attended Mass on the morning of his execution. (Copyright © Jack Kiernan)

The tunnel, located about two kilometres from the murder scene at the Springfield area of Mullingar, where Constable Rowlette alleged he found the murder weapon. (Copyright © Jack Kiernan)

Census of Ireland, 1901. Joseph Heffernan is listed as a farm servant in the Grimes household.

Dr Dillon–Kelly (seated centre wearing white coat) pictured with nuns and nurses from the Mercy Convent, Mullingar. (Courtesy of Davy Hynes and Westmeath Showcase)

The filter beds as you can see are still there, as sited in Joyce's map of the murder scene. The map puts the crime scene on the Mullingar side of the filter beds. However, the police and Joyce's measurements put the crime scene on the Athlone side of the filter beds. (Copyright © Jack Kiernan)

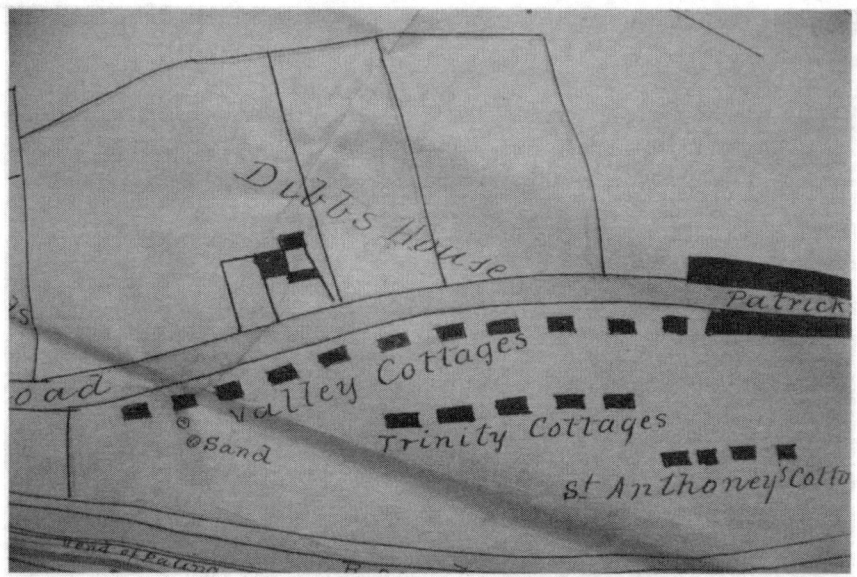

Map showing location of Dibb's house and surrounding fields. Note: St. Anthony's Cottages are incorrectly running parallel to the road. (Courtesy of National Archives, Dublin)

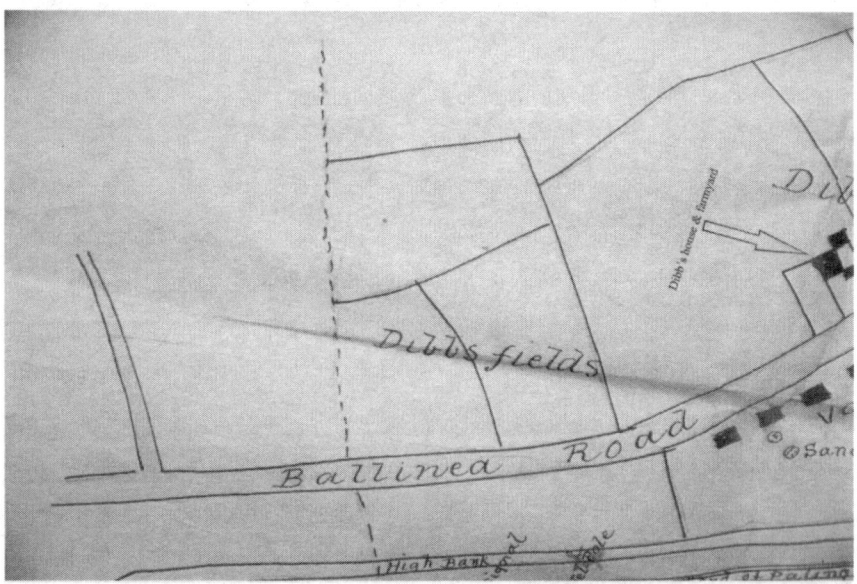

Dibb's field, where the prosecution alleged that Richard Monaghan was exercising a horse and witnessed the struggle. (Courtesy of National Archives, Dublin)

According to police and Mr Joyce's measurements, the cross on the right marks the scene of the murder. However, according to Mr Joyce's map of the crime scene, the arrow on the left of the picture also points to the murder scene. How did this happen and why was it not questioned by the defence? (Copyright © Jack Kiernan)

X on the left marks the spot where the Nooney's commenced fishing, approximately 200 yards from where they met Joe Heffernan (centre X) and approximately 300 yards from where they met the victim, Mary Walker (X on the right of the picture). Joe Heffernan and Mary Walker were on the opposite side of the canal. (Copyright © Jack Kiernan)

According to the police and Joyce's measurements, the arrow on the right points to where Miss Walker's dead body was found. However, Joyce's map places the murder scene approximately 150 yards closer to Mullingar. (Copyright © Jack Kiernan)

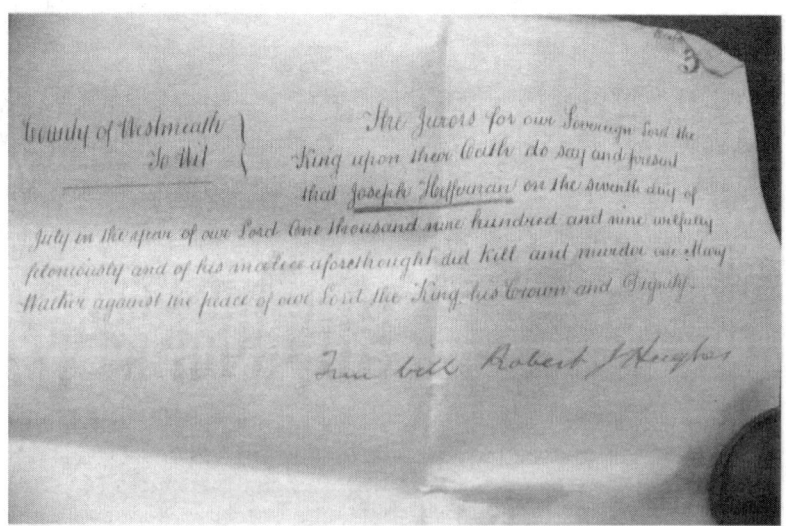

Confirmation of the jury's guilty verdict. (Courtesy of National Archives, Dublin)

THE NEW LORD CHIEF JUSTICE OF IRELAND,
MR. PETER O'BRIEN.

On account of his track record, and their inability to obtain guilty verdicts, Lord Chief Justice Peter O'Brien was retained by the British authorities for their prosecution in agrarian cases. It was during this period that he earned the name, 'Peter the Packer', for his ability to pack juries with men whom he knew would convict defendants. While O'Brien was a Catholic, he was also a Loyalist. Listed among his friends was none other than leading loyalist, Mr Edward Carson.

Mary Walker's relatives, from left: Joe Brennan, Marie Waldron, Kathleen Delaney, Johnny Brennan and Nicholas Brennan. (Courtesy of the Brennan family, Carlow)

the prisoner when he
said "It is a hard Case
but I suppose I deserve
it".

I submit this in
Compliance with instructions
Contained in the Second
paragraph of Circular (Copy attached)
No 479.

M.M. Gavan
Gov.

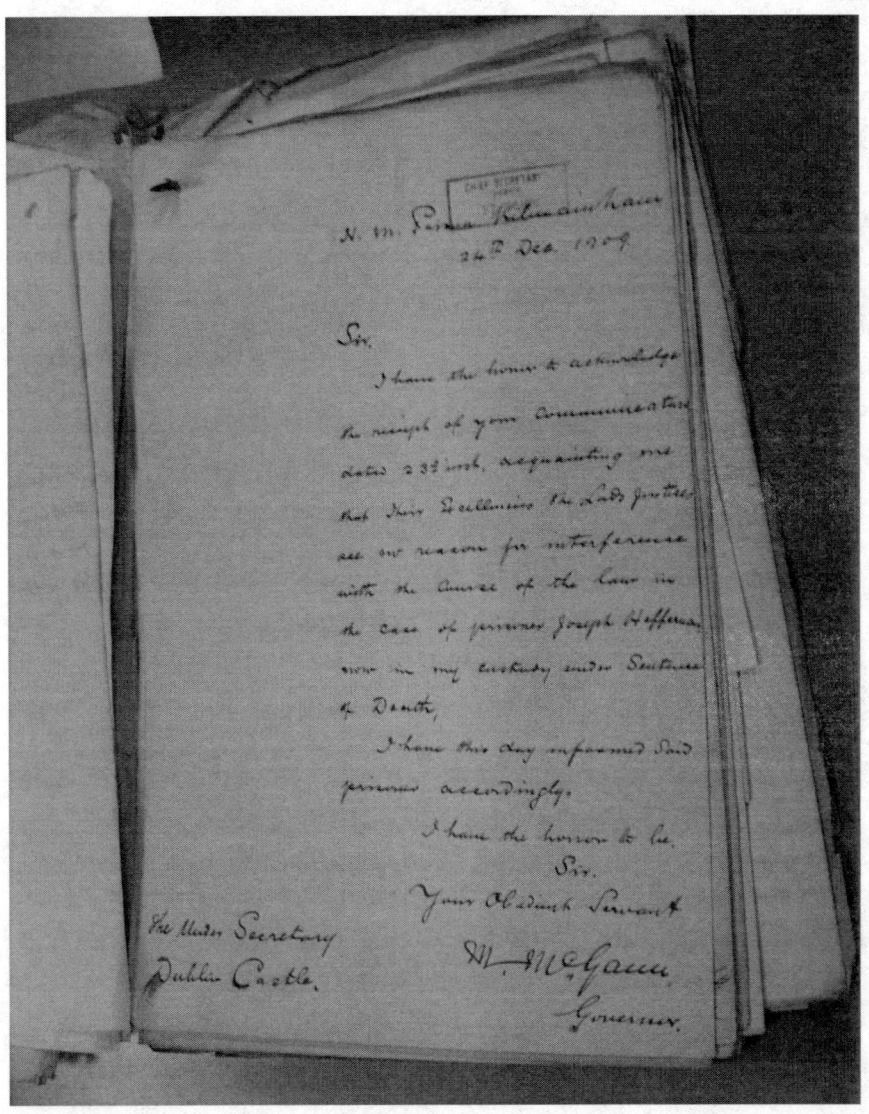

This page and previous: Two letters, each purported to have been written and signed by the Governor of Kilmainham on Christmas Eve 1909. But note the difference in the signatures.

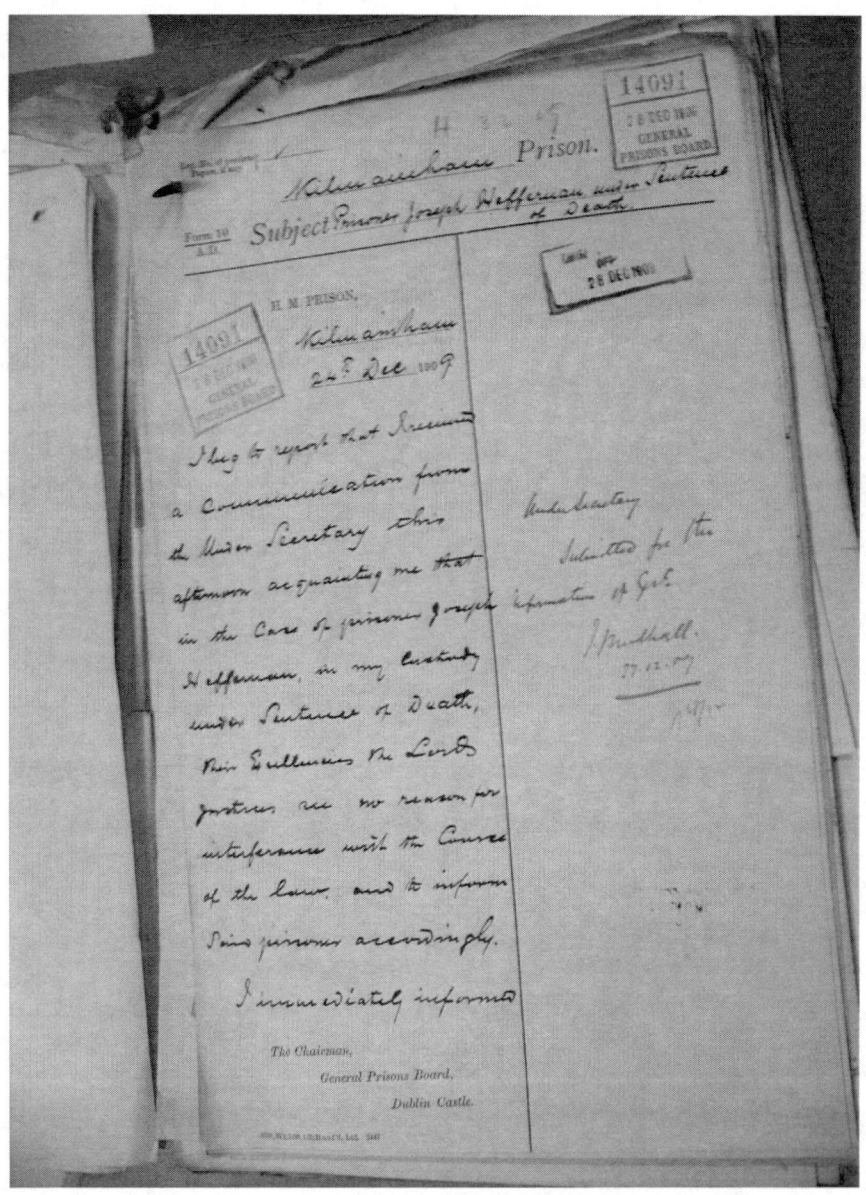

The missing file, H-32-09 (Heffernan's file)

10.

GREEN STREET COURT, DUBLIN, THURSDAY 2 DECEMBER 1909

The Judge was the Lord Chief Justice of Ireland, Lord O'Brien of Kilfenora. At 10.30am, the accused was put forward and pleaded not guilty. The court was densely crowded throughout the trial.

The following were sworn to try the case: Thomas Chambers, 30 Oakley Road; Lleylin T Powell, Dalkey; Henry Smallman, Ellemville; Valentine Whelan, Templeogue; Thomas Whelan; Thomas Bermingham, Corduff; Charles Hayes, Abbeyfield Avenue; James W. Whelan, Rathmines; Peter Fitzpatrick; Henry W. Robinson, Belgrave Square; James O'Reilly, Castle Street, Dalkey, and James Liliburn.

The following prosecuted: Sergeant Moriarty, KC; T F Maloney, KC; and Mr A. De Renzy (instructed by Mr P. Robert Kelly, Crown Solicitor, Westmeath).

The following appeared for the defence of Heffernan: Mr Wm J. Gleeson, B L (instructed by Mr O'Beirne of Hanmore & Co).

Mr A.E. Joyce, CS Mullingar, deposed that he was a civil engineer and in the habit of making maps, and that the map produced was made to scale and was an accurate map of what it purports to describe. At the suggestion of his Lordship, Mr Joyce was called before the other witnesses were taken, and for his Lordship's information pointed out several places such as the post office, railway station, and Ballinea Road.

To Mr Maloney: "It is 110 yards from Miss Walker's lodgings to the Green Bridge. It was 1,190 yards from the Green Bridge to where the body was found."

To his Lordship: "The canal path lies between the canal and the railway. From where Nooney stood and the scene of the outrage was 706 yards. From where the body was found to where the prisoner was alleged to have washed his hands is 52 yards."

To his Lordship: "The latter spot was pointed out to the witness by Nellie Woods, who alleged she saw the prisoner there. From where Richard Monaghan stated he was, to where he alleged he saw a man throw a girl down is 217 yards."

To a juror: "The place at which the tunnel is, to where the accused was arrested is about half a mile."

Mr Moriarty opened the case for the prosecution, saying the charge against the prisoner was one of murder and, as the jury were aware, the punishment for murder was death. That single statement was sufficient to bring before them the awful solemnity of the occasion. Mr Moriarty began to describe the murder:

> On the evening of that day, her dead body was found at 8.30 o'clock, lying in a hollow on the canal bank, between it and the railway line which runs along beside the canal path, and at the point about a half mile outside the town of Mullingar. The dead body, when found, presented all the appearance that Mary Walker had been murdered. There was a wound on the throat four inches long and deep just below what is called the Adam's apple. The face was covered with blood, the underclothes were stained and torn, and the ground around the place, which was marshy, presented evidence of a fearful struggle between the murdered lady and her assailant.
>
> Other indications, her torn blouse etc., disclosed also the fact that this poor young lady had died in defence of her virtue. The cause of her death was undoubtedly the wound on the throat, and that wound was undoubtedly, caused by a knife. The next question, and it was really the inquiry, which they [the jury] had to answer, was, who it was that murdered Miss Walker, and who it was who inflicted the wound. After they had heard the details of the evidence, which he [Mr Moriarty] would lay before them, they would have no doubt upon their minds, that it was the hand of Joseph Heffernan, the prisoner, who inflicted the fatal wound upon Miss Walker's throat.

Mr Moriarty then made reference to the movements of both Miss Walker and Heffernan on the day of the murder. Speaking of Miss Walker he said:

> She was well known to the people in Mullingar and respected as a result of being a most virtuous and well conducted young woman. On 7 July, Miss Walker was at her work in the post office, as usual, and left about 1.45pm to go to Mrs Daly's in Patrick Street, where she had been lodging. She had her dinner there at 2 o'clock and left the house at about 3.15 for her usual walk, and expected to be back at 6 o'clock as she was due back to go on duty at the post office at 7.30pm.
>
> On the same evening her dead body was brought home to her lodgings about 11 o'clock. They would know from the evidence which would be given that when Miss Walker left her lodgings at 3.15pm on that day, she walked to the Green Bridge and along the canal bank – that was her usual walk, and that was a beautiful day.
>
> She had left her lodgings at about 3.15pm and about 4pm she was seen on the canal bank by Thomas and Matthew Nooney, who were on the opposite side of the canal fishing, nearly opposite Merlehan's field. Thomas Nooney was himself employed as a postman, and both he and his brother knew Miss Walker perfectly well. She spoke across the canal to the Nooney's as she passed,

and bade them good afternoon. She was going in the direction of the racecourse.

At this point, his Lordship asked to be shown, on the map, the direction of Galway. This was done. Mr Moriarty said it was clear from the evidence that Miss Walker rested a little down the slope of the bank on her way in the direction of the racecourse.

Mr Moriarty stated that about 4.30pm, there was a man named Monaghan, a stable boy, who was exercising a horse in a field on the opposite side of the canal to that where Miss Walker passed. This field sloped up. Monaghan saw a woman run up the slope of the bank pursued by a man who overtook her and forced her down the bank. She and the man disappeared out of his sight. He stated that there was no doubt that the woman whom Monaghan had seen was Mary Walker, and that when the jury had heard the evidence, there would be equally no doubt in their mind that the man whom Monaghan saw was the prisoner Joseph Heffernan.

Monaghan did not say that it was Miss Walker whom he saw, as at the time the woman was some 200 yards from him and he knew her only imperfectly. But then there was no doubt that the dead body found the same evening, near where Monaghan had seen the struggle, was that of Miss Mary Walker. Counsel also commented on the fact that Monaghan had subsequently, without any communication from anybody and before hearing of the murder, came to the conclusion that the man whom he had seen was Joseph Heffernan. Continuing, Mr Moriarty stated that perhaps the time between Monaghan seeing the struggle and the time that Mary Walker was murdered on the slope of the canal bank, could be counted by seconds. As far as they could know, the person who last spoke to the murdered girl was Thomas Nooney and, with the exception of Heffernan, the last person to see her alive was this witness Monaghan.

The deceased's dead body was found that evening at 8.30pm. It was covered with grass and bore evidence, not only of the struggle and of the crime of murder, but that the crime of outrage – happily unsuccessful – had been attempted. About 4.30pm on the same evening, Father Magee, who was riding a horse along the Ballinea Road, heard screams of a woman and there could be no doubt that the scream was that of Mary Walker. Mr Moriarty addressed his Lordship again:

Let me now tell them something of the movements of the prisoner on that day, 7 July. The prisoner was a labourer, but had been occasionally employed by the post office to go on messages – not constantly – but if they were short of a messenger. His regular occupation was that of a day labourer, but from his occasional employment at the post office he had the opportunity of being acquainted – at least, with the appearance of Miss Walker. He was a native of Mullingar – at least he had lived there for the last five and twenty years. From 5 of July this year till the day of his arrest, he had been lodging with Mrs. Anne Moran, and was at the time out of occupation. On the day of the murder – 7 July – the prisoner left Mrs Moran's house at 7.45am, and he was then dressed in a dark blue suit, dark cap and wore brown leggings, a fact on which something turned, though not much. He stated he was going to look for employment. He returned on the evening of the same day, and in reply to a question from Mrs. Moran as to why he was so late, he said he had been up at the Green Bridge, that a girl had been killed there and that he had been looking on.

Well, there was no girl killed that day at the Green Bridge or any place about it except Mary Walker, and if the prisoner was looking on at what happened in the case. What will the jury think of the significance of that fact when taken into conjunction with the other facts which I will indicate to them as I proceed, for they must sink into their minds, and will the facts not go to prove that the prisoner was guilty of the death of her at the removal of whose body he was looking on at the Green Bridge? What had the prisoner been doing on that day, from 7.45am till 10pm at night. Between 10am and 11am he went into Mrs Sullivan's public house in Mullingar and the assistant, Charles Quinn, will tell the jury that Heffernan spent about three quarters of an hour or an hour in Sullivan's, and that whilst there he took out a knife and cut tobacco with it. The jury would see what an important part that knife played. I do not propose to trespass on the valuable time of the jury by going into details as to the public houses which Heffernan visited on 7 July, but all the porter he consumed amounted to about three pints – a pint and a glass at one place and a pint and a half–pint at another.

Mr Moriarty said he would pass on to tell the jury something about the prisoner's movements in the evening after he had come back from the scene of the murder. When speaking to Mrs Moran that night, he had some drink taken but was perfectly rational. After leaving Sullivan's public house, he was next found at the house of Charles Skelly, a wash–out man in the employment of the Railway Company, and the prisoner seems to have left Skelly's at 3.15pm and Miss Walker her lodgings at 3.15pm also.

Mr Moriarty: "Well, when the prisoner left Skelly's house, Skelly went with him, and at the Green Bridge they parted, the prisoner going along the towpath of the canal and Skelly going back to his work at the railway. The evidence would show that the prisoner, when going along the towpath was preceding Miss Walker, and it would indeed be proved that he was only a few yards in front of her going "up" towards the racecourse."

His Lordship: "I would like to know what you call up and what down."

Mr Moriarty: "I am calling towards the racecourse "up" and to Mullingar "down.""

Continuing, Mr Moriarty said the next who saw the prisoner was a man named Lyons, who was filling a cart at a place called the Valley, and who noticed him and the way he was walking. Thomas Nooney, the next person who spoke to him, also spoke to Miss Walker and would prove that she was only 20 or 30 yards behind him on the towpath. He had been fishing with his brother on the opposite side of the canal. Heffernan spoke to Nooney, and the jury could have no doubt from the evidence that Heffernan was there on the towpath and that Miss Walker was a little bit behind.

The next person to see Heffernan was Richard Monaghan, who also later saw the woman whom they must conclude was Mary Walker. That was about two or three minutes before the murder. Moriarty suggested that Monaghan's evidence should satisfy the jury that Heffernan was actually seen at the spot beside where the murder was committed, and was doing the deed of violence. Father Magee fixed the time at which he passed on the Ballinea Road and heard screams to 4.30pm. Then they had Ellen Woods, who went out to look for her young brother and heard a dreadful scream come from the opposite side of the canal.

On the plan, the spot where the body was found was marked in red. About five minutes after she heard the scream, Ellen Woods was practically opposite to the spot where the dead body was lying. She saw the prisoner sitting on the canal bank opposite her, washing his hands with his feet and boots in the water. At first, he endeavoured to conceal his face from her by pulling down his cap. He then asked Woods for a match. She replied that she couldn't throw the match across if she had it. Was not this a most terrific fact against the prisoner: that he was found there, within 52 yards of the spot where Mary Walker was lying with her throat cut?

Other witnesses would prove that they saw the prisoner on that evening going back to town, and that the way he went meant he had to cross hedges and ditches and actually to squeeze himself out under a gate. The jury would naturally ask why he came out so openly along the canal path and was to be seen washing his hands, at a time just after that of a murder. They might also ask why, rather than go back the usual way, he elected to go through the fields and under a gate.

Then there was Elizabeth Flanagan. At 6pm on the evening of the murder, a man whom she did not know, but who would be proved to the jury to have been the prisoner, came to her house, where she had been left by her parents in charge of some young children. This man made very free of the house, lying on the bed, for example. In cutting some tobacco for his pipe, he took out a knife. Charles Quinn, the assistant in Sullivan's, would prove that the prisoner had a knife before the murder, and Flanagan would prove that he had one afterwards. Flanagan would tell the jury that she noticed a red stain like blood on this knife, but this might not fix their attention were it not that afterwards, having occasion to use his pocket handkerchief, Flanagan remarked that it was stained with blood. Flanagan asked Heffernan to explain the bloodstains and he replied first that she was very inquisitive, but that if she did want to know, that he had been skinning a goat and that the blood had got on his handkerchief in this way by it rubbing against the flesh of the goat. The crown submitted that the fact was that the prisoner had not been skinning a goat.

Mr Moriarty referred again to the prisoner washing his hands and boots on the canal bank, near where the body was found and to his statement about the Green Bridge, when he returned home to his lodgings. He then referred to the inquest held the next day and the wound on Mary Walker's throat, which had been made by a knife. On the day after the murder, at 11.15am, Heffernan was arrested at Mr Callaghan's place, about half a mile from Mullingar. He had gone out before 8am that morning, having got up about 7 o'clock and before going out was in the kitchen at his lodgings.

Whilst there, a boy came with a besom to Mrs Moran. She bought it and gave it to the prisoner. He had a knife and began paring the besom. He had the knife about 6pm on the evening of 7th and in Sullivan's between 10am and 11am on the same morning. When arrested on 8 July at 11.15am, he had no knife. How did he get rid of it? He went through Austin Friars Street and on to near the canal, through a tunnel under the canal, and at 8.55am he was seen outside that tunnel. The tunnel was searched by the police and two days after the arrest, a policeman found a knife under a water pipe and buried in mud. The knife corresponds to that seen by witnesses on Heffernan.

Mr Moriarty then referred to the fact that the clothes that Heffernan wore when arrested were taken off him. No human hand tampered with the clothes, from the time they were taken until they reached the analyst. He would tell them on his oath that he found the clothes and leggings bore upon them bloodstains, and that the clothes were bespattered with human blood. Mr Moriarty referred to the fact that up to recent times, it had not been possible for science to distinguish between bloodstains made by human blood and those made by the blood of other mammalia. But a distinguished professor, Dr McWeeney, was able to tell them that he found stains that were of human blood on the clothes. The doctor had also made an investigation of the knife found in the tunnel, and was satisfied also that there were bloodstains and indications of blood upon it. Mr Moriarty stated that other evidence would be given, which was in the nature of a confessional statement, but he did not intend to refer to it at that moment.

His Lordship said it was the prudent, fair and proper course to let the jury judge whether such evidence, if given, was evidence that they could take, and that Mr Moriarty was acting with transparent propriety and fair play in adopting the course he had taken.

Mr Moriarty then concluded a "powerful address," which had lasted nearly two hours, by telling the jury that they would hear the evidence and would listen with anxiety to see whether or not it brought home the guilt to the prisoner. He would not venture to say what their conclusion would be. He only entreated their earnest attention to the evidence. If the evidence led them to conclude that the prisoner was the murderer of Mary Walker, then he knew no matter how painful the duty might be, they would discharge it by finding the prisoner guilty of the atrocious crime of homicide.

Mrs Anne Moran was called first and stated:

> *Heffernan got up at about 6.45am on the morning of the murder and went out at about 7.45am. When he returned that evening he was dressed the same way. The next morning, Heffernan got up at about a quarter to seven and went out at a quarter to eight. He had his breakfast and was sitting by the kitchen fire when a boy came to the door selling besoms and I bought one off the boy. The handle was badly made and rough and I asked Heffernan to pare it for me; he had a knife in his hand when doing so, a knife which he pulled out of his own pocket. I did not actually see the knife, but it appeared to be a blunt one and I remarked to him that it seemed to be blunt.*
> *Prosecutor: "Anyway, you saw him take the knife out of his pocket."*
> *Mr Gleeson: "Oh, I beg your pardon."*
> *Prosecutor: "Very well, but she said so."*
> *Cross–examined by Mr Gleeson: "What did you think that he meant by his remark that he was looking on when the girl was killed?"*
> *Witness: "I thought he meant that he went with the crowd to look at the murdered girl."*
> *Mr Gleeson: "Were there not table knives in your house?"*
> *Witness: "Yes."*
> *Mr Gleeson – "And none of them a bit too sharp?"*
> *Witness – "Oh, they are sharp enough for my purposes."*

Mrs Anne Daly was next examined. Her evidence was to the effect that she lived in Patrick Street and Mary Walker lodged and boarded with her for 15 months. Miss Walker was a strong girl and in good health. She came to her dinner on July 7 at about 2pm and left wearing a dark navy blue suit and light green hat. It was her custom to go for a walk each evening. She should have returned about 6pm. Her dead body was brought in about 11pm that night. Mrs Daly was not cross–examined.

Thomas Nooney, who lives in Trinity Cottages, gave evidence to the effect that he was employed in the post office. On the afternoon of the murder he was fishing with his brother on the opposite side of the canal to that on which the murder was committed. He saw Heffernan on the towpath and he spoke across the canal to the witness. Shortly after, he saw Miss Walker pass and she bid him good evening. That was about 3.30pm. There was about a five–minute interval between the time she passed and the time Heffernan passed. He stated that the prisoner walked slowly and did not seem in a hurry.

During the evidence, Mr Gleeson objected to anyone putting the prisoner on places on the map mentioned by Counsel in examination, before the witness pointed to the place. Mr Gleeson cross–asked where the witness and his brother put up the fishing rods when finished fishing. The witness stated that they fished up to Merlehan's field at the Green Bridge. That was as near to the Bridge as they could go. Mr Gleeson said he then understood that there were two Merlehan fields on opposite sides of the canal.

Matthew Nooney, a little boy and brother of the previous witness, gave evidence of a corroborative nature. Heffernan and Miss Walker were not within sight at the same time. When cross–examined by Mr Gleeson, the witness said that the police had been speaking to him about his evidence.

> Mr Gleeson: "I suppose you have been pretty well drilled by the police."
> Witness: "Yes, on the times."
> Mr Gleeson: "I thought so." (To a juror) "Heffernan was the only person who passed along the bank whilst witness was fishing."

The witness further stated there was a man whom he did not know who came along the canal when he was fishing near the Green Bridge. He asked across if this was the Royal Canal and witness said yes. This man was a stranger to witness. He then went off the canal bank.

> Mr Gleeson – "Could he get back another way to the canal without you seeing him?"
> Witness – "He could."
> Witness to the Judge: "The man seemed to come from the direction of the street of Mullingar and appeared to go back towards the town."

Mr John Fallon, publican, Mount Street, Mullingar, was next examined and his evidence was to the effect that between 11am and 12pm on the day of the murder the prisoner, with a man whom the witness did not know, came into his shop and drank a pint of porter. He got another pint, but drank only half of it. Heffernan was quite sober. Witness described Heffernan's dress, all but the lower part, which he could not see owing to the counter. He wore dark blue clothes and a blue cap. He had not read a newspaper description of the way Heffernan was dressed, nor had he heard anyone describe the way he was dressed prior to giving his evidence before the Magistrates.

Charles Quinn, an assistant in Mrs Sullivan's Public House, Greville Street, stated that he knew the prisoner. He deposed to Heffernan being in the shop on the morning of the murder. The prisoner got a pint and afterwards a glass of porter in the shop, where he remained for three–quarters of an hour. He took out a knife and cut tobacco with it, having just bought a pipe. He wore dark clothes and brown leggings. In the evening he came in again and had a glass of porter. A man named Judge came into the shop at the time and said a lady had been drowned in the canal. The prisoner left about 10 minutes after.

Charles Skelly, Patrick Street, wash–out man at the railway station, deposed to Heffernan being in his house at 2.30pm on the 7 July. When the witness came home
Heffernan said:

> "Hello, my brown son" when the witness came in. Heffernan had some drink taken. He asked for the loan of a razor but the witness did not give it to him. Heffernan said,
> "Anything at all that will tear the hair off my face would do." Witness to a juror: "He used occasionally come into my house and get something to eat. (To Counsel) About 3.15pm I went back to work. The prisoner came with me as far as the Green Bridge, where I turned down to the railway. I did not know where the prisoner went afterwards."
> Mr Glasson to the witness: "Could you suggest any reason why the prisoner, who lived at the time in Austin Friars Street, should come from there to Patrick Street to look for a razor."
> Witness: "No"
> Counsel: "Are you usually called "my brown son?" (Some laughter.)
> Witness: "No, it is a word he is in the habit of using to people."

Patrick Lyons, in reply to Mr Renzy, said he was working on 7 July, filling a load on a cart close to the canal bank at the Valley. He saw the prisoner walking slowly out from Mullingar, on the opposite side of the canal bank. He noticed that the prisoner had leggings on and was dressed in dark clothes with a dark cap. He was looking about him. According to the witness, it had been bright at the time and it was not far from where the witness was to the Green Bridge. When he was at the Green Bridge with his load, it struck 4pm.

Richard Monaghan was examined by Mr Moriarty and said that he was exercising a horse for Mr Dibbs in a field near the road. The ground there sloped upwards from the road. He was exercising the horse from 3pm to 5pm. While there, he saw a woman come up suddenly on the opposite side of the canal. There was a man close behind her. When the woman got to the top of the bank she turned and the man pushed her down. The woman appeared to be running away from the man. The man was dressed in dark clothes but he noticed something white like the tops of leggings. He shoved the woman down. He saw the place where the body of Mary Walker was found. He had known Joseph Heffernan for four or five years, as he lodged with his father.

Mr Gleeson objected that the learned Sergeant was about to ask a question as to an opinion the witness might to have formed afterwards.

> *Witness (to a juror): "The man I saw was not taller than the woman – he was not a tall man."*
> *Mr Gleeson: "If there were any screams about that time, would you expect to have heard them from where you were?"*
> *Witness: "No, the wind was blowing too strong."*

The wind was blowing from him across to the opposite side of the canal, and five or ten minutes after he saw the struggle between the man and the woman, he saw Fr Magee pass on horseback on the Ballinea Road.

Father Magee deposed that on the afternoon in question, he was returning from beyond Brotenstown, where he had been visiting a sick person. He was on horseback. When on the Ballinea Road at the Valley, he heard a shrill piercing squeal. For a moment he looked about, as it suggested something strange to him. He heard and saw nothing however, and concluded it might be children playing and shouting as they often do about there. He went onto the palace. From where he was, to the far side of the canal, might have been 80 to 110 yards and about 90 yards from where the body was found.

The witness said he noticed Mr Dibbs' boy in the field, and had spoken about the same time to a man about the horse. He could not say the exact time at which he arrived at the palace, as he did not look at the clock. When in Patrick Street, he saw a train slowly steam out of the station. It would have been about 4.30pm when he heard the shrill squeal. He calculated that in this way that he left the palace at 2.30pm. It would take about 55 minutes each way for his journey and perhaps an extra ten minutes, as he had been speaking to a few people. Fr Magee was not cross–examined.

Ellen Woods was next examined by Mr Moriarty. She said she lived in the Valley Cottages. On the evening of 7 July, she was looking for her brother Paddy. She went down to the canal line. She was down in the hollow under the canal bank, so she could not see anybody on the other bank. While picking watercress near the tunnel she heard a scream. She went along this hollow and then came up out of the hollow nearly opposite the spot where Miss Walker's body was found. She saw the prisoner sitting on the opposite bank with his feet tipping the water, rubbing his boots and leggings with the grass. The prisoner had a cap on him and pulled it down on his eyes. He spoke to her after doing so. She knew the prisoner because he used to work with her father and when she brought her father's dinner, he divided it with him. When she went away, she left Heffernan, still seated on the canal bank.

> *To a juror: "I saw no stain or colour on his hands."*
> *Mr Gleeson: "Could you show the way he pulled the cap down on his face without disarranging your hair?"*
> *Witness: "No." (To his Lordship) "Once he pulled down the cap he left it down. He had it down while speaking."*
> *To a juror: "How did you know him if he had the cap down?"*
> *Witness: "I knew him by his voice."*
> *Mr Gleeson: "Was there a strong sun on your eyes at the time?"*
> *Witness: "Yes."*

Michael Murray, Patrick Street, son of Patrick Murray, gave evidence to the effect that he had been confirmed. He left the town on the evening of 7 July to milk a goat on his father's land, near the canal line on the far side of the railway. It took about a quarter of an hour to walk from the Green Bridge to the place along the racecourse road. While milking the goat, he heard a cry from the direction of the canal. It was like a cry of distress, a screechy cry. It was the scream of a woman. He stopped milking the goat and looked around, but could see nothing. A part of the top of the canal bank was all that would be visible to him from where he stood. He continued milking the goat and heard other screams. He had heard four or five altogether. The milking occupied him about five minutes. On his way home, he saw a man crossing Scollin's field. The man was walking in the meadow and the witness could only see from the waist upwards. He could not recognise the man who was apparently coming from the direction of the canal bank, where the dead body of Miss Walker was found. The man was going fast. He wore dark clothes and a dark cap, but he was too far from the witness to enable him to recognise him.

Richard Merlehan deposed that he left his home about 4.30pm on the evening in question. He had seen the spot where the body was found and the nearest part he was to that place in the fields that evening, would be about 100 yards. Where the body was found was out of his view. He thought, when he was in the fields, he heard the voices of children. He went to his dinner in his house at 3.30pm and left the house again at 4.30pm. The gap where he was, was not very far away from the place where the dead body was found. If there were loud screams, he thought he would have heard them, as the wind was blowing in favour of him.

Mrs Elizabeth Feeney gave evidence, as in her deposition, of seeing from the window of her house on the Clown Road, a man squeeze out under a gate from one of the fields. He wore dark clothes and brown leggings. She did not know him. He was of medium height and was not unlike the prisoner. After getting under the gate, the man went down a laneway and crossed into another field. Later she saw the man move on. He did not seem in a hurry.

Mr Christopher Downes, Greville Street, Mullingar, deposed he was a merchant. He cycled out to the racecourse on the evening of the murder. It was 4.48pm as he passed the post office. At the Green Bridge he turned down towards the railway station. He knew the road over which the Clown Bridge went. He had known the prisoner to see him on the road for about a year. He met him on the evening in question near the well. Heffernan, was coming towards Mullingar. The well was about 50 yards from the Clown Bridge on the Mullingar side. Heffernan was dressed in dark clothes with dark cap. He did not speak to the witness. It was invariably his custom to speak to the witness when he met him on the road. He believed that to be the first occasion on which Heffernan had not spoken to him when passing.

Dr Joseph Dillon–Kelly JP, Mullingar, was called next. In reply to Mr Moriarty, he gave evidence on the superficial examination of the body on the evening of the murder, at the place where he was informed it was found. It was then about 9.30pm. It was covered with grass, which he would say was pulled. There was a wound on the throat 2 inches each side of the Adams apple, 4 inches in all. The superior thyroid artery was cut. The carotid arteries were not injured.

> Mr Moriarty: "Would a knife do it, Dr Kelly?"
> Witness: "It would."
> Mr Moriarty: "Would it be likely to do it?"
> Witness: "It would."

The Doctor further deposed that he found blood on the face and other signs of violence. The clothes, blouse, etc., were very much torn about the chest and the underclothing was also torn. On the following day, he made a post–mortem examination with Dr Ballesty. Death was due to the wound on the throat. The deceased was a well–fed, healthy, strong young woman.

> Mr Gleeson: "You say, Doctor, the poor girl was strong and well fed. Would you call the prisoner (pointing to Heffernan in the dock) a strong, well–made man?"
> Dillon–Kelly: "I would call him very muscular. He was used to labour. He may not look it now but he was then."

Mr Gleeson: "Do you believe the deceased girl would have offered great resistance to an assailant?"
Witness: "Yes (emphatically) I believe she did."
His Lordship: "So great that it would require a knife to quell her?"
Witness: "Yes, to put an end to it."

He went on to express the belief that the deceased had died in the defence of her virtue. At this point the Court rose and adjourned until 10.30am on Friday morning.

11.

GREEN STREET COURT, DUBLIN
FRIDAY 3 DECEMBER 1909

At the outset of the proceedings, His Lordship said he wished to have Ellen Woods and some other witness's recalled. Lord Chief Justice O'Brien recalled and examined Ellen Woods. She pointed out the Valley Cottages on the map.

His Lordship: "You went out to look for your little brother, did you not?"
Woods: "Yes."
His Lordship: "How far did you go?"
Woods: "To near the tunnel."
His Lordship: "Did you then turn back?"
Woods: "Yes."
His Lordship: "When did you hear the scream?"
Woods: "When I was coming back."
His Lordship: "Did you point out the place?"
Woods: "Yes, to the Head Constable."
His Lordship: "What sort of scream was it?"
Woods: "Like the squeal of a cat."
His Lordship: "You saw Fr Magee after that?"
Woods: "Yes, about five or ten minutes after."
His Lordship: "Did you see anyone after that?"
Woods: "Yes."
His Lordship: "Who?"
Woods: "Joseph Heffernan."
His Lordship: "How long was that after you heard the scream?"
Woods: "I could not exactly say. I was about ten minutes picking the watercress."
His Lordship: "He was sitting with his feet tipping the water?"
Woods: "Yes."
His Lordship: "And you say he covered his face?"
Woods: "Yes."
His Lordship: "But you knew him before he covered his face?"
Woods: "Yes, I had seen Heffernan's face, and recognised it before he covered it with his cap."
His Lordship: "That was after you saw Fr Magee?"
Woods: "Yes."
His Lordship: "Could you say how long?"
Woods: "No, I do not know exactly."

Elizabeth Flanagan, Barrack Street, Mullingar, was next examined. She deposed that a man whom she did not know came into her house on 7 July at about 5.45pm. She had seen him since and identified him as the prisoner. When the man came in, he asked for Molly Roddy. There was no such person in her house at that time, though previously a person of that name lived there. He sat on the bed. He was wearing black/blue clothes, yellow leggings and strong boots with nails. He lay down on the bed and put one hand over the front of his head and the other at the back of his head.

After a while he got up and cut some tobacco with a knife. The knife now produced was the very same as the one he used to cut the tobacco.

His Lordship: "Would that knife, Dr Kelly, be calculated to inflict the wound you saw on the throat of the dead body of Mary Walker?"
Dr Kelly (with emphases and slowly): "Yes, it would."

Mr Moriarty continued the examination of the witness, Elizabeth Flanagan, as to what she noticed on the knife, and she said there was a red stain like blood on it. The witness was sitting at the fire at the time. The bed was near the fire and Heffernan was sitting on the bed. After that he asked for a "readier" for his pipe, and afterwards went out and got it himself. He returned and lay on the bed again. He afterwards took out his handkerchief and the witness noticed stains like blood on it. She asked Heffernan the cause of these stains and he answered that it was news she was looking for. After a pause of about two minutes, he said that he had been skinning a goat and that the flesh had knocked up against the handkerchief. Subsequently, Heffernan got up off the bed and began to walk about, up and down the floor. The witness got a bit frightened and, for the purpose of getting rid of Heffernan, she said her mother was sick in another room, and that Father O'Farrell was coming. Heffernan then asked to see her mother. The witness went out into the hall and Heffernan came after her. He asked her to go for porter, but she refused. She was frightened and went out to get her cousin, Susan Giff, who came in and ordered him out. He then left. The witness was about 14 years of age. She was afraid of the man.

Mr Gleeson: "Did he look wild?"
Witness: "It was the look of him that was so queer that frightened me."

His Lordship examined witness about the time the prisoner made the pause after she questioned him about the handkerchief, and asked if he seemed to be thinking during the pause. The witness answered in the affirmative.

Witness to Mr Gleeson: "He was quite sober. He left at once on being told to do so."

Witness to His Lordship: "I noticed nothing about his appearance except that wild look."

Witness to Mr Gleeson: "I had never seen him before. There was no reason why he should ask me to drink porter."

Mrs Susan Giff deposed to Mr De Renzy, that when called in by Elizabeth Flanagan, she came to her house. Joseph Heffernan, whom the witness knew well by sight, was there. When she went in he put his hand in his pocket. The witness said, "What brought you in here, Heffernan, you blackguard?" He replied, "Excuse me, I am looking for Mary Roddy, I thought she lived here." He then left.

Witness to a juror: "The Flanagan's were about 12 months in the house. (To his Lordship) Mary Roddy left it about 2 years ago."

Luke Sullivan, a labourer from Barrack Street, Mullingar, deposed that on 8 July, he was going to Irishtown, which was about 2 miles from the town. He knew the prisoner well, and knew where the tunnel that runs under the canal was. Along the canal bank was the shortest way to Irishtown. He did not go through the tunnel. There was a path up from near it to the canal bank. The witness was the Mullingar side of the tunnel when he saw Heffernan about 25 yards from him. Heffernan was not in the tunnel. He was stooped, as if tying his boot. The witness said "Hello Joe," and Heffernan replied, "Hello my brown son, did you feed him yet?" The witness explained that "feed him" referred to a jennet in a field, which the witness possessed. It was then 8.55am by the cathedral clock.

Witness to Mr Gleeson: "Callaghan's farm is only a few fields across from the tunnel."

Witness to a juror: "Heffernan was looking about him and seemed excited."

Patrick Lyons, re–called by his Lordship, said he saw the prisoner between three and four o'clock on the day of the murder. It was nearer to four than to three o'clock. The witness was looking at him for about ten minutes, and it was because the prisoner was looking about him so much as he walked along that he observed him. From where the witness saw Heffernan, to where the girl was killed, it was about 200 yards.

Constable Charles Moore gave evidence concerning the arrest of Heffernan at 11.15am on 8 July at Callaghan's. The place where he arrested him was about 1½ miles from Mullingar. The witness cautioned him and told him the charge. Heffernan replied, "Is it me? What do I know about it? I know nothing about it." The witness brought the prisoner on for some distance, until he met Constable Rowlette. They searched him; there was no knife on him.

> His Lordship: "Did he repel the charge when you made it?"
> Witness: "Yes."
> His Lordship: "Did he seem in the full possession of his senses?"
> Witness: "Yes."
> His Lordship: "And he repelled the charge?"
> Witness: "Yes."

The witness then gave evidence as to the parcelling up the prisoner's clothes and knife when they were taken from him, and the delivery of the same to Professor McWeeney in Dublin on 15 July. The clothes were in the same condition as they had been when taken off the prisoner. The boots and gaiters were also included. The witness had also handed over the clothes that had been taken from the dead body of Miss Walker. When the prisoner was arrested he was working, thinning mangolds. He was between two men. When the witness came up Heffernan stepped three paces towards him. He was not in the least excited.

Constable Rowlette deposed to searching the tunnel at the canal on 10 July and finding a knife, which was produced in court. The knife was under an old pipe and was covered with mud and hay. The witness stated that on 15 July he was in charge of the prisoner in the cell at Mullingar Courthouse.

Mr Gleeson here objected to the witness saying anything about any statement made by the prisoner subsequent to his arrest. This was not the officer who arrested the prisoner or cautioned him, and the Crown tendered no evidence of the circumstances of the statement. It was a very serious matter if the Crown had to rely upon a statement made by a man in Heffernan's position. It was the law, that if a man made a statement subsequent to his arrest to a policeman, that it should not be accepted and that is especially important in Ireland, where the people, rightly or erroneously, credit the police with having great powers.

> His Lordship to Witness: "Did you say anything to him to bring about the statement, or did you hold out any inducement to him to make it?"
> Witness: "No."
> His Lordship: "I will allow the evidence."
> Constable Rowlette: "The prisoner stated, 'I'm afraid they will swear my life away. Do you think if I admitted it, and said I was mad from drink, would I get off with a couple of years? I am sorry when I got that petticoat of a

trousers on me, that I did not run out and down the town. They would say I
was mad and send me to the asylum.'
"I addressed no observation whatever to him. When arrested, the prisoner's
trousers were taken off him, and he got a very large trousers, which was much
too big for him. That was what he meant by 'petticoat of a trousers.'"

Sergeant Thomas Cooke, Mullingar, deposed that on 8 July he was in charge
of an escort bringing the prisoner to Dublin. The prisoner made a statement
to the witness. The witness had held out no inducement to the prisoner to
do so. He had no conversation with the prisoner previously, except to answer
a question put to him by the prisoner.

Mr Gleeson objected to the statement being put in evidence and, in raising
the objection applied to his Lordship for permission to question the witness
as to the circumstances under which the statement was made. Sergeant Cooke
said it was after the train left Mullingar for Dublin on the way to Kilmainham.
There had been a hostile demonstration at Mullingar station.

Mr Gleeson then submitted authorities on the subject. He quoted a decision
in the case of the *Queen v. Thompson* 1893 (2nd Queens Bench). In that
case, Mr Justice Cave said that a statement wrung from the mind by the
flattery of hope or torture, comes in such a questionable shape, that when it
was given as evidence of guilt, it should not be seriously treated. The statement
now offered to be put in evidence, was made at a still later period, when
public feeling against the prisoner had grown much keener.

> His Lordship: "I will reject what the previous witness has said on the question
> of a statement, and I will not allow the statement now offered to be gone into.
> Mr Gleeson, you are managing your case very cleverly and with great
> direction."

Mr Moriarty said that owing to his official position, he could not acquiesce
in his Lordship's ruling.

The witness then gave evidence as to being in a cab on 15 July with the
prisoner, where he made a statement. Mr Gleeson again objected. At this time,
the Sergeant was bringing the prisoner back to Mullingar, where he
previously had a very hot reception. His Lordship allowed the statement.

The witness then gave the following statement, which he said was made by
the prisoner on the occasion in question:

> "I suppose you have plenty of evidence against me now. You have got the
> knife and everything, but Tom Cole will prove I had no knife. Mrs Moran
> said I had a knife, and that I pared a besom for her with it, but I pared it with
> my fingers. If she got plenty of porter that's all she wants. I suppose her
> evidence will hang me. She should not tell lies anyhow, many a man was taken

in the wrong. They can hang me and if they do they will hang me in the wrong. I don't know the girl at all. I was not on the canal bank that day or had any business out there."

The witness stated that he made a note of statement from memory, less than half an hour after he had heard it. He stated that Mrs Moran was not examined the previous day. Later on the same day, the prisoner said:

"They might as well shut me up someplace because if I am left knocking about I will do the same thing again and be taken again. I want to be put someplace where I will be put up and minded."

On 19 July, the witness was again in charge of an escort from Kilmainham to Mullingar, when the prisoner said:

"I met Jack Doyle in Sullivan's public house that day. I gave him a glass of porter. I asked him if there was any work to be got and he said there was plenty, that Merlehan of Clown had plenty. I rambled out the canal bank that day but I did not see Merlehan and I did not go to the house because I was not great with the woman since the last time I was working there. If I was asked was I about Clown I would have said I was, but I was not asked."

Warder Joe Mansfield, Kilmainham Gaol, deposed that on 17 October he was in charge of the prison hospital and the prisoner was there with him. When alone with the witness in the ward, the prisoner made a statement. The witness said he had not spoken at all to the prisoner at the time, nor had he at any time held out threat or inducement.

Mr Gleeson objected and the judge allowed him to examine the witness relative to the circumstances of the statement he proposed to repeat.

Mr Gleeson: "On 12 October in Kilmainham, did the prisoner make a determined attempt to commit suicide in his cell?"
Witness: "He did."
Mr Gleeson: "On 17 October, when you say he made a statement to you, was he in the prison hospital as a result of the injuries which he inflicted on himself on the 12th?
Witness: "Yes."
Mr Gleeson: "Was he ever in a straight jacket?"
Witness: "No."
Mr Gleeson: "Was he then under restraint?"
Witness: "No."
Mr Gleeson: "Had he not been ordered to be put under restraint?"
Witness: "He had."

Mr Gleeson objected to the statement under the circumstances. Mr Moriarty said the matters elicited by Mr Gleeson from the witness were worthy of the greatest consideration by a jury, but the admissibility of the statement was beyond doubt all the same. His Lordship admitted the statement and, amidst the greatest sensation, the warder spoke as follows:

> *Witness:* "He was lying in his bed. He raised himself on his elbow, and asked, "What will I get, sir?" I said I did not know. He then said, "There is no use in denying it, I killed the poor girl right enough, everybody knows it. I don't know what came over me. The devil, I suppose. I was drinking all that day. I put my arm round her and knocked her down. I cut a hole under her ear; the poor girl died easy."
> *Mr Moriarty:* "Did he appear quite rational at the time he spoke?"
> *Witness:* "Yes, except sleepy; he spoke on wakening out of his sleep."
> *A juror:* "What o'clock was it at?"
> *Witness:* "About 8am."

Dr McWeeney was next examined as to the condition of the prisoner's clothing. He had four stains on the left trousers leg that were due to blood, but other parts of the trousers felt damp, as if an attempt to wash the garment had been made. All four stains were human blood. There were a number of dark stains on the outside of the leggings that were not due to blood. He also found a number of minute spatters that were due to blood. The largest of these was in a seam and was sufficient to enable him to apply the Precipitine Test, which showed the stain to be of human blood. There were a number of cup–shaped depressions on the surface, as if some larger stains had been scooped out with the point of a knife.

The shirt had a large number of minute stains, such as might have been produced from vermin, but the prisoner was not a person affected with vermin. Most of the stains were on the outside, but there were some on the inside. When the sleeve of the shirt was turned inside out, the witness found a blade of grass inside. He thought this peculiar and fastened it with a pin where found, near the shoulder in the sleeve.

The penknife originally had two blades; the larger was now broken off. He found considerable traces of human blood under the remains of the broken blade. The witness was not cross–examined.

Mr Moriarty then indicated that the Crown case was closed. The defence was then opened.

Amidst the deepest silence, Mr Gleeson rose to address the jury. He said that the opening statement of the learned sergeant detailed to them the nature of the evidence he would give. The description of the evidence he was about to produce, given by the learned Sergeant, revealed to them the history of the crime, shocking in its horror and brutality, a crime that must cause feelings of revulsion in the mind of any person with any respect for human life. The learned sergeant detailed the movements of the unfortunate lady on the fatal day, and also those of the wretched man, Joseph Heffernan. But in all the Sergeants address, a suggestion was never made to them as to the character and antecedents of this unfortunate man. Mr Gleeson would establish, without a shadow of doubt, most important matters about the history of the prisoner and his relatives, from which he thought the jury, would have no difficulty in coming to the conclusion that he was not a rational man, but an unfortunate maniac.

He did not intend to detain them by a lengthy address at this stage. He could put a witness in the chair who would tell them that this man's brothers are afflicted with mental disease: that one was an inmate of an asylum and that the other was in it and had escaped, and that one of his cousins was in the asylum at present. Having regard to this, and to the conduct of the prisoner ever since his arrest, they would have little hesitation, he thought, in coming to the only conclusion to which Christian men could come: namely, if it was possible that by any chance they decided he was guilty of the crime charged against him, that he was a maniac, and not responsible for his act.

Mr Gleeson now produced witnesses on the question of the mental condition of the accused and his family history. Warder Joseph Finnemore of Kilmainham Gaol, in direct evidence, stated that he was in charge of the prisoner on the previous 12 October in the prison. Heffernan "attempted to tear his throat with his left hand and to hammer his head against the wall." He did himself some slight injury and was not allowed to do it anymore.

> Witness to Mr Moriarty: "I was not always in charge of Heffernan, but had the opportunity of observing him from 8 July, when he first came to the prison, up to 12 October. He was the same as any other man. He, was no more mad than I am myself"
> Mr Moriarty: "You look quite sane."
> Witness: "I hope so, sir."

The witness further stated that there was nothing in the demeanour of the prisoner up to 12 October, to suggest any difference between him and any other prisoner charged with a similar offence. On 12 October, the prisoner tried to cut his throat with his fingernails. Prisoners committed for trial on a charge of murder were never left out of sight in the prison, at any time.

> Mr Gleeson: "My Lord, this witness was produced by me, he has given decidedly hostile evidence and I now ask permission to cross examine him."
> Permission was granted. Mr Gleeson proceeded to ask the witness whether

he would contradict the doctor if the doctor gave a contrary version of the prisoner's conduct and state in the prison. Mr Moriarty objected and instructed that the doctor was to be allowed give his own views on the subject when in the witness chair.

Mr Gleeson: "I submit, my Lord, I am right. This witness volunteers in the chair to give his opinion as to the mental condition of the prisoner – and says he is no more mad than he. That, I submit, is most improper."

Witness to his Lordship: "Such prisoners are put on "observation watch" and if a man does any act of violence a special eye was kept on him."

His Lordship: "Had you any means of testing his sanity?"

Witness: "Only just to see him."

His Lordship: "Did he show any signs of want of mental balance or anything else strange?"

Witness: "No."

Dr John O'Donnell, Medical Officer of Kilmainham Gaol, was examined by Mr Gleeson. He had Heffernan under Observation practically every day. On account of the serious nature of the charge against him, the witness examined the prisoner very carefully.

Mr Gleeson: "Did you notice any suspicious symptoms or mental signs about him?"

Witness: "Yes."

Mr Gleeson: "What did you notice?"

Witness: "The physical signs I noticed were temporary, for example a tremor of the lips. That was noticed on one occasion. To a medical man it might seem suspicious."

His Lordship: "A sign that would say "enquire further," and if there were other things it would be of some importance?"

Witness: "Yes My Lord."

To Mr Gleeson: "Witness made a report in the Prison Journal about the occurrence of 2 November."

At the request of Mr Gleeson, the Journal was handed in by Mr McGann. The report dated 3 November stated:

Joseph Heffernan is under restraint since yesterday. He had another violent seizure which lasted twenty minutes, during which he made some incoherent statement mostly of the immoral character. He kicked about. When I saw him he said I know nothing about it, but said there was a row going on in the hours of the morning in the hospital. From these, and other suspicious circumstances and considering the gravity of the offence with which he is charged, I would recommend that Sir Christopher Nixon be called in to consult.

Mr Gleeson: "Was he ever called in?"
Witness: "No."

In reply to Mr Gleeson as to why the recommendation was not carried out, the witness pointed out that unless prisoner was under restraint, the rules of the prison said there was to be no consultation.

Dr O'Donnell to Mr Moriarty: "Dr Russell was doing duty for me as I was on holidays at the time prisoner came first to Kilmainham. I first saw Heffernan about 20 July; I treated him as an absolutely sane prisoner. For the first week or 10 days after that, I saw and examined the prisoner every day. The prisoner was perfectly sane, he would know the difference between right and wrong.
Mr Moriarty: "Would he know that to attack a woman or use a knife was wrong."

Mr Gleeson objected and Mr Moriarty did not press the question.

Mr Moriarty: "Would he know the meaning and value of the act?"

Mr Gleeson objected again.

Mr Moriarty: "Was he like any other man?"
Witness: "Yes."
Mr Moriarty: "I notice that no attempt was made on his behalf to show that he was not able to follow the trial."

Mr Gleeson objected and the question was disallowed.

Mr Moriarty: "Is he perfectly sane at the present time?"

Mr Gleeson objected, but his Lordship overruled and the question was put.

Witness: "He is sane."
Mr Gleeson: "You noticed actual grounds for suspicion as to his condition?"

The witness spoke very low and hesitantly, and could not be heard.

Mr Gleeson: "Did you or did you not notice that there were conditions which excited your suspicions?"
Witness: "Conditions that I would like to have advice on."
Mr Gleeson: "Did you not ask that Sir Christopher Nixon be brought in because you had come to the conclusion that this man was insane?"
Witness: "Oh no."

Mr Gleeson:"What were your suspicions about, doctor?"The witness hesitated and mumbled some words, which could not possibly heard by the press.

Mr Gleeson (impatiently):"Did you think he was alright? Was that the reason you asked for Sir Christopher Nixon?"

Witness:"Oh no."

His Lordship:"You know that Sir Christopher Nixon is a very distinguished medical man and you thought that, as there was so much doubt about the prisoner's condition, that it would be well to have Sir Christopher Nixon. You were absolutely certain of your own opinion and wished him called in?"

Witness:"I was bound to do so, under the circumstances, my lord."

Mr Gleeson:"Is lunacy or madness consistent with great cunning in crime?"

Witness (after a brief pause):"Yes."

Mr Gleeson: Might a man, from brooding over a crime, develop symptoms which were like those of insanity?"

Witness:"Yes."

Mr Gleeson:"But in your opinion this man did not show any symptoms of insanity?"

Witness:"No."

His Lordship:"The doctor could not know what was in his mind."

The Court now rose for half an hour for luncheon and sat again at two o'clock.

Dr Rainsford, Medical Superintendent of the Stewart Institution, in reply to Mr Gleeson, stated that the report made in the prisons doctor's book would indicate temporary loss of sanity. He had since examined the man himself, but he could form no opinion as to what the condition of his mind was at the time of the alleged crime.

Mr Gleeson:"Do you consider him a man of average mental type?"

Witness:"He is a man of very low mental type."

The Lord Chief Justice:"His low mental type would not prevent him from distinguishing between right and wrong?"

Witness:"No."

Witness to Sergeant Moriarty:"I examined the man before the trial and came to the conclusion he was perfectly sane."

The Crown now proposed to call Dr Matthew Russell, who was acting as locum for Dr O'Donnell on 8 July when prisoner first came to the prison.

Mr Gleeson: "I object to the evidence of Dr Russell being taken – firstly, because it was not on the deposition; secondly, because the Crown knew that if they wanted him they could have had him, and thirdly, as no note was addressed to me."

Mr Moriarty said notice had been given two days before Dr Russell was called as a witness. When it was known that his evidence would be relevant to the case, the notice was given. Mr Gleeson said he did not get it. As an advocate, he must object to the evidence and asked his Lordship to note the objection. His Lordship allowed the evidence.

Dr Russell stated he examined the prisoner on 9 July for bruises and scratches. He found none on him. He found no symptoms of insanity. The man was the same as an ordinary prisoner charged with murder.

> *Witness to Mr Gleeson: I examined prisoner for scratches because I learned there was a history of a struggle."*
> *Mr Gleeson: "You thought it would be more important to find out a scratch than to find out if he was a lunatic?"*
> *Witness: "There was time enough for that."*
> *His Lordship: "Did he display any symptoms of insanity whatsoever?"*
> *Witness: "No."*
> *Mr Gleeson: "Have you any particular treatment to apply to the insane?"*
> *Witness: "Only a few words."*
> *Mr Gleeson: "No other examination?"*

Dr R.A. Lepper, Medical Officer at St. Patricks, deposed that he saw Heffernan for the first time on 1 December in Kilmainham. He was a total stranger to him up to that time. He tested the prisoner as to whether he was sane or whether he would be able to plead there. He came to the conclusion that the prisoner was sane.

> *Mr Moriarty: "Was he sane and able to act in the way I have asked you?"*
> *Witness: "Generally speaking, yes, I believe he is sane, but I believe he is degenerate, a low mental type of man – either as a result of defective evolution or from degeneracy."*
> *His Lordship: "Would that prevent a man being able to distinguish between right and wrong?"*
> *Witness: "In exaggerated cases, yes; in this case, no."*
> *Witness to Mr Gleeson: "Fitness to plead was my first concern in the examination I made. The prisoner's head was not exactly normal. The frontal area was slightly flattened and the head was asymmetrical – that is, different at one side to the other. That would be due either to congenital defect or neurotic processes in connection with the mental state."*
> *Mr Gleeson: "Would he be peculiarly liable to impulses?"*
> *Witness: "The Degenerate always are."*
> *Mr Gleeson: "And the impulses might be uncontrollable?"*
> *Witness: "Possibly."*
> *Mr Gleeson: "Would you swear that?"*

Mr Moriarty objected, saying there was no basis in evidence for the questions; Dr Lepper could not speak to the prisoner's condition on a particular day.

> Mr Gleeson: "I am dealing with Heffernan. Do you agree, Doctor, that this man would be peculiarly liable to an uncontrollable impulse?"
> Mr Moriarty: "I object. (To witness) Could you speak to the mental condition of the prisoner on 7 July?"
> Witness: "No."
> Mr Moriarty: "During an impulse of that description, would this man be capable of distinguishing between right from wrong?"

Mr Gleeson objected and the question was not allowed.

> Mr Gleeson: "Assuming that the evidence given is true about his commission of this crime, would you regard it as evidence of an impulse?
> Witness: "All degenerates are, unfortunately, particularly liable to impulse."
> Mr Gleeson: "Would he be able to distinguish between right and wrong if seized by one of these impulses?"
> Witness: "That would depend on the nature of the impulse. It might arise from sudden terror, or hallucination or delusion."
> His Lordship: "There are a good many people with abnormal–shaped heads, doctor?
> Witness: "There are."
> Mr Gleeson: "Would the prisoner be incapable of offering resistance to an impulse?"
> Witness: "I have, so far as I can, given information to you. I could not find out what his father and mother died of."
> Mr Gleeson: "Did you not think that if the family history was bad and other appearances suspicious, it might enter into a consideration of this man's sanity?"
> Witness: "Yes."

Mr Gleeson asked if such a man's condition might not be influenced – one day one way, and a month hence different.

> Witness: 'Oh yes. He is, I would say a potential lunatic."
> Mr Moriarty: "Are we not all potential lunatics, doctor?
> Witness: "I don't think you are."
> Mr Moriarty: "That is the entire case, my lord."

Mr Gleeson then addressed the jury on behalf of the prisoner. He said that if the accused were to be found guilty, he would be liable to pay the penalty with his life.

No duty can be more serious than the duty which places it within your power, should you think fit, to take away the life of a fellow man – the life which is given by God, and which we are told, God alone has the right to take. But, for the protection of society, if a man is responsible for what he does, and, being responsible, commits the abominable crime of murder, the law allows that he be punished with death. I would like to say that, apart altogether from the perpetrator of that abominable crime, it was not an Irish crime, and not the crime of any country that has a regard for chivalry or manhood.

I recognise that there had been a great deal of public feeling in the case, and I would appeal to the jury not to be influenced by anything they had heard, or any opinion that had been expressed. I am not here to admit the accuracy of the case for the Crown, and although I take issue in the case on the plea of insanity, it must not be assumed that I admit that the man in the dock is the perpetrator, but if you should come to the conclusion that the evidence you have heard proves the man to have been Heffernan, I would ask you to take up the consideration of the question as to what manner of a man Heffernan really is.

He thought he could establish to their satisfaction, that Heffernan was a person mentally irresponsible for his actions:

Now, what was the evidence? What would be the conduct of a sane man who had committed a murder? He knows the punishment and what would he do? He would naturally make some endeavour and save his skin. But what was the Crowns case? That having been seen by the girl, Woods, washing his boots within a few yards of the scene of the murder, that he goes back to Mullingar and resumes work the next morning. What was his conduct on the night of the murder, when he is in the public house when the news is brought in? Does he clear out and try to get away from Mullingar? No, is that the conduct of a discriminating man? I think you will come to the conclusion that it is not.

With regard to the evidence of the doctors, he would ask them not to put much reliance on it:

The experts might deny congenital insanity, but as men of the world did they not know, in spite of the medical evidence, that if a man has a brother and other relatives in the asylum, that he himself is likely to be tainted? The experts are only giving their opinions, they are theorising, and one ounce of fact is worth a ton of theory. Dr Lepper admits that he found congenital disease, and that was enough to show them that they were not dealing with a normal man, but with a man afflicted by the Almighty. He is a man weaker than you, and because he is weak and mentally afflicted, the Crown says that he shall be hanged. Gentlemen, that would be a crime worse that the murder of Miss

Walker. If that was how the law was carried out, half the lunatics in criminal asylums would be dead men today.

The point has been raised that though mentally afflicted, the prisoner still knew the difference between right and wrong. His Lordship said on that point he would put the following question to the jury: If you find on the evidence that he is guilty, at the time he did the act, was he labouring under such a disease of the mind as not to know what he was doing? He would ask a further question as to whether he knew it was wrong.

As His Lordship told you, the issue they had to try was, was he aware of the nature and quality of his act – that is of course, assuming he did it. To decide that, they must know the history of his family; they could not decide it without that. When they considered his family history they would decide that his mind was in an irrational state – an abnormal state… It is all very well for the learned Sergeant to joke about a person being insane one day and alright the next. The point is, what is your opinion of the state of his mind at the time of the murder, if he committed it? If you find that the opinion of these experts is a little too finely drawn, you will decide the case on your own opinions, and will be guided by no theories except those of common sense. I hope by putting the case before you that I have shown you that the man was not rational at the time of the murder, and that Ireland can, therefore, still retain her reputation for freedom from this sort of crime, and that it can still be proudly boasted in the poet's words, that any girl or woman in this country can walk along and say, "No son of Erin will offer me harm."

Mr Maloney, KC, then addressed the jury for the Crown. He said:

Mr Gleeson has done everything possible for his client in the case, and has asked you to use your own cold–drawn common sense, but you must do so on the evidence put before you, and be guided by it, and not by any fanciful theory or exaggeration. The evidence he submitted proved that Mary Walker was murdered by the prisoner, and that he was responsible to God and the law for what he had done.

Counsel then reviewed the evidence given:

One witness knew him and recognised him, and when she saw him he pulled his cap over his eyes. What did he do that for? Was that evidence that he was irrational, or did it show a cunning mind? He knew what he had done and he did not want to be recognised. Did he know the nature and quality of the act he was doing? There had been wild talk of degeneracy. There were a great number of abnormal and degenerate people, and the law was used to keep them in restraint. It had been said that two of Heffernan's brothers had been in the asylum, but he himself had been in Mullingar for twenty–five years and no one suggested he should be put in the asylum. Did he not know the nature and quality of his crime when within fifteen minutes he was removing the evidence of his guilt from his clothing, when he hid the knife, or when he was asked by Elizabeth Flanagan, why there was blood on his handkerchief and he said he had been skinning a goat? There had been no suggestion by the defence or no attempt at evidence that he had skinned any goat that day. Then he had been arrested and the cunning mind began to work to get him out of the toils, and he said he should be put in some place where he would be looked after.

Dr Russell tells you he examined him on the day he came in, and no thought of insanity ever entered his head. Then, after two months in gaol, the prisoner attempted to commit suicide. Is that the evidence of insanity? He knew the terrible nature of his act and the evidence that would be brought against him, and that there was no escape. There is no doubt at present of his sanity. Everyone admits that he is able to follow the evidence and instruct his solicitor. No doubt, he is a low mental type. Most of our criminals are. It is sometimes different in England and America, but in Ireland almost all our criminals are men of deficient intelligence. Dr Lepper told them that though a man is passionate and degenerate it is no proof that he is not able to distinguish between right and wrong. The attempt to prove insanity is like the last desperate blow of the gamester, the last resort which the prisoner and his counsel are driven to by the inexorable logic of the case made by the Crown against him and the evidence which it contains. Gentlemen, you are not here to consider vague theories of degeneracy, you are here to protect the public, and to protect poor lone women who have to walk the path of life and whose only protection is the law.

The Lord Justice then charged the jury. He said the case had been very ably conducted on both sides. It had been defended with extreme skill by Mr Gleeson. Mr Gleeson had asked the witnesses few questions in cross–examination. He continued:

Gentlemen, my experience is that the man who asks few questions is able to conduct his case skilfully, as he avoids letting in a lot of evidence.

He congratulated himself and the jury on the attentive way, the most becoming way they had followed the evidence. Their example would be worth following by other juries. The recent case was one that had created a great deal of feeling in the country, and it was a case in which the jury should dismiss from their minds everything they had heard before they came into court. There was another point: it was a very atrocious crime and juries were sometimes inclined in such a case to hurry their decision and fasten on any man brought forward as a criminal. If they had a doubt, they will give it in favour of the prisoner. He did not mean a trivial doubt but one they would act upon in their daily business. With the exception of the confession, the evidence was circumstantial. Circumstantial evidence was considered as conclusive as direct evidence – it was the evidence that was usually produced in a Court of Justice.

If direct evidence of seeing the crime was essential, most criminals would get off. What the jury had to decide was, did all the circumstances taken together satisfy them of the guilt of the prisoner? The first point they had to decide was, whether Miss Walker was murdered. He did not think they would have any doubt about that. They had heard the evidence of Dr Kelly that she died from a gash in her throat, four inches long. The next point was the time, and he would be inclined to rely on Fr Magee's evidence on that point. Fr Magee said he heard a scream, and he put the time at about 4.30pm. Another boy said he heard four or five screams coming from the direction of the canal, so they might be satisfied Miss Walker was murdered, about where the body was found, at between four and five o'clock. Now he would come to the person who did it. Was it the prisoner at the bar?

Whose testimony was most important? He thought it to be that of Ellen Woods: she saw him there, she gave her evidence in a creditable manner, she said she heard a scream and that she saw Fr Magee. Fr Magee says it was 4.30pm. She then came up to the canal bank and whom did she see? She knew the prisoner Heffernan well and they spoke across the canal. Where she saw him sitting on the bank was 52 yards from where the body was found. He continued:

> You heard what the excellent witness, Dr McWeeney said: He discovered blood on the trousers, and described one part of the trousers as having been washed. At one time doctors could not distinguish between the blood of mammals, but science has advanced so far that they can now distinguish between the blood of other mammals and human blood. Dr McWeeney, as an exponent of science, tells you that he has no doubt that the stains on Heffernan's trousers were caused by human blood.
>
> All these are circumstances that certainly point to the guilt of the prisoner. Had he a knife? You heard what the girl Elizabeth Flanagan said, she told you about a knife and pocket handkerchief. You heard what he said when she challenged him about the blood on the handkerchief. He said she was looking for news, and then, after thinking for a moment, he said he had been skinning a goat. Was that true? If it was, it would be easy to prove it, for there was money in court in such cases (for expenses of witnesses), but no evidence had been produced to prove it. If it was a falsehood, why did he tell it? Was it because he was an innocent man?
>
> He had a knife on the morning of the murder and on the following morning. When he was arrested he had no knife. What had he done with it? Was it because it was an instrument used in an innocent act that he had not now got it? He was near the place at the time of the murder. The witness Lyons saw him passing near just before the time. He described him as walking slowly

and looking about him, and he was seen going home by a torturous way, if he was the man seen going home. Then, with regard to the prisoner's own statement, he said, "I killed the poor girl right enough." Was that confession true?

His Lordship then dealt with the plea of insanity, which had been raised on the prisoner's behalf. He said Mr Maloney made one observation in his well–reasoned speech with which he entirely agreed. He said most criminals were of a low mental type. That is true, but they are answerable to the law. It would be giving a great licence to crime if they were not to be held responsible for their acts because they were degenerate or of a low mental type. Why did he put his cap over his eyes? Did he know the nature of his act and try to disguise himself so that he would not be convicted with the act, if he had committed it? Why was he washing his hands? Why did he hide the knife, if he did hide it? Did he do it in order to prevent all identification of the murderer with himself? Why was the grass pulled and put over the body? Was it in order that it might not be discovered for some days, and to prevent evidence being brought to prove he was in her company that day?

The poor girl, gentlemen, was about 30 years of age and strongly built; she fought for her virtue. The man was comparatively small, and when she resisted, he may have taken out the knife and cut her throat. If you are satisfied he did it, the onus of proof lies on him to show that he was insane. Of course there may be some of the family in the asylum, but does it then follow that he is mad? You will consider the whole case, gentlemen, and bring to bear on it that becoming attention with which you followed the evidence. If you are satisfied beyond a reasonable doubt that he did it, you will then consider the other question which I told you of with regard to insanity: whether he was responsible or so afflicted by disease of the mind that he could not know the nature and quality of the act, or distinguish between right and wrong. If he has not satisfied you of that, it is your duty to bring in an unqualified verdict of guilty.

★★★★★

Joseph Heffernan, the town fool, had been in the wrong place at the wrong time. He displayed no physical evidence of being involved in the vicious attack on Mary Walker. In every case I studied, the perpetrator of similar attacks displayed scratches such as the kind Dr Russell hoped to find on Heffernan's body. His boots and clothes displayed no evidence of being anywhere near the victim while she was being brutally murdered. However, when the police took custody of the defendant's property, they soon displayed the corruption that sent Heffernan to his death. The shirt, for example, displayed all the hallmarks of being worn by someone infected by parasites, fleas, ticks etc. Dr McWeeney, a forensic expert for the prosecution, confirmed that Heffernan's body showed no sign that he was infected by such bugs. Therefore, one must conclude that he was neither the wearer nor owner of the shirt. The trousers were clearly interfered with by a police officer, who definitely did not know what he was doing in contaminating the left leg only, in such a way that it would transfer blood to the other leg as soon as the wearer of the trousers walked. It is clear that the trousers were never worn after they were contaminated with blood.

As regards the leggings, McWeeney said in his statement, "near some of the small droplets of blood were little cup shaped depressions where the surface of the leather was of a brighter colour than elsewhere and seemed to have been scooped out." Adding, "this; may have been done with the object of removing the more obvious spots of blood." However, Mrs Moran, Heffernan's landlady, while testifying at the Magistrates' hearing on 19 July, stated that when Heffernan left her house on the morning of the murder, he was wearing yellow or brown soft leggings "not of leather," and he was dressed the same when he returned that night. McWeeney, the so—called "excellent witness," on hearing Mrs Moran's description of the leggings as "not of leather," refrained from using the word "leather" while giving evidence at the assizes.

When he was arrested, Heffernan was not carrying a knife, he did not have matches, a pipe, or tobacco – there were not even tobacco particles in his pockets. He had no handkerchief and he was not wearing bloodstained or wet clothes (except the left knee, the result of thinning mangolds). Heffernan was wearing newish looking boots less than an hour after the killer walked through 22 feet of boggy moist ground, boots that were larger than the discredited cast taken from the scene of the murder.

The famous handkerchief, as spoken about by Elizabeth Flanagan, which she alleged Heffernan used to blow his nose, remains a mystery. Throughout the day of the murder and indeed the morning after, nobody witnessed Heffernan blow his nose. The prison officers and the doctor who carried out a medical examination mentioned nothing about the defendant suffering from a slight head cold. During his entire incarceration, nobody mentioned seeing Heffernan blow his nose or sniffling. If he had a handkerchief, why would he use grass to clean his hands and boots? Grass blades are very sharp, and there is a good chance he would have cut himself if he used grass in the manner as alleged by Woods. At the Magistrates' hearing, Heffernan disputed Flanagan's estimation of the amount of time he spent in her house, saying that someone could have seen him come and go and could prove that he had only been there for two minutes. Five months later at the assizes, Flanagan decided to counter this by adding, "Heffernan left her house to get a readier and returned and lay on her bed."

I feel at this stage that I must mention the prosecution's decision, with the assistance of the defence team, not to mention the times, and what an important part this decision played in the conviction of Heffernan. Heffernan was seen, and positively identified entering Mount Street, at least fifteen minutes before three witnesses saw a man (whom nobody positively identified) walk away from the scene of the crime. The prosecution placed a lot of importance on the route Heffernan took while returning to Mullingar. However, if Heffernan wanted to conceal himself, he had better options at his disposal. He could have stayed in the fields and entered the town under the railway bridge, which is about a three–minute walk from Clown Bridge. This would bring him into the centre of town via the Blackhall/Grove Street area. He also had the option of walking through the fields for another three or four minutes, and enter the town from the Kilbeggan road.

Then we had Murray's uncontested evidence. Had this child been cross–examined by the defence, he would certainly have become their star witness. The fact that he had a definite time at which he arrived at the Green Bridge, and the time he and Merlehan saw an unidentified man leave the murder scene, would have been invaluable if he had been properly cross–examined. If it had been taken together with Christopher Downes' identification of Heffernan near Scoutail Bridge, along with Grogan and Duignam's sighting of him a couple of minutes later in the town centre, it would certainly have warranted a dismissal of all charges against Heffernan.

Incredibly, none of the above was taken on board by Gleeson. He totally ignored everything and anything that pointed towards his client's innocence and instead attempted to impress upon the jury his perception of Heffernan's mental state. It seems this man was encouraged by the prosecution to ensure a guilty verdict was returned by the jury.

12.

THE JUDGE'S REMARKS

1

The Judge at the outset, praised Mr Gleeson for asking few questions in cross–examination, adding, "Gentlemen, gentlemen. My experience is that the man who asks few questions is able to conduct his case skilfully, as he avoids letting in a lot of evidence."

2

He congratulated himself, despite his obvious negligence. If he had been doing his job as he was paid to do, he would have studied the prosecution's case before the trial and put a stop to the charade that cost an innocent man his life.

3

He congratulated the members of the jury, whom I believe must have noticed something was awry. The jury should have questioned a lot of the evidence, especially after witnessing the judge force Ellen Woods to perjure herself.

4

He said, "With the exception of the confession, the evidence was circumstantial. Circumstantial evidence is considered as conclusive as direct evidence – it is the evidence that is usually produced in a Court of Justice." In this statement, he is telling the jury that he believed all of the prosecution's evidence, especially Woods and indeed Mansfield's testimony concerning the alleged confession. The jury was more or less informed by the Lord Chief Justice that he deemed Heffernan guilty.

5

O'Brien continued, "If direct evidence of seeing the crime was essential, most criminals would get off. What the jury had to decide was: did all the circumstances, taken together, satisfy them of the guilt of the prisoner?"

They had heard the evidence of Dr Kelly that Mary Walker died from a gash in her throat. He failed to mention the lack of defensive wounds on her arms etc. and the fact that Heffernan's body displayed no physical evidence of him being involved in a desperate struggle, such as scratches or bruises.

The Judge was inclined to rely on Fr Magee's evidence on the time of the murder. Fr Magee said he heard a scream, and he put the time at about 4.30pm. Actually, Fr Magee thought the scream to be that of children playing in the area. Richard Merlehan also mentioned the fact that he thought he heard kids playing in the area. Magee said he calculated the time, unlike Downes, Merlehan and Murray, who looked at a watch or clock to confirm the exact time.

He then spoke about young Michael Murray's evidence. Murray's evidence clearly takes Fr Magee out of the picture, because at the time he alleged he heard the screams, Magee was in the priests' palace. The time that Murray said he saw an unidentified man walk away from the murder scene, was confirmed by Merlehan. At the same time, Heffernan, was positively identified by three reliable witnesses, as he walked through Mullingar. Incidentally, young Murray said the screams frightened him; this does not sound right. We have an eleven–year–old child who said he heard screams that frightened him. A few minutes later, he meets Richard Merlehan, an adult, and says nothing to him. As a matter of fact, he totally ignored Merlehan. Murray was 154 yards further away from the crime scene than 35–year–old Merlehan, yet Merlehan, a young man in his thirties, heard no screams.

Of course, if Gleeson had done his job properly, and studied all the evidence given by the witnesses from day one, he would have extracted the vital information that would prove Heffernan's innocence. Whether O'Brien, a man baying for Heffernan's blood, could accept his innocence is another story. I really believe he intentionally assisted the prosecution throughout the trial to acquire a guilty verdict.

6

The judge next asks, "Whose testimony was most important?" He thought it was that of Ellen Woods.

She gave her evidence in a creditable manner; she said she heard a scream and that she saw Fr Magee and Fr Magee says it was 4.30pm [Woods stated she left home at 4.50 or 5pm]. *She then came up to the canal bank, and whom does she see? The prisoner Heffernan* [this is where Woods perjured herself, giving two versions as to how she identified him], *she knew him well, and they spoke across the canal. Where she saw him sitting on the bank was 52 yards from where the body was found* [this is not what she said at the magistrates' hearing in Mullingar]. *There had been screams heard; did Heffernan hear them? What was he doing? He was washing his hands and seemed to be cleaning his boots* [she contradicted her own statement concerning the leggings]. *Was there blood upon them?*

Again, the judge is informing the jury that he believed everything Woods said. Woods perjured herself under his guidance. The timing in her evidence just did not make sense. Nobody saw her on or at the canal bank at the time of the murder, simply because she was not there at that time.

7

The judge continued, "You heard what the excellent witness, Dr McWeeney said." He discovered blood on the trousers and described one part of the trousers as having been washed clean of all bloodstains. Why would Heffernan wash just one side? How could he do everything he is alleged to have done in such a short period of time? There is no doubt that the real killer's clothes would have been saturated with blood, and the blood on the trousers would transfer from one leg to the other as soon as he walked.

O'Brien went on:

One time doctors could not distinguish between the blood of mammals, but science has advanced so far that they can now distinguish between the blood of other mammals and human blood. Dr McWeeney, as an exponent of science tells you that he has no doubt that the stains on Heffernan's trousers were caused by human blood.

He, like Dr McWeeney, failed to inform the court that the Precipitin Test at that time was far from accurate. It was his wish to mislead the jury and indeed the country with inaccurate claims about modern science. Unfortunately, he succeeded. The Precipitin Test was not used as reliable evidence in British courts until the 1930s and only after numerous improvements to its accuracy. He failed to remind the court that Woods, on the first day, said she identified Heffernan by his voice (sound) and then, the following day, she changed her story to say that she identified Heffernan "as she saw his face" (sight).

O'Brien also failed to remind the jury about the fact that McWeeney, the excellent witness, let the cat out of the bag when he spoke about the bloodstained shirt, and the fact that Heffernan's body did not display the evidence needed to prove it was his shirt. In fact, McWeeney proved the shirt was not worn by the defendant. Then of course we have the leggings. Mrs Moran swore that they "were not of leather". However, a week later, when they arrived at McWeeney's laboratory, they mysteriously turned into leather. How did that happen?

The discovery of the knife, which Constable Rowlette alleged he found, was unknown to the other members of the search party. It was the same knife that he kept in his possession until the following evening, when he arrived for duty. The same knife that he said was "pretty sharp" while Mrs Moran stated the knife she alleged Heffernan had, "wasn't a sharp knife". McWeeney stated that he found starch grains, such as would be contained in bread, on the knife, adding they were adhering to minute traces of blood. He neglected to explain how this came about, as no such starch grains were found in Heffernan's pockets. The only time this could happen was when the defendant had breakfast the morning after. There is a problem here, as minute traces of blood would dry shortly after staining the knife. It would be out of the question to suppose that tiny spots of blood would be wet enough for the starch grains to adhere to them nineteen hours later. Any fair–minded, right thinking judge would have thrown out this evidence.

Why the knife, the pipe and other evidence such as, the umbrella, handbag, belt, watch (if Miss Walker had one) and shoes were not dusted for fingerprints is a mystery to me. Perhaps, the fear of establishing the identity of the real killer had something to do with this. I also believe Heffernan's cap should have been tested for bloodstains, because Woods stated that Heffernan, while washing his boots, etc., pulled the cap (with wet hands) over his eyes in order to hide his face from her. Or maybe Richard Merlehan was right when he stated that the person he saw wore a "small black cap, or black hair, or ne'er a cap at all." The judge should have commented on the delay of seven days before the evidence was handed over to McWeeney for analysis, and the fact that McWeeney kept the articles for another six days before he analysed them.

8

O'Brien next mentioned Elizabeth Flanagan:

> You heard what the girl, Elizabeth Flanagan said. She told you about a knife and pocket handkerchief. You heard what he said when she challenged him about the blood on the handkerchief. He said she was looking for news, and then, after thinking for a moment, that he had been skinning a goat. Was that true? If it was, it would be easy to prove it for there was money in court in such cases (for expenses of witnesses), but no evidence had been produced to prove it.

Heffernan mentioned numerous witnesses to authorities and not one was called to give evidence on his behalf. Why would he tell a frightened child anything? This story about the goat just did not happen. O'Brien went on, "If it was a falsehood, why did he tell it? Was it because he was an innocent man? He had a knife on the morning of the murder and on the following morning."

Flanagan was a young girl and this strange man walked into her home while she minded her siblings. She stated that he took out some tobacco, not in a pouch, and filled his pipe. She described the pipe. She said she saw a knife and described that also. (Heffernan's right hand was deformed yet she said nothing about this). She said he then asked for a readier to ready his pipe, which he then lit and smoked.

This just does not make sense. Nobody, no matter how daft he may be, would attempt to clean his pipe after filling it with tobacco. If Charlie Quinn is to be believed, the pipe would not need to be cleaned as it was purchased just a few hours earlier. Flanagan said nothing about Heffernan using the fire to light the pipe. She said he lit the pipe. If Ellen Woods is to be believed, Heffernan had no matches. Then we have the loose tobacco in his pocket. Surely, if this were true, there would have been tobacco particles found in his pockets.

Flanagan said he openly displayed the knife while he cut the tobacco. She then went on to say that he tried to hide it quickly when she returned with Susan Giff. This just does not make sense either. Also, Flanagan and Giff had to walk through a hallway before they reached the kitchen door, thereby giving Heffernan plenty of time to allegedly put a knife into his pocket at his ease, and not "quickly", as the witnesses said. O'Brien then stated, "You heard what he said when she challenged him." Is this man for real? The girl also said she "was getting frightened as he was getting wicked looking." It is difficult to believe a fourteen–year–old girl would dream of challenging a complete stranger about such things, especially a stranger who simply walked in off the street and carried a knife. She would be doing her best to get him to leave or she would go for help straight away.

O'Brien mentioned the "bloodstained handkerchief". However, he failed to mention the fact that this piece of prosecution evidence was never found. With the exception of Flanagan, no witness gave evidence to the fact that they had seen the defendant use a handkerchief on the day before the murder, the day of the murder or any time after. He spent almost six months in Kilmainham Gaol and not one prison officer or member of the medical staff, or indeed the nuns from Basin Lane, gave evidence that he required the use of a handkerchief during all that time.

Flanagan then stated that Heffernan "paused" for about two minutes when she challenged him. O'Brien helped out here and gave her a reason for the "pause", which she readily accepted. This "pause" was not mentioned by Flanagan while giving evidence at the Magistrates' hearing in Mullingar, or indeed in her statement given to the police on 19 July 1909. This is the young girl who alleged she saw bloodstains on the knife from a distance. The forensic expert stated he had to use a powerful lens to see what Flanagan saw, without the aid of any equipment whatsoever. After describing the knife and the pipe in an observant, but rehearsed manner, she failed to mention anything about the defendant's clothes being damp from bloodstains, or water, as they would have been if he had very recently washed the blood away. However, O'Brien failed in his duty as the Lord Chief Justice and ignored all this in his summary.

This man was not interested in administering law or justice. When he said, "all these are circumstances that certainly point to the guilt of the prisoner," he was informing the jury that he believed everything this child said, even though nothing made sense. Addressing the alleged confession, O'Brien failed to mention the medical evidence of both doctors who confirmed that the knife entered the victim through the Adam's apple and not under the ear, as the alleged confession states. He should have mentioned this.

Next on his agenda was the plea of insanity. While no plea of insanity was lodged, Gleeson actually led the court to believe that Heffernan was guilty but insane. O'Brien stated, "I agree with Mr Maloney's observation when he said most criminals are of a low mental type." He added, "Did Heffernan know what he was doing?" Here he convicted Heffernan before the jury deliberated. He then asked, "Why did he pull the cap over his eyes? Did he know the nature of his act when he wanted to disguise himself, so that he would not be convicted of the act?"

He then said, "Why was he washing his hands? Why did he hide the knife? Did he do it in order to prevent all identification of the murderer with himself? Why was the grass pulled over her body? Was it in order that it might not be discovered for some days, and to prevent evidence being brought to prove he was in her company that day?" He went on, "The girl was strongly built. She fought for her virtue. The man was comparatively small and when she resisted he may have taken out the knife and cut her throat." As the victim had no defensive wounds, the evidence does not support this, and as Heffernan's body contained no scratches or bruises, it surely suggests that this man was not involved in the type of struggle as described throughout the trial. The fact that his right hand was deformed would certainly make it difficult for Heffernan to hold the victim, and at the same time remove the knife from his pocket and open it in the manner O'Brien led the jury to believe.

O'Brien's summary was actually a shambles. He went out of his way to instruct the jury to bring in a guilty verdict, probably to put the case to bed and lessen the chances of the guilty party being identified. As the Lord Chief Justice, one would assume O'Brien was the leading legal brain in the country, yet in his summary he missed all the important evidence that would lead to the dismissal of the charge of murder against Joseph Heffernan. This incompetent judge got the blood he craved when he signed Heffernan's death warrant.

At about 4.53pm, the jury returned to the court and, amidst the most awful silence, the Clerk of the Court looked at the issue paper handed down by the foreman and pronounced the words, "You find the prisoner "guilty".

In a clear voice, the Clerk of the Court then addressed the prisoner:

> *Joseph Heffernan, when this charge was first made against you in this court you pleaded not guilty and put your cause upon your God and your country, and your country has found you guilty. What have you to say why the sentence of the law should not be passed upon you?*

His reply could not be heard and a warder repeated his words for him, "He says he hopes your Lordship will give him a few days. The judge made no reply, but then spoke, addressing the prisoner:

> *Joseph Heffernan, you have been found guilty by the jury who tried you of the crime of murder, and it is only right to that jury to say that their verdict claims and meets with my entire concurrence.*
>
> *Mary Walker, the heroic girl slain by your ruthless hand, died nobly in defence of her virtue. Her pure soul has gone before the tribunal of God to receive at His hand her great reward. She has gone before that Great Being whose principal attribute is Mercy.*
>
> *Joseph Heffernan, hold up your hands in supplication (here the prisoner raised up his hands) to Him, the wideness of whose mercy is likened to the wideness of the sea, and to whom judge and convict must at the last day answer for their conduct here.*
>
> *It now becomes my duty as the humble minister of the law to pass upon you the sentence of death, which is the most distressing duty incident to the life of man.*

The Judge then pronounced the most awful sentence of man on man – that of death – fixing the execution date for 4 January 1910. In a dazed condition, the condemned man walked from the bar of the court with the warders.

13.

CONSTABULARY SKULDUGGERY

CONSTABLE ROWLETTE

Constable Rowlette stated:

I know the tunnel that runs under the canal where the water pipe passes to the engine house. I remember 10 July 1909. I went to this tunnel on that day at about four o'clock pm. I went to it through Gas Lane and down the Mill Road. Constable Moore was with me; Sgt Brennan met us at the tunnel. I searched the tunnel and I found a knife in it. I see the knife produced; it is the knife I found. The knife was covered with mud under the water pipe – it did not appear to be long there. The mud around it seemed to have been recently moved and there was no rust on it. The knife has a metal handle; the large blade was broken, the small blade was intact. It is pretty sharp. I kept it in my possession until the evening of 11 July 1909. I then handed it over in the exact state I found it to Constable Moore.

Rowlette's statement is unbelievable. However, he – and the entire investigating team – got away with it to such an extent that Rowlette was promoted to the rank of Acting Sergeant shortly after Heffernan's execution and, on 1 June 1912, he was promoted to the rank of full Sergeant. Rowlette stated that when he took part in the search of the tunnel he was accompanied by Sgt Brennan and Constable Moore. Brennan, as a sergeant and senior man was in charge of the search party. Constable Moore was in charge of all evidence relating to this case, and as far as this investigation was concerned, Rowlette was merely assisting with the search.

Rowlette said in his statement, "I searched the tunnel and found a knife in it." That is all very well, but neither Sergeant Brennan nor Constable Moore mentioned anything about anyone finding a knife at the tunnel. I do not believe Rowlette found a knife in or near the tunnel. If he had, according to regulations, he should have immediately brought it to the attention of the officer in charge.

He then stated, "I kept the knife in my possession until the evening of 11 July 1909. I then handed it over in the exact state I found it to Constable Moore." Rowlette, by his own admission, kept the knife in his possession for twenty–four hours or more. This unusual behaviour was never clarified. Because of Rowlette's "cloak and dagger" behaviour, I feel I am correct in my assumption that he lied and fabricated the entire story. I also believe, while Brennan and Moore did not back him, they certainly knew what he was doing when he produced the pocket knife the following evening. Incidentally, Rowlette produced the pocket knife a few days after the inquest where Dr Dillon–Kelly stated, "The wound was probably caused by a pocket knife."

We also have two descriptions of the knife's capabilities. The first description from Mrs Moran, Heffernan's landlady. She swore she saw it in action on the morning after the murder and, as Heffernan was unable to cut the besom, she alleged she said to him, "That's not a sharp knife." (Mrs Moran, while giving evidence at the assizes, admitted that she did not actually see the knife.). Rowlette, who alleged he found the knife more than fifty hours later, swore the knife was "pretty sharp". He also said the knife was covered with mud. The forensic analyst, in his report, stated that, "There was some brownish matter resembling a mixture of soil or earth with rust." Rowlette, while giving evidence at the Magistrates hearing in Mullingar said, "There was no rust on the knife."

He also stated at the Magistrates hearing, as he did in his statement, "the knife was covered with mud." However, at the Assizes he said, "The knife was covered with mud and hay."

CONSTABLE CHARLES MOORE

Constable Moore said in his first statement, taken on 8 July 1909, "From information I received, I arrested Joseph Heffernan, the prisoner now present on this date, on the charge of murdering Miss Walker on the canal bank yesterday evening." Moore actually admitted that he arrested Heffernan on the charge of murdering (not on suspicion) Miss Walker before he interviewed him. From the very start, the authorities had Heffernan tried, convicted, and executed. The normal procedure was then, as it is now, that a suspect is arrested on "suspicion" of committing the crime and is then taken to the station and questioned. He is allowed to tell his story by way of a statement and his version of events is checked out, after which the police decide whether to charge or release the suspect.

Constable Moore, in his initial statement, said, "From information I received, I arrested Joseph Heffernan." Mr Gleeson, the Defence Lawyer, failed to question this and extract from Moore the exact time or even an estimated time that he received this information. Thomas Rattigan, a paid informer, in his statement, said that at least one person in the queue outside the dispensary was in possession of this information prior to Heffernan allegedly passing the dispensary sometime between 8.30am and 8.45am. Rattigan, if he can be believed, said someone in the queue asked Heffernan as he passed by, "Were you not taken yet, Joe."

Moore, in his second statement taken on 26 July 1909, said:

> *I brought him to the Police Barracks of Mullingar and his clothes and boots were removed from him in my presence. He had no knife on him. I saw a list made out of his clothes, and I then had them made up in a parcel and sealed. I did not in any way interfere with them. I noticed that the left knee of the trousers was damp. I conveyed those clothes to Dublin myself, and handed them over to Dr McWeeney myself on 15 July 1909. I also handed over to him a parcel of the clothes of the deceased, which I received from Sgt Brennan on the 11th last.*

His evidence during the magistrate hearings was much the same as his statement.

At the assizes, in response to a question from the judge, Moore said that Heffernan was in "full possession of his senses". He gave evidence about the "parcelling up of the prisoner's clothes when they were taken from him, and also of the knife, and bringing of the same to Professor McWeeney in Dublin." He added, "The clothes were in the same condition as when they were taken off the prisoner; the boots and gaiters were also included."

If everything was, as he said, sealed on the morning of the arrest and not interfered with, how did D.I. Ruttledge and Moore take the boots out to the murder scene afterwards, and how was the knife added to the parcel three days later?

According to Moore, when Heffernan was arrested, he "had no knife on him". As Moore never mentioned tobacco, a pipe, matches or indeed a handkerchief, we must assume that he had no such items in his possession either. Far from not interfering with Heffernan's property, Moore actually assisted the Inspector in at least contaminating the crime scene with the prisoner's boots. Moore also stated that the left knee of Heffernan's trousers was damp, but really, if, as Moore said, Heffernan was thinning mangolds, this was just the result of a left-handed person kneeling down while he worked.

Moore also informed the court that on 15 July 1909, he brought both Heffernan's and Mary Walker's clothes to Dublin and handed everything over to Dr McWeeney. Why did it take seven full days to get the evidence to Dublin to be forensically tested? Constable Moore, unlike other witnesses, stated that Heffernan was in "full possession of his senses" and "not in the least excited" when arrested, and remember, he was not being arrested when the other witnesses alleged they observed his "nervy" behaviour.

CONSTABLE HOLMES

At the inquest on 8 July, Holmes stated that he noticed "two tracks from where the body lay, to the drain," thereby putting the tracks on the canal side of the drain. He also stated he remained in "charge of the body till it was removed to Mullingar." Constable Holmes's statement on 15 July deals with the evening of the murder and the murder scene itself. He goes on to talk about the dead body of Miss Walker, the marshy ground with long grass, the areas where the grass was flattened, the water ditch, the boot tracks he saw "on the far side of the water ditch" (railway side) as if "someone had jumped across the water ditch."

He mentioned blood and said, "There must have been a great struggle." He stated that he took charge of the tracks and allowed no one to interfere with them. He went on to say that he saw Constables Foskin and Harrington pick up gloves, a belt and a pocket of a skirt from the ground close to where the body was lying. Holmes was not called to give evidence at the assizes.

Holmes's evidence concerning the murder scene was mostly in line with what other witnesses had to say in terms of the trampled grass in certain areas and blood, and so on. However, giving evidence at the inquest, he stated that it was "as if someone had jumped down in the drain." If this is correct, and someone had "jumped down in the drain," the prosecution, in my opinion, wrongly led the court to believe that it had been the defendant. If Heffernan really had "jumped into the drain" on his way from the murder scene, how could he have cleaned and dried his boots to look new in less than an hour? Elizabeth Flanagan swore Heffernan's boots appeared to be newish when she saw them about an hour later.

Why did Holmes change his story from one week to the next? He knew in his heart and soul that this kind of skulduggery would certainly send an innocent man to the gallows. I believe District Inspector Ruttledge to be the instigator, as he was at the scene that was littered with boot prints as the locals thronged to the area. Of course, this is one of the reasons for moving, on paper, the alleged prints to the railway side of the drain. As District Inspector Ruttledge, who surveyed the murder scene, questioned the witnesses at the inquest and failed to query Holmes's evidence, we must assume that what Holmes had to say then was simply what they agreed between them. However, shortly after the inquest the police decided that this had to be changed as they began to copper-fasten a case against the defendant. The people in charge of the case sat around the table in a cosy incident room in Mullingar Police Station, and, in my opinion, began to plot the murder of local man, Joe Heffernan.

One week later, on 15 July 1909, while making a statement at the police station in Mullingar, he said, "On the far side of the water ditch, I found, under the fence, two boot tracks as if someone had jumped across the water ditch." Incidentally, during the inquest, Holmes called the ditch "the drain" which of course is all the same, but that was the term he preferred to use. A week later he changed this to the inspector's wording, and called it "the ditch." He had probably been listening to Ruttledge too much. He also said at the inquest and one week later, in his statement, "I remained in charge of the body till it was removed to Mullingar." In his statement and in his evidence he said, "I took charge of the tracks and allowed no one to interfere with them." Is he saying that he remained at the scene all through the night? Remember, he was not on duty; he was out for a stroll and would be improperly dressed for night duty – it gets very cold through the night, even in July.

During the inquest, while speaking about the "two tracks", he never mentioned anything about "taking charge of the tracks and not allowing anyone to interfere with them." I am curious about the belt and gloves; were they made of leather? If they were, were they dusted for fingerprints? Also, was the umbrella found at the scene dusted for prints? Holmes was in the bad books with the District Inspector. On 15 August 1907, he was warned about his conduct and fined 20s, the equivalent of £1, a hefty deduction from his wages at that time. It seems that D.I. Ruttledge, who knew the boot prints never existed, offered Holmes a golden opportunity to get himself back into the good books. All he had to do was run with the boot–print story. I believe that D.I. Ruttledge told Constable Holmes that he would not be cross–examined at the inquest or at the Magistrates', and he would not be required for the assizes.

HEAD CONSTABLE CRUDDEN

In his statement, Head Constable Crudden mentioned the measurements relating to the case. He was assisted by the relevant witnesses as required. He said he walked from the "murder scene to Clown Bridge by the way the man was seen by the witnesses." The problem with this is, the unidentified man seen walking from the murder scene was heading towards the back of Railway Cottages. However, we know the unidentified man seen by Mrs Feeney came from the direction of Merlehan's house. We do not know which route Crudden timed. Maybe he timed a bit of both. If so, did he crawl under the gate, almost trapping himself? Did he sit under a tree for a period of time? Did he walk slowly as he was passing Merlehan's house? We know Heffernan wanted to talk to Merlehan about the possibility of obtaining some work, and passed his house. Crudden also walked and timed the journey between the Green Bridge and Murray's field. He was accompanied by young Michael Murray. He said it took them about fifteen minutes to complete the walk. I also timed this walk and estimated that fifteen minutes would be about correct for an adult. In my opinion, young Murray would have to trot to keep up with Crudden.

Murray was eleven years of age at the time, and kids of that age do not really walk like adults, they just saunter along at their ease. Crudden took charge of timing the walk and I am sure that young Murray never got a look at the watch. It seems to me that no matter what he timed it at, he would say exactly what suited his case at the time. It is difficult to believe that Murray was capable of walking that distance in fifteen minutes.

Head Constable Crudden was a very domineering person when it came to pleasing and indeed protecting his masters in London, Dublin and indeed his immediate boss in Mullingar, D.I. Ruttledge. It seems he was prepared to do almost anything to secure a conviction. He knew, like every other policeman stationed in Mullingar, that Heffernan was innocent. You read how he threatened the local media for carrying what one would describe as an ordinary news article that showed his friends in a bad light. The article also embarrassed the authorities in the House of Commons at Westminster.

Murder is a different kettle of fish, however, and it demanded all his attention to ensure the arrest, trial, conviction and execution of an innocent man. He certainly got at young Murray as they walked (in Murray's case, jogged) the distance from the Green Bridge to Murray's father's field. He was entirely responsible for Murray's memory loss and the alteration of his story as he gave evidence at the assizes. This man had access to all the vulnerable witnesses, including the children while he compiled his report. He looked on as various police officers blatantly lied and played their part in the murder of Joe Heffernan. In this way, the local constabulary ensured that the British occupying forces would not be answerable to anyone, despite the fact that I believe it was one of His Majesty's soldiers who murdered Miss Mary Walker.

SERGEANT THOMAS COOKE

In his statement, Sergeant Cooke said he was in charge of the escort that conveyed the prisoner Heffernan from Mullingar to Kilmainham Gaol on 8 July 1909. Cooke stated, "On the train between Mullingar and Broadstone Heffernan made a voluntary statement," which, according to Cooke, was:

> *This is a terrible thing to be charged with. I know nothing about it, I was not even out in that direction yesterday, or had no business out that way either. I never left the town yesterday. I did not take any drink for the past three months until yesterday and I should never take it because I am not accountable for what I do when I take it.*

On 15 July, Cooke was again in charge of the escort that brought the prisoner from Kilmainham to Mullingar. He said:

> When we brought him out of the prison and were conveying him to Broadstone Station he made a voluntary statement. He said, "I suppose you have plenty of evidence on me now; you have got the knife and everything, but Tom Cole will prove I had no knife. Mrs Moran said I had a knife and that I pared a besom for her with it, but I pared it with my fingers, if she got plenty of porter that is all she wants. I suppose her evidence will hang me. She should not tell lies anyhow, many a man was taken in the wrong. I don't know the girl at all. I was not out on the canal bank that day or had any business out there."

According to Cooke, Heffernan afterwards said:

> They might as well shut me up someplace because if I am left knocking about I will do the same thing again. I want to be put someplace where I would be brought up and minded.

On 19 July, Cooke was again in charge of the escort that brought the prisoner from Kilmainham to Mullingar. He stated that between the prison and Broadstone Station, Heffernan made another voluntary statement. He alleged that Heffernan said:

> I met Jack Doyle in Sullivan's Public House that day; I gave him a glass of porter. I asked him was there any work to be got; he said, "Yes, plenty of work, Dick Merlehan of Clown has three or four acres of meadow down." I rambled out the canal bank that day and crossed up the fields. I did not see Merlehan, and did not like to go to the house, as I was not great with the woman since I left them last. I slept in Dibbs' field that day. I think it was in meadow. If I was asked about Clown ["about Clown" is crossed out] … was I out about Clown I would have told I was out there but I was not asked. Many a time I went out the canal bank and crossed up to Merlehan's when I was working with him.

Cooke's evidence at the Magistrates' hearing and the assizes was in line with his statement. However, as Cooke himself said, he was in charge of some of the escorts ferrying Heffernan between Mullingar and Kilmainham Prison. There were two daily trips bringing Heffernan to Mullingar and back to Dublin. It seems odd that Heffernan only spoke to Cooke and totally ignored the officer in charge of the return journey. Also, no other member of the escorts carried out on 8, 15 or 19 July heard Heffernan make any statement whatsoever. There is no record of corroborating statements being given by the other police officers, nor were they asked to give evidence at any of the court hearings. Stranger still, how did Heffernan know that a knife was found on 10 July, as he had no visitors or legal representation from when he was arrested to the date in question, 15 July.

How, on 15 July, did Heffernan know about Mrs Moran's statement concerning a knife when the lady in question did not make the statement until 19 July? It beggars belief that Sgt Cooke alleged that Heffernan came clean on 19 July about his presence on the canal line on the afternoon of the murder. Heffernan had already confirmed he was on the canal line that afternoon. During the Magistrates' hearing on 15 July, four days earlier, while questioning Thomas Nooney, who was fishing on the canal line, Heffernan said, "I don't remember talking to you." If one was to believe Cooke, Heffernan, had an ideal opportunity to deny being on the canal line while questioning Nooney four days previously.

If what Cooke said about the alleged statements was true, was he not duty bound to get at the truth? He should have ensured interviews and statements were taken from the following people: Tom Cole and his employees, Mr Gill (Farm Labourer), Jack Doyle and his company in Sullivan's pub, and of course Mrs Merlehan. The thing is, these people were certainly interviewed at some stage, but their evidence was deemed to have a negative effect on the police case resulting in a failure to take statements.

If Heffernan did mention these people, then he had to be telling the truth concerning what had transpired between him and them. He had no way of contacting them in order to get them to give credibility to his story. For example, Tom Cole could swear that while Heffernan worked for him a short time before, he had never seen him with a knife, or smoking a pipe. Jack Doyle would be in a position to verify Heffernan's story about why he was out at Merlehan's farm and Mrs Merlehan could confirm that she and Heffernan fell out and were not on speaking terms. It is also strange that Francis Judge, who did make a statement, was not asked if Heffernan had a knife and smoked a pipe while drinking in Sullivan's pub.

Dr EDMUND McWEENEY, ANALYST (FORENSICS)

Dr Edmund McWeeney, a Professor at the School of Medicine, Cecelia Street, Dublin, stated the following:

> On 15 July 1909, I received from Constable Charles Moore a parcel containing two sealed packets. In one packet there were articles of clothing, stated to have been found on Joseph Heffernan when he was arrested on 8 July 1909 and a list of the same. In the other packet there were articles of

clothing stated to have been taken from the body of the deceased Mary Walker on 7 July 1909, with a list of same. I examined these articles on 21 July 1909.

We know that the murder occurred on 7 July 1909, and the relevant evidence was in the possession of the police, allegedly packaged and ready to be moved to Dublin on 8 July 1909. Why did it take a week to arrange this? We also know that McWeeney examined the evidence on 21 July 1909, allowing another six days to elapse. Why the delay? McWeeney said he carried out the entire examination in one day. Bearing in mind the amount of evidence he gave throughout the case, it is difficult to believe that he could get through a thorough examination of all the evidence in such a short time.

He dealt with the trousers first and said:

> *I found stains of blood on the left leg, about the left knee, and situated 12 inches above the lower end was a diffused dark coloured stain to which mud was adhering. I found this stain to be due to blood; it is marked number 1. Higher up the leg of the trousers and more to the inside I found a dark superficial indistinct stain about 2 inches long situated 16½ inches above the lower end of the garment; it was due to blood. About 13 inches above the lower end of the same leg, I found a third stain due to blood. Much higher up the same leg, 22 inches from the lower end and 7 inches from the fork situated towards the back and inside of the leg, I detected another bloodstain. All the bloodstains, which I discovered on this garment, were on the left leg. The stains responded to all the usual tests and by means of the new Precipitin Re–action Test. I was enabled to determine the stain marked number 1, the only one to which I applied this particular test, was due to human blood. The lower part of the body of the trousers in front and the adjoining of both legs looked and felt damp. The original colour of the stuff was fresher in this place and there was an absence of stains. This moisture and freshness may have been caused by an attempt to wash the garment.*

At first glance, this evidence looks very compelling. On closer inspection, a number of his findings just do not add up. The first thing that jumped out at me was that all the bloodstains were on the left leg. The two–inch bloodstain he found higher up (16½ inches) on the leg of the trousers and more to the inside, and the stain much higher up (22 inches) on the same leg towards the back and inside of the leg, should have transferred the fresh blood to the right leg when the wearer of the trousers commenced walking. McWeeney also said, "The lower part of the body of the trousers in front and the adjoining of both legs looked and felt damp." This is very strange because Constable Moore stated that when he arrested Heffernan, "I noticed that the left knee of the trousers was damp." This is a far cry from what McWeeney discovered thirteen days later. You do not need a degree in forensic science to notice dampness on the leg and front of a pair of trousers. McWeeney further suggested, "This moisture and freshness may have been caused by an attempt to wash the garment." McWeeney used the word "may" – if he did not know this for sure why did he add this rider to his evidence?

When McWeeney spoke about the new Precipitin Re–action blood testing system, he was being economical with the truth. At that time this test was far from accurate. It was not until the 1930s, more than twenty years later and following numerous improvements to its accuracy, that this system was used as compelling evidence in British courts. Having said that, I believe the blood on the trousers to be human blood, which was put there after the garment was taken off Heffernan, if indeed it was his garment.

The bloodstains on the clothing produced in court do not indicate that the wearer was present when the horrendous bloody attack was inflicted on the victim. Dr Ballasty, at the inquest, stated, "I agree with Dr Kelly's evidence, except in regard to the question of how the wound was likely made." He thought the man leant on the centre portion of her throat more than any other, and that it was not a stab at all. He added, "The centre portion was the deepest part of the wound, which pointed to this, and it would be necessary to lean heavily on the knife to do this." As there were no defensive wounds on the victim's hands or arms, I believe this. I believe that while she was unconscious on the ground, the killer straddled her, took out a knife and killed her in the manner described by Dr Ballasty. As Mary was still alive and her heart functioning at the time, blood would be pumped straight onto the killer's chest, neck and face. His upper clothes and sleeves would have been saturated with blood. If one was to believe the prosecution, Heffernan's jacket and waistcoat escaped all this: not a drop of blood was detected on either garment.

McWeeney's opinion that the trousers may have been washed is way off the mark. The prosecution produced numerous witnesses, most of them eager to send Heffernan to the gallows, and not one of them noticed damp patches on his clothing. The perpetrator's clothing would have been heavily stained with fresh, damp blood, or if he washed the blood away, he then had the problem of concealing multiple damp patches on his clothing. There were four sightings (three positive and all before 5.05pm) of Heffernan making his way up to Barrack Street. He was then seen by Elizabeth Flanagan and Susan Giff (he actually lay on Flanagan's bed) and afterwards by numerous people in a number of pubs. None of these people mentioned that his clothes were damp. If his clothes were washed, Heffernan just did not have the time to dry them off prior to meeting Christopher Downes at 4.50pm. It is very easy to come to the conclusion that some police officers stationed in Mullingar tampered with the evidence. They wanted Heffernan executed at all costs.

As regards the leggings, McWeeney again mentioned finding minute bloodstains. Partly hidden in the seam, he found the largest quantity of blood to be a small encrusted stain. He said, "From this stain I succeeded in obtaining sufficient coloured extract with which to carry out the Precipitin Test, which at once yielded the reaction characteristic of human blood." At the Magistrates' hearing in Mullingar he said, "More examination is sought." Why did he say this, as "more examination" was not sought? He also said he found minute droplets and that "near some of these small droplets were little cup–shaped depressions where the surface of the leather was of a brighter colour than elsewhere and seemed to be scooped out. This may have been done with the object of removing the more obvious spots of blood." I do not know how McWeeney convinced the jury of this. Heffernan simply did not have time to carry out the amount of cleaning, drying, and scooping out required. The police had Heffernan's clothes and leggings in their possession for a whole week; this gave them plenty of time to do whatever they wanted to do. McWeeney also said that the blood droplets caused cup–shaped depressions in the leather. I actually tried this myself and discovered what I already knew; human blood will not cause cup–shaped depressions in leather. The strangest thing about the leather leggings is that Mrs Moran, Heffernan's landlady, swore while giving evidence at the Magistrates' hearing, that Heffernan wore leggings "not of leather." This, of course, registered with McWeeney, as he avoided mentioning the word leather while giving evidence at the assizes.

He analysed the shirt next and reported as follows:

> As regards the shirt, this presented a great number (dozens) of minute bloodstains, none bigger than a pin's head. They were scattered over the garment and not confined to any special part. They were mostly on the outside but some were on the inside. As regards the mode of origin of these minute stains, many of them resemble those often seen on the undergarments of verminous individuals.

Giving evidence at the assizes, McWeeney said:

> … but the prisoner was not a person affected with vermin. Moreover, some of the stains appear to be rather too large to be produced in this way. I have not tested these stains as regard the origin, human or otherwise. The lower part of the shirt presents a good deal of diffused greyish discolouration. The discoloured places have not the stiffness which is characteristic of seminal stains and even on careful microscopic examination I have failed to detect Spermatozoon.

McWeeney said, none of the droplets were bigger than a pin's head and resembled those often seen on the undergarments of verminous individuals.

He then, it seems to me, ruled out Heffernan as the wearer of the shirt, when he added, "But the prisoner was not a person affected with vermin." The fact is, it was not Heffernan's garment, as the insects in question definitely bit the wearer of the shirt and left little red spots on his body. After saying none of the droplets were bigger than a pin's head, McWeeney then said, "some of the stains appear to be rather too large (is rather too large bigger than a pin's head?) to be produced this way." So, who owned the shirt? The evidence proves it certainly was not Heffernan's. The shirt itself, it seems, was not worn during a sex attack, or at least it did not contain evidence that it was. Where did this shirt come from? The only conclusion any right–thinking person could come to, after reading McWeeney's evidence, was that the shirt was never worn by Joseph Heffernan.

Dr McWeeney next dealt with the knife, he stated:

> *At first sight, no marks resembling bloodstains were to be seen on the knife or outside of the handle. Closer inspection with a powerful lens, however, revealed suspicious reddish or brownish incrustations in the following places: inside the handle, hinges of the blades, the sides and grooves of the tin opener and most of all on the turned side of the broken–off blade. On microscopic examination I was enabled to see the individual red blood corpuscles in these incrustations and I noticed in size, shape and appearance they corresponded with those of human blood. With some trouble I was able to obtain enough solution to apply the Precipitin Test and I then found that the blood was of human origin.*

On the small blade he "found starch grains such as would be contained in bread; they were adhering to the minute traces of blood." McWeeney admitted that no marks resembling bloodstains were to be seen on the knife or outside of the handle. He said he needed to carry out a "closer inspection with the aid of a powerful lens in order to detect signs of blood." However, Elizabeth Flanagan swore in her testimony that she saw the knife and "it had a stain like blood on the handle." Mind you, Elizabeth also said that Heffernan was cutting tobacco at the time she saw the handle of the knife, a difficult task indeed. She would have been at least three or four feet from Heffernan at the time. How did she see the blood? Why didn't she mention Heffernan's deformed right hand? I do not believe she saw a knife at all.

McWeeney said he found starch grains, such as would be contained in bread, they were adhering to the minute blood traces. To me, McWeeney is saying here that the grains came in contact with the blood, after the blood came in contact with the knife. From the evidence produced, the only time Heffernan had an opportunity to use a knife on bread was at breakfast the morning after the murder, and at this stage the blood would be dry. His landlady, Mrs Moran and the "walkabout tramp" gave no evidence that Heffernan used a penknife to cut bread. McWeeney said nothing about finding starch grains in any of Heffernan's pockets so we must assume that there were not any. Another interesting fact was that there were no bloodstains in his pockets from the knife or indeed his hands, and no dampness to suggest he washed the pockets.

McWeeney stated, "I examined Miss Walker's clothing, especially the undergarments, and they bear the aspects of having been violently rent asunder. Beyond the obvious evidence of violence having been applied to the undergarments, my examination did not yield any additional evidence of outrage." Why he failed to mention the amount of blood that was obviously soaked into her clothes, beggars belief. In comparison to Heffernan's alleged garments, her clothes, no doubt, displayed evidence of being present during a bloody, vicious, fatal assault. The murder scene, the area where the body was found and the surrounding areas were saturated with blood. However, Heffernan and his clothes displayed no sign of him being at the crime scene. Not one witness who saw him in town, from 4.50pm until he arrived at his lodgings after 10pm, mentioned anything out of the ordinary about his clothing.

Fingerprinting was used at that time (Scotland Yard set up their Fingerprinting Bureau in 1901), but there was no evidence that the police dusted the knife or other pieces of evidence found at the murder scene for fingerprints. The knife, together with a copy of Heffernan's prints, would have to be sent outside of the jurisdiction for a comparison check. It is one thing to transfer blood to a garment, but transferring a person's fingerprints onto the knife etc. is a different story. Unless, of course if Heffernan assisted the authorities to achieve this, and actually handled the knife. Their problem was fingerprint evidence could not easily be tampered with. This procedure would be under the control of people they did not know. This could not be allowed to happen, as a true and honest fingerprint report coming back to Mullingar would certainly cause problems for the local police authorities. This is the only conclusion I could come to when I realised that fingerprints were not taken from anything in relation to this case. So it seems the truth would be very damaging to the prosecution case.

Dr JOSEPH DILLON–KELLY

Dr Dillon–Kelly, dispensary doctor and local magistrate, Mullingar, stated the following at the inquest, held on 8 July 1909. There was no wound or injury on the body except on the throat; it went clean through the larynx, or Adam's apple as it is sometimes called. This wound was four inches long. It divided a number of blood vessels, the super thyroid and a number of other vessels, which, with shock would account for death and he believed death was caused by haemorrhage and the shock of the wound. The wound was caused by a sharp instrument, probably a pocket knife. He thought there was a push, or a stab and also a draw on the knife when it was used in making the wound. Dillon–Kelly also described the torn condition of the deceased clothes and underclothing. From the appearance of the clothes, it seemed that the deceased had been subjected to very great violence.

In his statement taken on 15 July, Dillon–Kelly said:

> *There was no wound or injury on the body except on the throat; this wound was four inches long. It penetrated clean through the larynx, dividing it almost. The carotid arteries were not injured; the superior thyroid arteries were severed. The haemorrhage from these arteries and shock were the cause of death. I believe a pocket knife would cause this wound. The blouse was torn open, and also the upper part of the corset; the lower part of the corset was torn open and torn into ribbons, particularly on the right side. The deceased was wearing bloomers, and underneath, knickers. The bloomers were torn from the waistband down to the knee and the knickers similarly torn. I formed the opinion that the deceased had been subjected to great violence and I have no doubt that outrage was attempted.*

Dillon–Kelly went into more detail when he mentioned the condition of the deceased's clothes. At the inquest, when giving his opinion on how the wound was inflicted, he mentioned a "push or stab". His assistant, Dr Ballasty, stated that he agreed with Dr Dillon–Kelly's evidence, except in regard to the question of how the wound was likely made. He thought "it was a draw in which the man leant to the centre portion more than any other and not a stab at all." It seems Dillon–Kelly agreed with this, as in his statement taken one week after the inquest, and indeed throughout the entire court proceedings, he does not mention the word stab again. At the assizes, Dillon–Kelly agreed with the Judge when His Lordship asked if the violence was "so great that it would require a knife to quell it." However, the lack of defensive wounds on the victim's arms and hands contradicts Dillon–Kelly's opinion on this issue. The evidence shows that the perpetrator was strong enough to rend the victim unconscious with his bare hands, and he then proceeded to attack the defenceless body with the knife. At the assizes, Dillon–Kelly expressed an opinion that the victim "was strong and well fed," and when asked by Mr Gleeson for the defence whether he would call Heffernan "a strong well–made man," he replied "I would call him very muscular. He was used to labour, he may not look it now but he did then."

Dillon–Kelly never medically examined Heffernan, so how could he lead the court to believe that Heffernan was a well–made man? How could he say he was very muscular when arrested and not look it now, when in actual fact, Heffernan was very run down when arrested in July? He lost 12lbs. in weight since the previous March. That is a lot of weight to lose in a four–month period, especially if, like Heffernan, you do not have it to lose. Heffernan weighed 144 lbs. in March (Kilmainham Gaol records), and when arrested in July he weighed 132lbs. (using the same scales). He improved while on remand in Kilmainham and actually put on 8lbs. by December, when Dillon–Kelly expressed his incorrect medical opinion. Dillon–Kelly either deliberately lied or he was just a first–rate, second–rate doctor. Being badly run down, having a deformed right hand, weighing 9 stone 4½lbs., and standing 5ft 4¾in would certainly rule any man out of the suspect list, especially when one considers the severity of the damage that was inflicted on the victim and her clothing.

This horrific murder was carried out by a strong, cool, calculated killer – a clever man who killed before, using a bladed weapon, whether it was on the field of battle or in civilian life. The murder displayed all the hallmarks of someone trained in this sort of thing. It was a clean, professional example of how to carry out such an attack. It was not a frenzied, out–of–control assault, carried out by the town idiot; there were no other stab wounds, or indeed any other injuries inflicted to her unfortunate body. This man was experienced in the art of unarmed combat. He was a strong individual; strong enough to tear her clothes into ribbons. It is one thing to tear her clothes along the seams but it is a different story to actually tear clothes into ribbons; and we know that garments at that time were made of heavier materials than they are today. The victim was a healthy, strong woman, who, as the evidence suggests, put up a tremendous struggle and no doubt would have left, at the very least, scratches on the perpetrator's arms and face. However, on 9 July 1909, Dr Matthew Russell, locum for Dr O'Donnell, Kilmainham Gaol, Dublin, examined Heffernan's body for bruises and scratches, and, as he said, "I found none." I have studied a number of such cases in the past two years and every perpetrator's body displayed the evidence that Dr Matthew Russell failed to find on Heffernan's body.

Dr JOSEPH MICHAEL BALLASTY

Dr Ballasty, who was honest and truthful, stated in his evidence at the inquest:

> *I assisted Dr Kelly–Dillon in the post–mortem. I agree with Dr Kelly's evidence; except in regard to the question of how the wound was likely made. I think it was a draw in which the man leant on the centre portion more than any other, and not a stab at all. The centre portion was the deepest part of the*

wound, which pointed to this, and it would be necessary to lean heavily on the knife to do this.

When taking all the evidence into consideration, Dr Ballasty's theory of events is as close to being accurate as you will get. The victim was not stabbed; she was unconscious when the knife was pushed into her throat. The killer, straddled her body, and with the weight of the upper part of his body pushed the knife into her throat, killing her in cold blood.

SERGEANT MORIARTY

Sgt Moriarty opened the case for the prosecution. He stated that the ground around the murder scene, which was marshy, presented evidence of a fearful struggle between the murdered lady and her assailant. However, he failed to mention that there was no physical evidence of the struggle which Richard Monaghan alleged took place, between the towpath and the little bush 18 feet below. He also failed to mention that there was no evidence of anyone sitting on the canal bank, washing boots. The prosecution mentioned nothing about the reeds or long grass being trampled down. He said nothing about finding tufts of bloodstained grass allegedly used by Heffernan to clean his hands and boots. There was no sign of blood in that area.

Moriarty informed the court that the canal line was Miss Walker's usual walk. He did not inform the court that her landlady, whom she had lived with for the previous fifteen months, did not know where she went for her stroll.

Moriarty next spoke about Fr Magee's evidence, stating, "He was riding his horse along Ballinea Road and he heard the scream of a woman and there could be no doubt that the scream could be that of Mary Walker – perhaps her death scream." However, Fr Magee swore in court in Mullingar that on reflection, "it might be the cry of children playing on the opposite side of the canal." At the assizes he said, "I concluded it might be children playing and shouting as they often do about there." Richard Merlehan also thought it was the sound of children playing in his field.

Sergeant Moriarty next informed the court that Heffernan was at the Green Bridge, looking on at what happened in the case and then asked what the jury thought of the significance of that fact, when taken into conjunction with the other facts. "Would the facts not prove that the prisoner was guilty of the death of her, at the removal of whose body he was looking on at the Green Bridge?" What was that all about?

Mr Moriarty told the court that the morning of the murder, Heffernan went into Mrs Sullivan's public house and "whilst there he took out a knife and cut tobacco with it," adding, "the jury would see what an important part the knife played." While we know the prosecution's story about where the knife was allegedly found, he failed to admit that, when Heffernan was arrested and searched, there was no pipe, tobacco, nor indeed tobacco particles found in his pockets (one witness stated that the tobacco was loose, not in a pouch).

Moriarty, in what turned out to be a successful attempt to convince the jury, stated that the victim and perpetrator were in very close proximity to one another:

> The next man who saw the prisoner was a man named Lyons, who was filling a cart at a place called the Valley, and who noticed him and the way he was walking. Then the next person who spoke to him, and also spoke to Miss Walker, and who would prove that she was only 20 or 30 yards behind him on the towpath, was Thomas Nooney, who was fishing with his brother on the opposite side of the canal.

Matthew Nooney stated at the inquest that there was about ten minutes between them, but at the Magistrates' he revised that down to about five minutes. The prosecution concocted lies that were so blatant they defied common sense. In this paragraph, Moriarty distorted the evidence and fooled the court, the judge, the jury, the media and any gullible person in attendance. His problem was that the Nooney's met Heffernan prior to Lyons seeing Heffernan. Lyons stated, Heffernan was in his view for about ten minutes after the Nooney's saw him and he did not mention seeing Mary Walker at all. So what did Moriarty do? He changed the evidence and informed the court that Lyons saw Heffernan before the Nooney's saw him.

We know that Matthew Nooney swore at the inquest that there was gap of about ten minutes between meeting Heffernan and the victim. His brother Thomas stated, "Mary passed him a short while after Heffernan." He also said that he did not pay much attention to Miss Walker or Heffernan, and he forgot about the other man who was on the towpath around the same time. So, on the face of what Thomas said and forgot to say, I believe Matthew was more accurate when he put the gap at about ten minutes. The evidence leads me to believe the gap was at least twenty minutes, because as Lyons saw Heffernan after the Nooney's and never mentioned Miss Walker during the ten minutes Heffernan was in his view, the distance between them had to be greater. Lyons also had a clear view back to where the Nooney's were fishing and he did not see her.

Moriarty stated that Lyons noticed Heffernan by the way he was walking (Lyons statement says, "As I never saw Heffernan wear leggings before I noticed him on that account."). In his evidence, he stated that Heffernan was walking slowly and looking about him. However, Moriarty admitted, that Heffernan left his lodgings on the morning of the murder to look for employment. There was also evidence that Heffernan asked Jack Doyle if there was any "work about." Heffernan stated that Doyle replied, "There is if you go to Dick Merlehan in Clown; he has a meadow down," and as the police failed to take a statement from Jack Doyle, I feel Heffernan told the truth. He went out the canal line to look for Merlehan in one of his fields. Merlehan had land on both sides of the canal and I believe anybody on a similar mission would be walking slowly and looking around, scanning both sides of the canal.

The next piece of evidence Moriarty dealt with was that of Richard Monaghan. He told of Monaghan witnessing a struggle, and how he realised later it was Heffernan by the way he swung his arms. He failed to mention that the long grass from the bush up to the towpath showed no evidence that such a struggle had taken place in that area. (In July, grass all over this locality stands more than 38 inches in height). A struggle, that Monaghan allegedly witnessed for a split second as he galloped or trotted the horse. Nor did he mention the fact that Monaghan continued to exercise the horse for a full hour (at the assizes Monaghan reduced this time to a half an hour) after the alleged struggle. In addition, Mr Moriarty neglected to mention the fact that Monaghan did not see a man wash his boots at the side of the canal bank and there was no evidence of blood, or that anyone had disturbed the reeds or long grass as they allegedly washed their boots. Monaghan did not see Ellen Woods either. Incidentally, the train guard, Joseph O'Connell, also swore that he saw no one on the canal line. Moriarty failed to mention the discrepancy between Monaghan's statement, and the evidence he gave at the Magistrates' court. In his statement he said, about ten minutes after he witnessed the struggle, he saw a woman come up along the canal line and at this time he saw Fr Magee. His statement was interfered with and changed to read that he saw Fr Magee "before" he saw the man push the woman down the bank, and Monaghan stuck to this amendment while giving evidence at the Magistrates' hearing. While giving evidence at the assizes, he stated that he saw Fr Magee five or ten minutes "after" he saw the man push the woman down the canal bank.

Next, the jury heard the unbelievable evidence of Ellen Woods. Moriarty had to be deceitful again and misled the court as he addressed the attendance. Times were very important here, and Moriarty avoided mentioning them, except for Fr Magee fixing the time at which he passed on the Ballinea Road and heard a scream, as nearly as he could to 4.30pm. However, Woods stated she left her house at 4.50pm or 5pm. Moriarty said Woods heard a "dreadful scream" coming from the opposite side of the canal that was "possibly the death scream of Mary Walker." He never mentioned the fact that the time she alleged she heard the scream, she said she saw Fr Magee riding his horse on the Ballinea Road and then altered this as required by the police. In her statement and at the magistrates' hearing, she swore she saw Heffernan washing up on the canal line at the time she heard a train travelling towards Mullingar station. The train logbook put the train arriving at the station at 4.25pm, thereby passing the murder scene at 4.22pm. According to young Woods, Heffernan was cleaning his boots about eight minutes before Fr Magee passed by. Woods' timing would put the killing of Miss Walker at about 4.10pm. So, what do we have here? We have Michael Murray leaving the Green Bridge to walk the fifteen minutes to his father's field. This was at the same time that Woods alleged she saw Heffernan washing up after killing Miss Walker. If what she said was true, then young Murray heard and saw nothing. Merlehan saw nothing, Monaghan saw nothing and Fr Magee heard nothing. However, she changed this part of her story on a number of occasions. Moriarty failed to ask Ellen why she had not asked Heffernan, a man she knew, whether he had seen her brother; after all, she said the reason she left her house was to look for him. Moriarty informed the court that where Woods alleged she saw the prisoner was 52 yards from the murder scene. Woods informed the Magistrates' in Mullingar, that this distance was the same distance between the Chairman and the defendant in Mullingar courtroom. Mullingar courtroom is nowhere near 52 yards in length, breadth or indeed diagonally. The distance between the Chairman and the defendant would be no more than four yards. The attendance at Green Street was not informed of this.

Ellen Woods lived quite close to Michael Murray. Her time, between 4.50pm and 5pm is very close to Murray's times when he was milking the goat. She then alleged she saw Heffernan spend some time washing up on the canal line. Murray saw a man walk away from the murder scene somewhere between 5.05pm and 5.15pm. The problem is, Heffernan, was positively identified in town by three reliable witnesses from 4.50pm. I really believe Murray did see a man walk away from the scene of the crime but that he didn't hear any screams, because neither Richard Merlehan or Bridget Nugent (who were much closer than Murray at the time), heard a scream. However, he had been well drilled by the police. I also think Ellen Woods, due to the inconsistency of her evidence, was not at the crime scene at the time Miss Walker was murdered; not one witness saw her there. She was merely talking and listening to her very close neighbours Murray, Matthew Nooney and Monaghan and wanted some of the limelight.

Moriarty went on to say that other witnesses saw Heffernan on that evening going back to town; and that he crossed hedges and ditches and actually squeezed out under a gate. If Moriarty knew his job and had studied all the evidence, he would know the reason why Heffernan went back to town the way he did. He also knew that Heffernan was positively identified in town by three reliable witnesses; he was seen by Christopher Downes at 4.50pm. This was a full twenty minutes prior to Murray and Merlehan witnessing someone they couldn't identify leave the murder scene and walk towards the back of Railway Terrace. Another person saw Heffernan on Grove Street, and a third person saw him entering Mount Street from Blackhall (more than a mile from the crime scene). Merlehan walked home after the man he saw leaving the murder scene went out of his sight. This was about 5.10pm, as he arrived at his house at 5.15pm and looked at his watch. This time concurs with Michael Murray's version of the sighting. The witnesses that Moriarty mentioned gave Heffernan a foolproof alibi. It does not take a Sherlock Holmes to realise that the defendant could not be in two places at the same time. Moriarty deliberately deceived the court. He was, of course, assisted by Gleeson, with the blessing of the judge. These people knew in their heart of hearts that Heffernan was innocent.

He then said that Elizabeth Flanagan stated that Heffernan lay on the bed in her kitchen, "and in cutting some tobacco for his pipe, he took out a knife." Now, Charles Quinn, the assistant in Sullivan's, would prove the prisoner had a knife before the murder, and Flanagan would prove that he had one afterwards." However, he failed to mention the fact Jack Doyle was in Sullivan's pub and the police failed to take a statement from him. I must assume he was questioned and had a different story to tell. To my mind, Doyle failed to corroborate Quinn's statement concerning the purchase and smoking of the pipe. The prosecution needed this evidence to put the knife in Heffernan's possession, so whatever Doyle had to say was discarded. Flanagan wanted to make the case that Heffernan openly displayed a knife, which she alleged she saw clearly enough to give a complete description to the police; while at the same time, she wanted to prove Heffernan done his utmost to hide the knife from her and Susan Giff.

The prosecutor talked about a bloodstained handkerchief but no handkerchief was found in Heffernan's possession. Flanagan alleged that Heffernan told her he was skinning a goat, and that the blood got on his handkerchief in this way, by its rubbing against the flesh of the animal. Except for what Flanagan said, there was no proof that Heffernan had a handkerchief. Nobody else saw it and he never mentioned to anybody throughout the day that he was skinning a goat: so why would he tell a frightened young girl anything?

Moriarty then referred to the prisoner washing his hands and boots on the canal bank near where the body was found. Again he failed to explain why the killer neglected to wash up in the hidden five–foot drain located between the railway line and the canal bank. Nor did he explain why Mr O'Connell the train guard, and Monaghan, who had a clear view of the canal line and still exercising Mr Dibbs' horse, failed to see anybody sitting on the canal bank, washing boots, not to mention failing to see Woods.

Moriarty talked about 8 July, the day after the murder: at 11.15am Heffernan was arrested at Mr Callaghan's place, about a mile and half mile from Mullingar. Moriarty stated Heffernan had gone out to Callaghan's before 8am that morning. He talks about Heffernan's landlady, Mrs Moran, handing him the besom to pare for her, adding, he "had a knife, and was paring the besom." Of course, he never mentioned that Mrs Moran also said that the knife was not very sharp, and later, at the assizes she that, "she didn't actually see the knife." Moriarty then asked how Heffernan had disposed of the knife. He told the court that Heffernan went through a tunnel at "8.55am and is seen outside the tunnel by a man named Patrick Sullivan (this should be Luke Sullivan)." He continued, "The tunnel is searched by the police, and two days after the arrest, on 10 July, a policeman finds in the tunnel under a water pipe and buried in mud, a knife which corresponds in all degrees to that seen by witnesses with Heffernan." Moriarty intentionally led the jury to believe that Sullivan's evidence instigated the search of the tunnel. As Moriarty said, "The search took place on 10 July." However, Sullivan, a paid informer, made his statement almost three–and–a–half months later.

The problem here is that the prosecution accepted that Heffernan was on Callaghan's farm since before 8am. Then they brought in a paid informer, Luke Sullivan, in an attempt to place Heffernan at the tunnel. This was done because the evidence of the previous witnesses, Creevy, McCormack and Veldon was either very dubious or they got cold feet. However, according to the prosecution at the Magistrates' hearing, Heffernan was seen hiding a knife down at the tunnel at 10.30am, while at the same time he was on the Harbour Bridge. At the assizes they brought in Luke Sullivan to put Heffernan at the tunnel, this time hiding the knife at 8.55am, yet the prosecution accepted that Heffernan was on Callaghan's farm since before 8am.

Sullivan, a man I personally knew, came forward three–and–a–half months after the murder and actually changed his evidence. He gave a different and clearly untrue account of the distance between him and Heffernan at the tunnel. Sullivan also said that after work that day 8 July he heard about the murder of Miss Walker and immediately thought of seeing Heffernan at the tunnel that morning. This is very strange, because the police said the knife was allegedly found on 10 July, two days later at that tunnel (not the tunnel at the murder scene). It also took him three–and–a–half months and an informer's fee to come forward. Sullivan gave two different accounts of the distance he was from Heffernan. His statement said that Heffernan was about 25 yards from the far side of the tunnel. At the assizes however, he swore that the prisoner was 25 yards from him, thereby leaving out the width of the canal and both towpaths. In reality, neither estimate could be correct. Heffernan, who Sullivan said was stooping down as if to tie his lace, would have to have been at least 120 yards from the tunnel, in order to be seen from the far side of the canal. The court was not appraised of any of the above.

Moriarty dealt with forensics next and referred to the fact that up to recent times, "It was not possible for science to distinguish between the bloodstains made by human blood and those made by the blood of other mammalia." He mentioned the Precipitin Test and as we have seen, this system was far from accurate at that time.

As far as the leggings were concerned, McWeeney said the following: "I found small minute droplets" adding, "near some of these small droplets were little cup shaped depressions where the surface of the leather was of a brighter colour than elsewhere and seemed to be scooped out. This may have been done with the object of removing the more obvious spots of blood." However, Mrs Moran clearly stated that the leggings were not leather. In my opinion, none of the articles analysed by McWeeney belonged to Heffernan.

I realise that Moriarty had a job to do here, which did not involve working on behalf of the defendant. However, like every other prosecutor, he should be duty bound to get to the truth. But his case reeked of skulduggery.

WARDER JOE MANSFIELD

Warder Joe Mansfield stated that Heffernan said the following: "There is no use denying it, I killed the poor girl right enough. Everybody knows it. I do not know what came over me, the devil I suppose. I was drinking all that day. I put my arm around her and knocked her down; I cut a hole under her ear; poor girl died easy."

He states that, Heffernan told him, that he cut a hole under the victim's ear, yet medical evidence proves that the entry wound was at the centre of the throat, straight through the windpipe. It is plain to see that Mansfield was lying. I also have a problem with police and prison officers making allegations of a very serious nature while their colleagues refused to verify these allegations with supporting statements. Mansfield said the alleged statement was given over the course of a conversation in the prison hospital. It is unbelievable that in such a small hospital nobody overheard it. I am sure there were members of staff, or patients within earshot of the alleged conversation.

Mr GLEESON

Mr Gleeson, Heffernan's defence lawyer, stood up like some sort of Rip Van Winkle returning after a long sleep. He appears to have been asleep since the murder was committed, or if not he had taken his orders from the prosecution and completely ignored the inquest report, the witness statements, the Magistrate transcripts and the evidence presented at the assizes. Despite numerous contradictions, and indeed evidence changing on behalf of the prosecution, Gleeson challenged nothing of importance. Moriarty and his cronies literally got away with murder. As far as I can see, the evidence proves that two people were murdered – Mary Walker and Joe Heffernan – and all because the defence gave the prosecution a free run.

The only witnesses Gleeson produced gave evidence on the question of the mental condition of Joseph Heffernan and his family history. As a matter of fact, if he cross–examined the prosecution witnesses, he would have extracted more than enough evidence to prove the case against his client was a set–up.

Every single shred of Ellen Woods' evidence was up in the air; nothing made sense. Young Ellen Woods actually perjured herself in his presence. The first day in the witness box she stated that she identified Heffernan by the sound of his voice. The second day, she said that she recognised him by his face, before he pulled his cap down. If Gleeson was awake and went through everything with her while she was giving her evidence, the whole prosecution case would have collapsed. Ellen actually gave two accounts of when she saw Fr Magee. In her statement she said she saw him "when" she heard the screams; at the assizes she said she saw him "after" she heard the screams. Young Michael Murray's evidence was the same. He, like Ellen, perjured himself, either in Mullingar or in Dublin. He also left out important times such as the five–minute delay on the Green Bridge, the ten minutes he spent mending the gate and the reduction of the time he said he spent milking the goat from ten minutes to five. If Gleeson had cross–examined Murray on his activities, between the time he arrived at the Green Bridge right up to the sighting of a man leaving the crime scene at 5.10pm, the prosecution case would have collapsed, simply because between 4.50pm and 5.10pm, Heffernan was positively identified by three reliable witnesses as he walked through the town. A short time later he was in Flanagan's house in Barrack Street. Gleeson certainly hung Heffernan out to dry. However, I do not for one minute blame these children; they were put under severe pressure by the police.

Why did Gleeson fail to call Jack Doyle (who could prove that Heffernan did not purchase or smoke a pipe in Sullivan's pub on the morning of the murder) and indeed all the customers drinking in the various pubs Heffernan was in on the day of the murder? There were others, like Tom Cole, Mrs Merlehan, the man the Nooney brothers met on the canal line, Elizabeth Flanagan's father, the man Fr Magee spoke to at the Valley, Patrick Grogan, John Duignam, the group of people outside the Dispensary with Thomas Rattigan, the walkabout tramp in Heffernan's lodgings, Mrs Skelly, Mr Gill (farm labourer), etc. He also failed to call Francis Judge to the witness box.

This man was in a position to prove that Heffernan was not smoking a pipe while in Sullivan's pub on the evening of the murder. Then of course, he had at his disposal, Mrs Bridget Creevy, Mrs Christina McCormack and Michael Veldon, whose evidence, had been used (in an attempt to place Heffernan hiding a knife at the tunnel at 10.30am) by the prosecution at the Magistrates' hearings in Mullingar and not used in Green Street. Their evidence was later scrapped. The time was changed, from 10.30am to the earlier time of 8.55am. The evidence they swore during the Magistrates' hearings in Mullingar should have been queried by Gleeson.

Gleeson decided to allow Heffernan to be convicted. He actually stated on a number of occasions that his client was not a rational man, but an unfortunate maniac who was not responsible for his act. What act was he talking about? At this stage Heffernan had not been convicted. However, when the jury members heard this, they no doubt assumed that even the defence team deemed Heffernan guilty. He also failed to study the Nooney's times. He knew from where and when they commenced fishing. He knew they swore that they fished slowly and he knew where they met Heffernan after fishing for about one–and–a–half hours. The fact is, it took them that length of time to fish about 200 yards, or three quarters of an hour per hundred yards. However, it seems the police (and Matthew admitted that they were well drilled on the times by the police) convinced them that they had fished the hundred yards (police measurements) between meeting Heffernan and Miss Walker, in five minutes, thereby putting Miss Walker about five minutes behind Heffernan.

A crown prosecution witness actually handed Gleeson fantastic evidence concerning his client and he totally ignored it. Dr Matthew Russell stated, "I examined the prisoner on 9 July for bruises and scratches, I found none. He had no symptoms of insanity. The man was the same as an ordinary prisoner charged with murder." In reply to Mr Gleeson he said, "I examined the prisoner for scratches because I learned there was a history of a struggle," to which Gleeson replied, "You thought it would be more important to find a scratch than to find out he was a lunatic?" Mr Gleeson should have concentrated on the absence of bruises cuts and scratches on Heffernan's body.

There was so much conflicting evidence that Gleeson could have focused on: the evidence in relation to Heffernan's boots and alleged boot prints, Rowlette's story about finding the knife, or the huge discrepancies in the times given by the various witnesses. Had he studied the case, Gleeson would have known why Heffernan was on the canal line, walking slowly and looking about him.

DISTRICT INSPECTOR RUTTLEDGE

District Inspector Ruttledge gave his account of the murder scene. He mentioned the condition of each area where the struggle had taken place. The grass from the bush, he said, was, "all dragged down to the foot of the sloping bank for 12 feet as if someone had been dragged down it." So apparently, the grass from the bush to the top of the canal bank (18 feet in distance) was undisturbed. If what Richard Monaghan said was true, then surely the grass from the top of the canal bank should have been flattened the whole way down to the bush. Monaghan alleged that the attacker, whom he later identified as Heffernan, ran up the canal bank behind Miss Walker, then threw her down head first and disappeared after her.

Ruttledge also stated that, "At a place across the water ditch, (which he stated was five feet wide) it was evident that a man had stepped across heavily on the right foot and brought the left one after him; the tracks were sloping up against the bank." He went into a lot of detail about the tracks on the far side (or railway side) of the water ditch. However, giving evidence at the inquest, Constable Holmes stated the tracks were on the canal side and Ruttledge, whose job it was to cross–examine all the witnesses at the inquest, did not question this. There are very few men Heffernan's size, if indeed there are any, who could step across five feet of water, especially from, as Ruttledge himself said, "moist, boggy land, with a good deal of grass and sticks." His only hope of getting to the far side would be to run up to the water's edge and attempt to jump across. Of course he would need solid ground to have any chance of clearing the water. No matter who killed Miss Walker, the rims and soles of his boots would have collected a lot of dirt. I am speaking as a former Irish soldier who, like every other trained soldier, encountered this problem after patrolling through similar terrain. It would be very difficult for him to entirely wash away traces of walking on boggy land and jumping to the muddy bank, in the short space of time before Elizabeth Flanagan deemed his boots to appear "newish". As stated by the Inspector, there was 22 feet of marshy ground with long grass and rushes bordering the canal side of the water ditch. Conditions such as these would make it impossible for someone like Heffernan to successfully clear the ditch. It would be a difficult enough task for a fit man with no alcohol in his system. Ruttledge stated that the "tracks were sloping up against the bank. At this place, there is a gap in the hedge; it is quite easy to get up on the bank, cross the paling and get out on the railway line." He then seems to contradict himself when he says, "The ground in which the right track was, was a difficult place to get at; the tracks sloped upwards, the ground was boggy and moist, and there was a good deal of grass and sticks."

The two tracks pointed out to Ruttledge by Constable Holmes were caused, as the Inspector said, "by a man stepping heavily across the water ditch on his right foot and bringing the left foot after him." If this was correct, then more than likely, the tracks were made by a right–handed man. Evidence was given by Constable Moore and Dr McWeeney concerning the damp left knee of "Heffernan's trousers". Heffernan, you may remember, was thinning mangolds on Callaghan's farm when arrested. Anyone who has performed this type of work will tell you that the natural way to do this is to get down on one knee. As Heffernan's trousers, if they were his at all, showed evidence of him using the left knee to perform this task, the chances are, he was left–handed.

The right track was, according to Ruttledge, a "difficult place to get at; the tracks sloped upwards, the ground was boggy and moist and there was a good deal of grass and sticks." He went on to say he took exact measurements of the right track. How in the name of God could he get exact measurements from this track? In any case, all men's boots of the same size would have exactly the same measurements. How many men in Mullingar that evening wore the same size boots as Heffernan? We know that he did not get a satisfactory cast from the print. There appeared to be no evidence whatsoever to prove that the boot track, if there was one, belonged to Heffernan. Ruttledge's actions afterwards prove this. He was a senior police officer yet, by his own volition, he contaminated the murder scene by bringing Heffernan's boots out to where the crime was committed. He then had Constable Moore step across just where the first track was taken. He next, as he said himself, "took a third track of the prisoner's boot in prepared clay at the barracks."

According to Ruttledge, "the sole of the original track is slightly shorter than the boot itself. I attribute that to the fact that the footprints sloped upwards, and the hot solution shortened it a little." Ruttledge said that the track contained "grass and sticks" and I believe this would make it impossible, even today, to take a true and accurate cast of that track. Despite all this, the inspector issued the following statement to the *Westmeath Examiner*, "the police… have had moulds taken of the prisoner's boots and of foot tracks near the place of the murder and that these correspond very closely." Ruttledge then stated, "I left police in charge of the scene with instructions to watch the tracks and allow no one near them." However, he failed to name the officers in question and I really believe, after studying Constable Holmes' evidence given at the inquest, that the tracks referred to by Ruttledge did not exist.

A few days later, Ruttledge informed the *Westmeath Examiner*, "A young girl informed the police that on the afternoon in question she saw Heffernan, now under arrest, engaged washing his hands and leggings in the canal on the opposite side to where she was, and that, she added, he shouted over to her 'Good evening', or words to that effect." Incidentally, "Good evening", or words to that effect soon changed to, "After pulling his cap over his face" Heffernan said, "Have you aira match?" This was done to suggest that Heffernan, as a smoker, had a knife, as all pipe smokers carried a knife. Nothing was mentioned about hiding his face with his cap. The *Westmeath Examiner* published this statement on 17 July 1909, right in the middle of the Magistrates' hearings.

These statements were clearly designed to turn the townspeople against Heffernan, and to allow the British authorities time to move the real perpetrator back to England. I say this because a second suspect was arrested on the morning after the murder, and no doubt this was the man the Nooney brothers saw on the canal line on the afternoon of the killing. I believe he was British and most likely a soldier. If this had got into the public domain, it would certainly have destroyed the British authorities' good relationship with members of the local middle–and upper–class population.

The murder itself was not carried out the in the fashion the police and the media led everyone to believe. Mary Walker was not initially attacked by a knife–wielding killer. The unfortunate girl was attacked and thrown on the ground. The killer straddled her; she was unconscious at this stage. He calmly took out his knife and, in a very professional manner (that of a trained soldier using his bayonet) he "coolly", as Dr Ballasty said, "pushed the knife" into the centre of her throat. He then slashed her throat from one side to the other. I came to this conclusion after researching numerous knife attacks in Britain, eastern Europe and the United States. In each of these cases, the victim sustained defensive wounds however, Miss Walker's dead body displayed no such injuries. Incidentally, exactly one month after Heffernan was executed, D.I. Ruttledge was presented with a "Good Service Pay Award" of £30 per annum from 4 February 1910. That equates to double a labourer's annual wage at that time. The same month he was commended without record for "Good Police Duties" in a murder case.

Mr JOYCE'S MAP

Mr Joyce, a civil engineer, sketched the map of the murder scene. The map shows two witnesses (Monaghan and Lyons) closer to the murder scene than they actually were. In my opinion, this was a deliberate attempt to mislead the judge and jury, who would not know the area. For example, the Valley Cottages are stepped back off the road and St Anthony's Cottages are running parallel to the canal and the road. Joyce also failed to show that Merlehan had land on both sides of the canal. However, he had to come clean about this when questioned by Gleeson. Joyce also sited the signal pole where the telegraph pole was and vice versa.

Joyce described himself as a civil engineer and "in the habit of making maps". This statement and the quality of his work are, to say the least, not very encouraging. In today's world, the quality of his work would not be up to junior cert standard. How in the name of God could he swear in a court of law that the map was "an accurate map of what it purports to describe"? Mr Joyce's address was given as Mullingar. If this was correct, I cannot understand how or why he got it so wrong, especially when a man's life was at stake. He was an educated man and, in my opinion, even he was well drilled by the police.

14.

WHO KILLED MARY WALKER?

Of course, it is impossible to actually name the person responsible for the horrific murder of Mary Walker. However, after taking all the evidence into consideration, I have no hesitation in saying that he was not a local. Having said that, he certainly knew his way around the area very well. He knew the different ways he could access and egress the Royal Canal without being noticed, and if he had been noticed, he had a Plan B to take care of that situation. He kept a cool head while he went about his sordid business. He knew how to kill and did so in a very professional manner. Make no mistake; this man killed before. He was a strong, healthy, fit man – a man familiar with the tactics needed to set up and carry out the crime.

Let us take another look at what transpired on the canal line that horrible evening, starting at 3.15pm. Miss Walker left her lodgings for an afternoon stroll. Patrick Lyons left the building site at the Valley Cottages at about 3.55pm and arrived at the Green Bridge at 4pm. He was paying particular attention to the canal line and he did not see Miss Walker. From where Lyons was working at the Valley Cottages, he had a clear view back to where the Nooney's were fishing. Mary should have arrived opposite to where the Nooney's were at about 3.20 pm. So where was she?

The only conclusion I can come to is that she went into town first, maybe to a shop or to meet a friend. She may have met some people and the police would have known this, but if the times did not suit their theory of events, this evidence was simply scrapped. As Mary was a very friendly lady, it is more than likely she spoke with her killer and, in my opinion, it was the stranger who later met the Nooney's and asked if "this was the Royal canal." After speaking with the Nooney's this man did an about turn and put his Plan B into action. He walked back towards the town and re–entered the canal from a different route. If he asked Mary the same question, she would no doubt have informed him that it was a lovely place for a walk and she would shortly be going out that way for her afternoon stroll.

Once leaving the Nooney's, this man would come to an opening in the wall between the canal line and the racecourse road. Unseen by the Nooney's, he then took a u–turn to the right and straight away he had two options open to him. The first option was to walk under Clown Bridge and pass Railway Cottages (also called Railway Terrace), entering the canal bank via the railway line at a place of his choosing. His other option was to enter the Galway cattle platform via the gate on the right–hand side, located at the fork on the road. This would give him the concealment he needed to successfully carry out his horrible deed. He simply walked up the side of the line, the hedgerow hiding him from the Nooney's, and indeed anyone else who might be strolling along the canal line.

He selected his ambush site and entered this area by jumping the drain and leaving his boot prints on the canal side of the drain. This was backed up by Constable Holmes (if Holmes was being truthful) in his evidence at the inquest on the day after the murder. After crossing the drain, the killer climbed the canal bank as far as the much talked about small blackthorn bush, and lay in wait for his victim, who he knew was on her way.

As Mary approached, the maniac spoke to her and probably asked for assistance, perhaps giving her some story about spraining his ankle. Mary, being the kind person she was, went to his assistance and presented her killer with a golden opportunity to satisfy his sick craving for her blood. As soon as she came close to him she was doomed. She had entered his trap; there was no way out. The killer was a very strong man. He grabbed her round the throat. Of course she would have fought a fierce battle; no doubt his arms and hands were scratched and torn, but this did not deter him. While Heffernan's body displayed none of the signs of a violent struggle, I am sure the police discovered cuts, scratches and bruises on the real killer's body.

He kept the pressure on her throat until she fell to the ground. He then straddled her, took out his knife and pushed it into the centre of her throat. He drew the knife to the left and right, leaving a four–inch cut across the front of her neck. Next on his agenda, was to satisfy his sick, sexual impulses and he began to tear her clothes into ribbons. When he finished, or maybe he was disturbed (which I doubt, as he had time to cover her body with grass), he crossed the drain and entered the railway line. He then made his way back to town from the crime scene, walking towards the back of the Railway Cottages (Michael Murray and Richard Merlehan confirmed this). He entered the road at a place of his choosing and simply walked into the sunset. Incidentally, the man Mrs Feeney saw in the field, passed by the front of the Railway Cottages.

Who was this stranger? How did he know the area so well? What did he do for a living? Where did he kill before and why did the British authorities choose to murder Heffernan, in order to protect the real killer? This man was arrested on the morning after the murder. He was quickly released because his alibi allegedly checked out. To this day, his identity remains a mystery, despite the fact that he was seen by, and spoke to the Nooney's. Thomas Nooney was a local postman at that time and therefore would be likely to recognise anyone from the area. Taking everything about the crime itself into consideration, and adding to that the refusal of the authorities to charge a man they knew full well was responsible for the crime, I feel that the man was a British soldier, attached to the 4th Battalion, Royal Fusiliers and stationed at Wellington Barracks (Columb Barracks) Mullingar. This battalion was stationed in Mullingar for about two years and left in September 1909, approximately two months after the murder of Miss Walker.

As a trained and experienced soldier, he would have been capable of overcoming an unarmed lady without any bother. It was a calm, calculated attack. He was no amateur. He killed his victim in cold blood. He knew exactly what he was doing and when he finished he coolly walked from the scene. This man, as a soldier, would have taken part in numerous foot patrols throughout the area. Prior to these patrols, soldiers were briefed and familiarised with the relevant terrain.

Soldiers are adept in the art of map reading and can locate any area with the use of a compass. Soldiers can be dropped into any country or city in the world and locate their area of responsibility without any trouble. This killer, no doubt, patrolled the greater Mullingar area on countless occasions. He was a stranger with a difference. He knew the area inside out, while at the same time a local postman did not recognise him. The post was not delivered to the barracks by the postman. The mail was collected from the post office by the Orderly Room Runner, who was based at H.Q. Mullingar Barracks. He collected the mail from the sorting office where Mary Walker was employed, and brought to the barracks in bulk. This soldier would have come into contact with Miss Walker every working day of the week. He would have known her very well. There is another scenario, which is worth considering. Mary was by all accounts a very friendly lady, and no doubt she would be on speaking terms with the soldier whose job it was to collect the post from the sorting office. They could have arranged to meet on the canal line. They could have sat down at the famous blackthorn bush. Mary thinking, "This could be the beginning of a relationship, we'll probably talk about one another for a while and hopefully take it from there." This could not be done in the sorting office, as her co–workers would, no doubt, be listening in. However the predator wanted more than a chat and was having none of it. As a sex predator, he was not able tolerate Mary's expectation of what should take place. He had to be in control at all costs and we know what happened.

Quite a number of British soldiers stationed in Mullingar at the time fought with Kitchener during the Boar War in Africa. They were experienced men who were trained to kill. These were hard, battle–worn men, some suffering from ailments such as post–traumatic stress disorder. In the last hundred years, we have learned a lot more about the effects warfare can have on combat soldiers. Many of the soldiers suffering from such disorders were moved to garrison towns and cities throughout Ireland, instead of being discharged from the forces.

Miss Walker's killer was known to the British authorities, and this presented them with a massive problem. By and large, the British had a good relationship with middle–class locals in Mullingar. If it became known that Miss Walker's killer was a British soldier, the consequences would have been dire. How would it affect the British government, and indeed the Royal Family? The situation throughout the country was like a time bomb, waiting to explode. The police knew that if the murder of Miss Walker was not handled properly, this crime would serve as the detonator to ignite that bomb. The aftershock would be felt as far away as Westminster, the heart of the British Empire.

The morning after the murder, the authorities had a stroke of luck. Thomas Nooney arrived at the police station and informed the officer on duty that he remembered Joseph Heffernan walking out the canal line the previous evening, adding that he was ahead of Miss Walker. If a local man had to die to preserve what was left of their already tarnished reputation, then so be it. Without further ado, the police organised an arrest party and walked out to Robinstown to apprehend Heffernan. They immediately arrested him and charged him with the murder, based solely on the evidence that he had been seen on the canal line. Their next step was to feed the concocted evidence of their plan to the locals via the media and the Church.

They messed up somewhat during the inquest when Constable Holmes explained where he allegedly found the boot prints. His evidence was recorded and published in the local papers but the arrogance of the senior police officer did not allow this hiccough to derail their cover–up plan. During the following week, they decided, on paper, to move the boot prints to the far side of the drain, adding, "This is the how the killer made his escape." This too was published during the Magistrates' hearing and seemingly, nobody noticed. They got away with it. They also got away with the fact that the plaster casts of the boots were actually smaller than Heffernan's boots.

With the assistance of the local media and the Church, the police were now on a roll. Heffernan, was now despised by the entire population of Mullingar. This is borne out by the actions of locals, as large numbers attempted to snatch him from the police as they escorted him between the courthouse and the railway station. Others queued up to give false evidence in order to secure his conviction and execution. These people soon found themselves under pressure from the police. They chopped and changed their stories as required to ensure there was no way out for the unfortunate Heffernan. Several prosecution witnesses changed their evidence. Some simply fabricated evidence as the legal process progressed – people like Michael Murray, Ellen

Woods, the Nooney brothers, Elizabeth Flanagan, Mrs Creevy, Mrs McCormack, Mr Veldon, Mr Luke Sullivan and so on.

The British authorities felt they had no option but to bring the local population along for the ride. They knew they needed the confidence of the local media and the Church to achieve their aim. It is difficult to criticize the media and indeed the Church. Realistically speaking, when a senior police officer walks into a newspaper office and hands over an up–to–date progress report on a murder investigation, it is only natural to believe him. Local people believed everything they read in the local newspaper and soon people actually queued up to say whatever the police wanted them to say in order to ensure that Heffernan paid the penalty for Mary Walker's death.

Why did people in Mullingar get involved in corrupt police activities? Why did they allow themselves to be used as a weapon to murder Joe Heffernan? Firstly, they were very fond of Miss Walker. They trusted her and would do anything for her, just as she obliged them time and time again down through the years. Secondly, the compelling campaign orchestrated by the police with the assistance of the Church and media was very convincing.

My family on my father's side is from Mullingar, as is my grandmother's family on my mother's side. It is reasonable to believe that some of my family members were part of the mob that tried to grab Heffernan from the police with the view of lynching him. Indeed, after I read the article in the *Westmeath Examiner* in July 2009, and before I really went through each piece of evidence, I formed the opinion that Heffernan was indeed the guilty party.

But my granddad's words played a part in my decision to shake the tree just to see what would fall out. He said that he was informed, before he ever came to Ireland, that Heffernan was innocent. He never clarified the situation. I imagine that he did not know any other details, but was merely told by a comrade soldier back in England.

15.

HEFFERNAN'S PREVIOUS CRIMINAL RECORD

Heffernan had been known to the police before Mary Walker's murder. He had three previous convictions that saw him serve three prison sentences. In March 1909 he was sentenced to two months in prison for stealing a hair mattress, valued £1. In January 1907, Heffernan was sentenced to three calendar months with hard labour for stealing two clocks, and in February 1904, after spending 6 weeks on remand, he was sentenced to 9 calendar months with hard labour for indecent assault. By order of the Lord Lieutenant, the sentence was to take effect from 16 January 1904, when he was first taken into custody.

He was found guilty of indecently assaulting Jane Garry. Garry's statement was as follows:

> *I came into Delvin yesterday, 15 January to attend the market where I buy eggs. I was accompanied by Joseph Heffernan, my servant boy. About five o'clock in the evening we left Delvin to return home. We had a trap and a jennet and Heffernan drove. We went the Mullingar road as far as Mr Behan's, where there is a cross roads, one road leading to Mullingar, and the other towards Bracklyn. Our direct way home was the Mullingar road. Heffernan, however, turned the jennet up the Bracklyn road. I at once said to Heffernan, "This is the wrong road you are going" and he said, "I will go anyway I like." I said, "No Joe, you must go to the right." He said, "No, I shall go this way." I then tried to take the reins but he would not let me. I then tried to get out of the trap saying I should try to overtake my brother, who had gone on in front with a load of eggs and then he might go whatever way he liked. He would not let me get out of the trap; he then hit me in the mouth and knocked me out of the trap. He then dragged me to the side of the ditch and knocked me down. He pulled up my clothes as far as the knee and I struggled to prevent him. I shouted for police and Pat my brother and Father Dillon. Heffernan afterwards attempted to have [illegible] with me and struck me several blows in the face when I would not let him. Heffernan had his person exposed at this time. Just then, two men came up. I did not know they were there until I heard them say to Heffernan, "What are you doing there?" Heffernan then got up. I said to the men that Heffernan had insulted me and that I was on my wrong road.*

> *The man, whom I now know to be John Dunne, said he would go back with me to Delvin and that I should report the matter to the police. Heffernan then said he did not care what steps I took. I then went back to Delvin with Dunne and to the Police Barrack. I did not see Heffernan again until I saw him today. I was quite sober but Heffernan was under the influence of drink. We had gone about three hundred yards from the crossroads when Heffernan assaulted me. Heffernan had been in our employment since last November but had never been to the market with me before.*

This statement was not signed, dated or stamped. All statements at that time, as is now, must be signed by the witness. However, either Miss Garry elected not to make a statement or did not agree with the content as written by the police constable. The content of this statement, because it is not signed or legally endorsed by the usual 6d "Ireland Petty Sessions" stamp, means absolutely nothing. The statement at the outset states, "I came into Delvin yesterday 15 January." This of course leads one to believe it was taken the day after the incident. However, near the end of the statement it reads, "I did not see Heffernan again, until I saw him today." This leads one to assume the statement was written on the day of the trial. This, together with the fact the statement was not signed, stamped or dated, surely points to skulduggery on the part of the British authorities. As the court transcripts are missing, I do not know if Miss Garry gave evidence or indeed, was in attendance at the trial.

Heffernan's statement is as follows:

> *I wish to say that I did not go to do her any harm. She thought not to let me drive and gave me some clouts. I was never here before and did not know the roads and she did not tell me that I was on the wrong road that I remember. I done her work that day, as she could not be got the whole day, and Pat told me he would not bring her to the markets any more, as she would do nothing. Before we started she brought me into Corcoran's and gave me a half whiskey* ["I think" is added here, initialled but not by Heffernan] *and herself the same. It was all her own fault, from first to last.*

Heffernan pleaded not guilty. Heffernan's statement is not signed. I believe that even if he knew anything about the statement, it was his prerogative whether he wanted to sign it or not. However, the statement was not stamped and the arresting officer, Constable James Treacy, in his statement said, "Heffernan made no statement." So where did his alleged statement come from?

John Dunne, who arrived at the scene at about 6.30pm, stated:

I heard shouting; Thomas Gavin was with me. We met a trap and jennet on the road and three or four perch further on we found a man and woman in the ditch. The woman was shouting and appeared to be calling for assistance but I could not understand what she said. It was very dark and Gavin struck a match. As well as I could see, the woman was lying on her back with her head on the road, and her feet to the ditch, the man appeared to be kneeling beside her as if he was in the act of rising up. The woman complained that she had been assaulted.

Dunne said nothing about Heffernan's person being exposed. Dunne's statement was signed, stamped and dated.

In his statement, Thomas Gavin said:

I heard what appeared to be a woman's shout on the road in front. We met a jennet stuck up tight against the fence. The shouting still continued. I remarked some bulk on the opposite side of the road to which the jennet was and then I shouted out, "Hello, what's that?" At once I got a reply from the woman. She said, "Save me from this party, he is trying to take my character." I then struck a match and saw the woman lying on her back with her head to the road and her feet to the ditch. The man was apparently sitting with the woman lying across his knees. I noticed that the woman's clothes about her chest were tossed. I remember her face was all blood. Heffernan said nothing except to call her bad names. Dunne drove the trap back to Delvin and Heffernan followed on foot."

Gavin said nothing about Heffernan's person being exposed. Gavin's statement was signed, stamped and dated.

We have two witnesses who in reality saw nothing of a sexual nature. Both said they heard the shout of a woman. When they first heard the shout they hurried towards it to see what was going on. As they approached, Gavin said he heard the woman calling for assistance. Dunne said he could not make out what she was saying. Gavin said the woman then said, "Save me from this party, he is trying to take my character." Dunne said, "The woman complained that she had been assaulted" (not sexually assaulted), while in Garry's statement, she is alleged to have said, "He insulted me." Dunne said, "The man appeared to be kneeling beside her as if he was in the act of getting up." Gavin said, "The man appeared to be sitting with the woman lying across his knees." In reality, that is two entirely different versions of what Heffernan was doing when the match was struck.

Garry's unofficial, unsigned and unstamped statement means absolutely nothing. If she made a complaint about indecent assault she would have no trouble whatsoever signing the witness form. Likewise, if she made a complaint about common assault, and only common assault was written into the statement, she would have no difficulty signing it. Remember, Dunne stated that she said she was assaulted (not sexually assaulted). However, according to Garry and Heffernan's "statements", they agree that they took a wrong turn, and this created the problem. I decided to go out to the area, to see for myself. Quite frankly, I can understand how Heffernan took the wrong turn on that dark January evening, with no lights, road markings or road signs to assist. He was unfamiliar with the area and the small, narrow road. What I cannot understand is why Miss Garry did not travel with her brother, or at least follow directly behind him. She is alleged to have said in her statement that she was calling for her brother, but she knew full well that he was miles ahead of her. Surely, the normal reaction from a lady being attacked is to scream at the top of her lungs – and not to call out for various people. Why did she stop for a drink at Corcoran's pub? Was she drinking? Did she become aggressive while under the influence? Why did the police fail to take a statement from her brother Pat? Surely he was in a position to answer some of the questions. I have done some research and discovered that at that time, maids and boy servants were verbally and physically abused on a regular basis by their employers. In a letter to the Lord Lieutenant, Heffernan stated that Miss Garry verbally abused him and hit him some clouts. He also said he could not take any more and he, in turn, hit her a few clouts.

According to the statements, they both agree that a scuffle broke out on board the trap, this resulted in her falling out on the road. Nobody gave evidence of seeing him indecently assault her. It seems he was coming to her assistance. For all he knew, she could have been killed or seriously injured. Gavin said Heffernan had her body lying on his knees. He was not on top of her or indecently assaulting her; his hand was not inside her clothing. He said the breast part of her dress was tossed, but in reality, she was involved in a scuffle – a scuffle that, according to her "statement," she admitted she instigated, as she tried to pull the reins off Heffernan. According to Gavin, her face was "all blood" (Dunne said nothing about this). Was this a result of the "few clouts" she got off Heffernan, or was it a result of the fall? It seems to me Miss Garry made no indecent assault complaint against Heffernan. She may have lodged a common assault complaint. The unsigned statement also states, "Heffernan had his person out." Could she have known this if it was so dark that Gavin had to strike a match in order to see what was going on?

While serving his sentence for indecent assault, Heffernan wrote to the Lord Lieutenant, he explained his case and asked for credit for the six weeks he was held on remand while awaiting trial. This was granted. Only one page of the letter remains on file. What became of the remainder of the letter and why did it vanish? Perhaps Heffernan mentioned Miss Garry's absence on the day of the hearing and he therefore felt he had no charge to answer.

Strangely enough, his case, along with six others, was listed for hearing on 29 February 1904. However, the *Westmeath Examiner* never mentioned the trial, except Judge Madden's remark when addressing the Grand Jury. Madden stated the following:

> *Gentlemen, there are seven cases before you; one of these was before you on a previous occasion, so you are not likely now to have any difficulty in considering it. There are six other cases, but none of them of any great importance. There is one case of alleged attempted rape, which is a rather curious one, but none of these cases require any special remark from me to you.*

The *Westmeath Examiner*, while publishing a report on the remaining six cases, failed to cover Heffernan's trial – if there was a trial. The Midland Reporter and Westmeath Nationalist used ninety words to cover the trial. The report is as follows:

> *A man named Joseph Heffernan, The Downs, Mullingar, was charged with attempted rape, indecent assault and common assault on a girl from the same place. The prisoner, who was not professionally represented, pleaded guilty to the charge of common assault and not guilty to the two other charges. Mr Denis Henry K.C. prosecuted. Evidence having been given in the case, the jury retired and after an absence of a few minutes, returned with a verdict of indecent assault and the prisoner was sentenced to nine calendar months with hard labour.*

This is very strange. A case reported in the same newspaper, with a guilty plea actually received a lot more coverage. I believe that Miss Garry made only one complaint, that of common assault, and as the statement as written by a policeman touched on indecent assault/attempted rape she refused to sign it and refused to appear in court to give evidence against Heffernan. The facts point to the prosecutor merely reading out the "statements" and the jury being asked to consider the "evidence."

While records show that Heffernan had a deformed right hand in 1907 and 1909, as a result of a bad burning, this accident happened sometime after the indecent assault case. I do not know exactly what happened on that January evening in 1904, but I know this: there was more than enough evidence to warrant a dismissal of all charges of a sexual nature against the defendant. Of course, five years later this conviction was of great assistance to the authorities. It meant they could say what they liked about Heffernan and the vast majority of locals would swallow it.

16.

UPDATE: THE MISSING FILE

In the first edition of *Is It Me?* I explained the situation regarding a missing file. This file was held at Dublin Castle. In October 1923, The Ministry of Home Affairs (now the Department of Justice) wrote to Dublin Castle requesting five files; among them was H–32–09, which was Heffernan's. His file was delivered to the Ministry of Home Affairs where it lay until 2011 when I submitted a request for same. After searching through the archives, the Department of Justice finally located the file. I was then asked drop in to the Department offices and invited to browse through the file. At this stage I delayed the publication of the first edition of Is It Me?

After studying the content, I selected a number of documents I deemed to be worthy of closer examination. An official undertook to photocopy and post the documents to my address. However, after five weeks, and no sign of the documents, I decided that I could not delay publication any longer.

The documents are now in my possession and the Department of Justice kindly gave me permission to publish whatever information I deemed relevant to the Joe Heffernan case. I retrieved numerous documents and newspaper clippings from the so–called missing file.

The newspaper clippings were all national. There was nothing from the Mullingar media. They filed nothing from the inquest or Magistrates' hearings. The British Authorities seemed to be very worried about how the media would report the trial. The Governor of Kilmainham Gaol was tasked with the job of delivering favourable newspaper clippings to Dublin Castle; he also submitted a cover note with same. This man took delight, and deemed it an honour to report to the Castle, the news that Heffernan was convicted and sentenced to death. His letter, dated 3 December 1909 was as follows:

3 December 1909
Case of Joseph Heffernan
Convicted of murder

The Under Secretary
Dublin Castle

Sir

I have the honour to report that the above named prisoner was found guilty of the murder of Mary Walker near Mullingar on 7 July last and sentenced this morning by the Lord Chief Justice to be hanged on 4 January 1910. The jury made no recommendation.
I have the honour to be

Sir
Your Obedient Servant
M. McGann
Governor

The wording of this letter speaks volumes for the delight these people felt when the jury delivered the guilty verdict.

I also came across a number of mercy pleas. One plea came from Scotland and the rest came from various bodies based around Ireland. They were all submitted to the Lords Justices for their attention. These gentlemen responded in the negative to the relevant bodies. Lord Chief Justice O'Brien, the man who imposed the death penalty on Heffernan, stated the following in his letter of refusal:

"In my opinion, there are no circumstances which would render the prisoner a proper object of mercy."

He went on to say:

"The prisoner attempted to violate a most respectable girl and when she made a heroic resistance, cut her throat."

Another document I unearthed was headed "General Prisons Board for Ireland" and dated 9 December 1909. The content was as follows:

Subject
Joseph Heffernan, Kilmainham Prison, sentenced to be hanged on 4 January (proximo), having been convicted of murder on 3 December 1909, at the Leinster Winter Assizes held at Green St, Dublin.

Minute
Under Secretary,

We beg to submit a copy of the Rule of Court in the case of convict Heffernan. The sentence passed in this case would in ordinary course be carried out at Kilmainham Prison. But having regard to the fact that it is proposed to evacuate this prison from the 31st instant, and that if the execution were to be carried out there, it would necessitate structural alterations in the

Execution Chamber, scaffold etc, owing to altered regulations since the scaffold was erected there, which we consider should not now be undertaken owing to the approaching evacuation of the prison. Under the circumstances we recommend, if there is no legal objection, that the convict may be moved to Mountjoy Prison where the sentence may be carried out, and removal orders similar to those approved of in a somewhat similar case are attached for this purpose.

Signature
Chairman

The request was denied and as such, Heffernan was executed in Kilmainham Gaol. Incidentally, Heffernan was the last prisoner to be hanged in Kilmainham; our 1916 heroes were shot.

The most disturbing information I extracted from the file was contained in two signed letters using the Governor of Kilmainham's name; both letters were written on Christmas Eve 1909. The content of the letters clearly shows the pressure this man was put under, as certain elements of the British Government covered their tracks.

The second letter was written, as the authorities were not satisfied with the content of the initial letter. Dublin Castle immediately flexed its muscles and returned the initial letter to the prison with instructions to add an enclosed rider to the second letter.

The content of the initial letter was as follows:

H.M. Prison, Kilmainham
24 Dec 1909

The Under Secretary
Dublin Castle

Sir

I have the honour to acknowledge the receipt of your communication dated the 23rd inst, acquainting me that their Excellencies the Lord Justices see no reason for interference with the course of the law in the case of prisoner Joseph Heffernan now in my custody under sentence of death.

I have this day informed said prisoner accordingly.

I have the honour to be

Sir
Your Obedient Servant
M. McGann
Governor

This letter was immediately rejected and together with a directive returned the same day to Mr McGann. The content of McGann's second letter was as follows:

H.M. Prison, Kilmainham
24 Dec 1909

The Chairman,
General Prisons Board, Dublin Castle.

I beg to report that I received a communication from the Under Secretary this afternoon acquainting me that in the case of prisoner Joseph Heffernan, in my custody under sentence of death, their Excellencies the Lords Justices see no reason for interference with the course of the law and to inform said prisoner immediately.
I immediately informed the prisoner when he said, "It is a hard case, but I suppose I deserve it." I submit this in compliance with instructions contained in the second paragraph of Circular No. 479.

M. McGann Gov

On studying both letters, I discovered a number of issues that in my opinion reek of official skulduggery. For example:

The tone of the second letter was completely at odds to that of the first. It is difficult to believe that both letters were written by the same person. The initial letter begins with the world '*Sir*' and ends with, "I have the honour to be, *Sir, Your Obedient Servant*, M. McGann, Governor." The second letter dispenses with the words 'Sir' and 'Sir, Your Obedient Servant.' This letter simply ends with 'M. McGann, Gov.'

The first letter then reads as follows, "I have this day informed said prisoner accordingly." The second letter reads, "I immediately informed the prisoner when he said, *It is a hard case, but I suppose I deserve it.*"

The writer stated in the second letter that Heffernan more or less admitted he was guilty. He then adds that, he submitted this in "compliance with the instructions contained in the second paragraph of Circular No. 479."

There is no trace of Circular No. 479; it has simply disappeared. The most disturbing difference I noticed between the two letters is the signature. While there is no doubt the name of M. McGann is clearly written on the bottom of both letters, the name was either signed by two different people, or Mr McGann went out of his way to disguise his signature on one of the letters. Later, according to McGann, Heffernan, while standing on the gallows, waiting to die, said nothing. One would imagine this would be the platform on which to admit guilt; that is of course if he was guilty.

All of the above was done in an attempt to cover up any problem or difficulty that may crop up in the future. When the British moved out of southern Ireland something did crop up. On 26 October 1923 the Ministry of Home Affairs requested Heffernan's file from Dublin Castle. While the entire file was not sent to Home Affairs, the file compiled after the trial was. This file contained both letters. I believe, as stated earlier, some of the child witnesses, now adults, were having difficulty coming to terms with the role they played during the trial. Their opportunity to do the right thing came when the British moved out of Ireland. They approached the new Irish government and poured their hearts out. In my opinion, the second letter was produced to all concerned, and they accepted the content as gospel.

I also discovered two letters dated 4 January 1910 the day of the execution, the content of the first letter was as follows:

H.M. Prison
Kilmainham
4 January 1910

Subject: Execution of prisoner Joseph Heffernan – a Westmeath Case

The Chairman
General Prisons Board
Dublin Castle

I beg to report that the execution of the above named prisoner was carried out this morning at 8 o'clock. The arrangements and result being in every respect satisfactory. Henry Albert Pierrepoint, 14 Cowgill, Clayton, near Bradford being the executioner. Assisted by Thomas W. Pierrepoint, Town End, Clayton near Bradford Yorkshire.

The prisoner, Heffernan made no statement this morning. I shall forward a copy of the verdict of the Coroner's Jury after the inquest has been held.

M. McGann Gov

The second letter, dated 4 January, was the coroner's jury verdict. The content is as follows:

ABSTRACT OF VERDICT

4 January 1910
County of the City of Dublin

To Wit
The body of Joseph Heffernan
At Kilmainham Prison
The verdict of the Jury was that,
The said Joseph Heffernan died in Kilmainham Prison on the 4th inst, from
asphyxia caused by hanging which was in accordance with the sentence
imposed upon him by the Lord Chief Justice of Ireland.

Louis A. Byrne
Coroner for the County of said City

The final letter in the file is dated 10 January 1910. This letter is a record of Heffernan's execution. The details concern the damage done to his body as a result of hanging, also the length of the drop before and after the execution. It does not make for pleasant reading and as such, I decided not to go into too much detail. Also, it has no relevance as to Heffernan's innocence.

17.

WITNESSES AND FAMILY MEMBERS

I decided to take a look at the calibre of the prosecution witnesses and their families. Some of these people produced by the prosecution were to say the least, hardened criminals. I did this as I wanted to establish what sort of a relationship existed between the police and the witnesses, prior to and after the murder of Miss Walker. With the exception of the publicans and Mr Callaghan (farmer), the information I unearthed was akin to something downloaded from Rogues Gallery. Quite a number of the witnesses, and/or family members, appeared regularly in the courts. The publicans also appeared in court but only for the minor offence of breaching the licensing laws. The thing is, quite number of the witnesses and their families were in constant trouble with the law, right up to the day of the murder of Mary Walker. From the date these people gave statements implicating Joe Heffernan in Mary's murder, to the passing of the death sentence, the police eased off. None of these people appeared in court during Heffernan's trial; it seems that they were given a free run to do whatever they wanted to do, during and after that time.

The fact that they were regular offenders left them open and easy to bribe as far as the police were concerned. There is no doubt that these criminals and the publicans gladly accepted the conditions as offered by the police.

PUBLICANS

During the four months prior to the murder of Mary Walker, Mullingar publicans regularly appeared in court charged with breaching licensing laws. I researched the reports of such cases from March 1909 until Joe Heffernan was convicted in December 1909. As a number of publicans gave evidence in the case, I decided to see if there was a change in police behaviour towards them as the Heffernan case progressed. I unearthed the following cases as reported in the *Westmeath Examiner*:

John Grimes, publican, Greville Street, Mullingar, was convicted of keeping his premises open for the sale of drink on a Sunday. He was fined £2 and costs.

John Lynch, publican, Earl Street, Mullingar, was convicted of keeping his premises open for the sale of drink on a Sunday. He was fined £1.

> *Patrick Murray, a spirit grocer and beer retailer, Patrick Street, Mullingar, was convicted of keeping his premises open for the sale of drink on a Sunday. He was fined 10s.*

I researched the name "Patrick Murray", Patrick Street, Mullingar. I discovered there was only one Patrick Murray residing in Patrick at that time, so the odds are that he was the father of young Michael Murray who gave evidence at the Heffernan trial.

> *Miss Martha Flood, Publican, Earl Street, Mullingar, was charged with keeping her premises open for the sale of drink on a Sunday. The case was dismissed.*
> *Mrs Bridget Sullivan, Military Road, Mullingar [Mrs Sullivan also owned a premises on Greville Street], was charged with keeping her premises open for the sale of drink on a Sunday. The case was dismissed.*
> *Mrs Bridget Sullivan, publican, Greville Street, Mullingar was convicted of selling drink at a prohibited hour of the night. She was fined £2 with the conviction to be recorded on the license.*
> *Mrs Bridget Sullivan [same lady], publican, Military Road, Mullingar, was convicted of keeping her premises open for the sale of drink on a Sunday. She was fined £2 with the conviction to be recorded on the license.*
> *John Colman, Earl Street, Mullingar, was convicted of keeping his premises open for the sale of drink on a Sunday. He was fined £1 and costs.*
> *Miss Margaret Brennan, publican, Dominick Street, Mullingar, was charged with selling drink to an intoxicated man. The case was dismissed.*
> *Matthew Murray, publican, Mullingar was charged with keeping his premises open for the sale of drink on Good Friday. The case was dismissed.*

From the date of Miss Walker's murder until after Heffernan's conviction, not one Mullingar publican appeared in the courts. A number of publicans gave evidence for the prosecution and as you read earlier, Charlie Quinn, Bridget Sullivan's barman swore that Heffernan had a knife in his possession while in Sullivan's pub on the day of the murder. He also swore that Heffernan purchased a pipe from him. From March until July, Bridget Sullivan, Quinn's boss, was charged on three occasions, and from July until Heffernan was convicted, she was left alone. It is very easy to come to the conclusion that some sort of a deal was done between some of the publicans and the police.

OTHER WITNESSES

ANNE MORAN
Prior to the murder of Mary Walker, Mrs Anne Moran, Joe Heffernan's landlady had numerous convictions for the following offences (I went back two years):

Westmeath Examiner, 1 June 1907

Patrick Melia and Denis Murray, Austin Friars Street, Mullingar, summoned Anne Moran for abusive and threatening language.

The chairman said he was satisfied that Moran used very improper language towards these two men. He would take the defendants own bail of £5. But if she appeared in court again, charged with abusing these two men, she would have to find sureties for her future good behaviour, or else she would be sent to jail.

Westmeath Examiner, 29 June 1907

The Mullingar District Council, as the sanitary authority, prosecuted Anne Moran, Austin Friars Street, Mullingar for keeping an unregistered common lodging house and also for allowing the sexes in the house to be mixed as prohibited by the bye laws. Moran was convicted and fined 10s plus 10s costs.

Westmeath Examiner, February 22 1908

Charles Doyle summoned Anne Moran for having assaulted and using threatening and abusive language towards him on the 8 and 9 February. The parties live at the Cross Keys (Part of Austin Friars Street), Mullingar. She was convicted of abusive behaviour and bound to the peace for 12 months, she was required to put up £10 herself and two independent sureties of £5 each and in default of finding sufficient solvent bail she would be sent to jail for one month. For the assault, she was sentenced to two months imprisonment with hard labour, the sentences were consecutive.

Westmeath Examiner, July 1908

Thomas Beglan and his wife, Mary Anne Beglan, Austin Friars Street, Mullingar, summoned Anne Moran for assault and abusive and threatening language. Moran was in custody, having been arrested on an information sworn by Thomas Beglan.

Thomas Beglan deposed that on the 28 June, Moran's husband broke down the mearing (fence) of his garden. At seven o'clock that evening Moran came to his back door and his wife to the front door and began to abuse him. Mr Moran fired a number of large stones into the house. The next day Anne Moran abused him and spat in his face. Thomas Beglan then stated that the reason Anne Moran abused him and his wife, was because he refused to go bail for her on a previous occasion.

Anne Moran was convicted, the chairman said they would deal leniently with her because they could send her to jail for two months without the option of a fine. They were not however going to do that. They ordered that she enter into bail – herself, £20 and provide two sureties of £10 each – to keep to the peace for twelve months. If she did not get the necessary bail she would have to go to jail for two months.

Westmeath Examiner, 1 May 1909

Mullingar District Council prosecuted Anne Moran, Austin Friars Street, for refusing to register a common lodging house. The District Council said that they had been trying at different times to get Moran to register but she refused to do it and she was heavily fined. The Magistrates' convicted Moran and she was fined £2 with the option of going to jail for two months. Throughout the duration of Heffernan's murder trial Moran was not arrested or interfered with by the police. Let's face it; she was a lady who could not control herself so the odds are she would have caused trouble during that time.

SUSAN GIFF

Westmeath Examiner, 13 April 1907

Bernard Giff [Susan's Husband] *was prosecuted for assaulting a man. The prosecution stated that the victim was in hospital and not able to attend the court. The court was also informed that Giff had left town. The prosecution asked for an adjournment for a week.*

Westmeath Examiner, 12 October 1907

Bernard Giff was summonsed for assaulting his wife Susan Giff on the previous Monday evening. The evidence states that on the day in question Susie Giff was given three guineas compensation from a gentleman in Navan for knocking down her child with his motor car. Her husband claimed that she drank the money.

The chairman: Were you under the influence of drink?
Susan replied, "I might have taken some drink."

A witness, Mary Roddy stated that Susie Giff brought her into her house that Monday night. Giff was fighting with her husband and she was "party full." Roddy added that Susie Giff flung her child under the table and her husband told her not to do it again. Susie then took down a jar and "Barney ran for his life." Finally, Roddy stated that the defendant never raised a hand to his wife.
The Head Constable informed the Magistrates' that the defendant had previous convictions, adding that he was a dangerous man.
The defendant was convicted and sentenced to jail for a month.

Westmeath Examiner, 10 October 1908

During a drinking session inside and outside Catherine Carroll's house, Barrack Street, Mullingar, a free for all broke out. The following were involved one way or another: Bernard and Susan Giff, Mary and John Roddy, Catherine Carroll, Dinah Giff (witness), James and Ellen Daly, Kate Anne Carroll. Most of the participants were drunk. There were quart cans of porter all over the house. People were beaten and some were thrown out on the street. Windows were broken. They were threatening to kill one another. It was an ugly incident. At the end of the trial, the Magistrates' couldn't figure out who was telling the truth. It was impossible under the circumstances to believe any of the evidence and it was the opinion of the bench that all cases should be dismissed with a caution.

Westmeath Examiner, 22 May 1909

Joseph Giff [Susan Giff's brother in law], *Barrack Street, Mullingar was charged with the larceny of one thousand cabbage plants, valued about 2s 6d the property of Patrick Shaw, Clonkill. The Head Constable stated that Giff's record was a very big one and his presence in the locality was a menace to the public and their property. The Chairman praised Sgt Brennan for the prompt manner in which he had dealt with the case. He hoped it would be the starting point in putting down the outrageous conduct carried on by men of the defendants stamp. What he described as a "Reign of Terror" existed in the town. He convicted Giff and sentenced him to jail for two months.*

Westmeath Examiner, 17 September 1910

Susan and Mary Giff were summoned for being drunk on 29 August 1910. The Chairman said it was perfectly disgraceful to see two young married women up in court charged with drunkenness and he thought they should be heartily ashamed of themselves. A fine of 1s and costs was imposed in each case.

DENIS CALLAGHAN

Westmeath Examiner, 15 May 1909

A farmer, Denis Callaghan, Robinstown, Mullingar, was prosecuted for ill–treating a number of cattle. Constable Twomey said Callaghan cruelly beat the animals about the head with an ash plant. He was convicted and fined 1s with costs.

Denis Callaghan was a brother and close neighbour of James Callaghan who gave evidence at the Heffernan trial.

THOMAS RATTIGAN

Westmeath Examiner, 5 October 1907

Thomas Rattigan (paid informer in Heffernan trial), a sweep, was charged with assaulting Mr Peter Wallace, DC, on the Irishtown Road the previous day. Rattigan was convicted. Mr Wallace, however, asked the Magistrates' to deal leniently with him. Rattigan was sent to jail for one month with hard labour.

LUKE SULLIVAN

Westmeath Examiner, 9 March 1907

Luke Sullivan (paid informer in Heffernan trial), Michael Creevy (Bridget Creevy's husband) and Patrick Gavan were charged with assaulting Edward McCormack on the 21 February last. The Head Constable stated that the defendants stood at corners of public houses and they intimidated people who were passing in order to get money for drink. They operated a sort of a highway business. The Head Constable stated that Creevy's wife informed him that Creevy could not attend the court as he was working. The Chairman enquired about Creevy's conduct, and was told that he was improving since he came out of jail last year. Despite the fact that Creevy and Gavan held the victim as Sullivan beat him up, the Chairman discharged them with a caution. The prosecution informed the court that Sullivan was in jail on a number of occasions. Sullivan was then sentenced to fourteen days in jail. At the expiry of that term he would have to enter into bail, himself in £5 and two sureties of £2.10s each to keep the peace for twelve months. If he failed to find bail he would have to go to jail for another fourteen days.

Westmeath Examiner, 24 July 1909

Luke Sullivan was prosecuted for poaching. A number of witnesses gave evidence of seeing Sullivan with three greyhounds and a number of rabbits in his hand. Mr Toomey, the gamekeeper said he was not three yards from Sullivan and he said to him "Stand Sullivan, your game is up." He said Sullivan then jumped through a hedge and ran away. He was found guilty and the prosecution handed in Sullivan's record, which showed that he had been many times convicted of poaching. He was fined £2 or one month in jail with hard labour. Sullivan asked for time to pay the fine; this was refused, he was taken into custody.

Sullivan was sentenced on Wednesday 21 July 1909, exactly two weeks after the murder of Miss Walker.

Westmeath Examiner, 10 September 1910

Luke Sullivan was prosecuted for stealing 6s, the property of Peter Lynch at his shop in Austin Friars Street. He was remanded in custody to Mountjoy jail.

Westmeath Examiner, 17 September 1910

Luke Sullivan, who had been remanded in custody last week on a charge of stealing 6s was then put forward. The depositions taken last week were read over. Sullivan entered a guilty plea. He was sentenced to four calendar months with hard labour.

ELIZABETH FLANAGAN'S PARENTS

Westmeath Examiner, 29 May 1909

Joseph and Lizzie Flanagan [Elizabeth Flanagan's parents] of the mendicant type were prosecuted for neglecting their children. After listening to all the evidence the Magistrates' deemed Joseph Flanagan fit to look after his children. The Chairman said that Lizzie Flanagan was in the habit of taking the baby away from Flanagan. She went tramping around the country, sleeping in fields. Her husband would report her missing to the police. The child was always healthy and strong when she took it away, when she returned it was nearly dead. He sent her to jail for a period of three months with hard labour.

Westmeath Examiner, 27 August 1910

Lizzie Flanagan was prosecuted for being drunk in charge of a child in a public place. Her husband stated that Lizzie was in Killucan and couldn't appear in court. The Chairman stated that, "This woman has been before the courts on different occasions. She is always going around the town begging. She is an awful nuisance.

Her husband said, "She has taken the pledge now your worship. She wasn't really drunk because she was able to carry the child."

The Chairman said, "I haven't a shadow of a doubt but that she was drunk and fined her 20s or 14 days in jail."

Her husband asked for time to enable his wife to pay the fine, this was refused and a warrant for her arrest was issued.

Who Gained What?

The publicans plied their trade hassle free, in most cases for more than twelve months. However, Bridget Sullivan's barman, Charlie Quinn vanished. I cannot trace him; he probably left town. Quinn was the barman who stated he saw Heffernan with a knife. He also stated he sold him a pipe on the morning of the murder.

Anne Moran, a serial offender was also left alone by the Council Safety Authorities and the police. This lady, who liked a drink, was regularly in trouble. There was no way she could stay out of trouble for more than a year and a half. Mrs Moran was Heffernan's landlady, she swore she saw a knife in Heffernan's hand the morning after the murder. However, she did come clean, while giving evidence at the assizes, when she stated that she did not actually see the knife. The police did not bother her for at least eighteen months after Heffernan's trial.

Elizabeth Flanagan, the young girl from Barrack Street. She swore she saw a bloodstained knife and handkerchief in Heffernan's hand shortly after the murder of Miss Walker. For assisting the police, her mother, who recently received three months with hard labour, was granted early release from jail. Just one week after Elizabeth gave evidence against Heffernan at the Magistrates' hearings in Mullingar, her mother was released. The strange thing about this is, prior to Miss Walker's murder, Elizabeth's father sent a petition to the authorities, pleading for the early release of his wife. The petition was signed by eighteen people, mostly businessmen.

The reasons he applied for her early release were as follows: Mrs Flanagan was the mother of five children, her eldest daughter Elizabeth was, at fifteen years of age too young to look after the family. Joseph Flanagan himself had received a warrant to form up with the army reserves, D Company, 3rd Leinsters, Birr, Co. Offaly. The petition was passed on to the Magistrate who tried and sentenced Mrs Flanagan. His response was as follows: "For the crime committed, I think the punishment inflicted was a reasonable one which should not be lessoned." His views were immediately delivered to the Chief Secretary's Office in Dublin. The Chief Secretary agreed and stated, "Let the law take its course."

So the petition failed, despite the fact that her husband was stationed in Birr and her fifteen–year–old daughter was left alone to care for herself and her four siblings. When that did not qualify for early release one would assume nothing would. Of course, giving evidence on behalf of the prosecution in Heffernan's murder trial changed all that.

Luke Sullivan, the informer who made a statement, three–and–a–half months after the murder of Mary Walker. Sullivan, who was a regular offender, appeared in court two weeks after the murder of Miss Walker. He was found guilty of poaching, he was fined £2 or one month in jail with hard labour. As he could not pay the fine, he was immediately taken into custody. If Sullivan knew what he said he knew, about seeing Heffernan down at the tunnel on the 8 July, why did he wait until October to come forward? He had an ideal opportunity to strike a deal with the police and avoid being summonsed for poaching.

From what I am told, an informer's fee in connection with a murder investigation was 30 shillings; this reminds me of Judas and thirty pieces of silver.

Susan Giff and her relations, Thomas Rattigan and the Callaghan family were not bothered by the police during the Heffernan trial and indeed for months after. With the exception of Callaghan, the remainder of the above witnesses were serial offenders, who regularly appeared in court.

It beggars belief that, from the minute the above–mentioned offenders or their family members gave statements implicating Heffernan in the murder of Mary Walker, their criminal activities were totally ignored by the police. These people may not have been regular churchgoers but they were definitely regular court goers.

18.

MILITARY SEX PREDATOR

As I researched the criminal activities of some of the witnesses and their family members I came across the following case report in a local newspaper. As this case could be linked to the Heffernan case, I decided to have a closer look at the evidence. It concerns a Lance Corporal attached to the 4th Battalion, Royal Fusiliers who was stationed in Mullingar. The Battalion had recently moved to Mullingar for a two–year tour of duty.

Westmeath Examiner, 28 September 1907

> *Lance Corporal Herbert Lambert was charged with, on 16 September 1907, at Walshestown Lower, Mullingar, indecently assaulting a young girl who was under 13 years of age. The accused pleaded not guilty. The official charge sheet read as follows:*
> *"Herbert Lambert on the Sixteenth day of September in the year of our lord one thousand nine hundred and seven unlawfully and indecently did assault one [I feel I shouldn't mention the child's name] a girl under the age of thirteen years and her the said child he did then beat, wound and ill–treat and other wrongs to the said child then did to the great damage of the said child against the form of the statute in such case made and provided and against the peace of our Lord the King his Crown and Dignity."*

The young girl deposed that:

> *"I live with my mother at Walshestown, Mullingar. On Monday, 16 September last, I left my mother's house at about 6.30pm to go to Mrs Ryan's. Mrs Ryan lives between my house and Walshestown chapel. It would take me about a half an hour to walk to her house. I arrived at Mrs Ryan's at about seven o'clock. I stayed for a short period of time at Mrs Ryan's and then turned back for home. On my way home I called to a neighbour's house to see my sister. I only stayed a few minutes and then continued on home. On leaving my neighbour's house I passed Geoghegan's and Fitzgerald's houses. I then passed Grehan's and after that Flanagan's. Shortly after passing Flanagan's I met a soldier on the road. He said "Good evening" and asked me was this the road to Mullingar. I said no, that it was back the other way to Mullingar. He said he was going to catch up with other soldiers. He gave me a penny and asked me to meet him tomorrow evening. I said no, that I would not be out. He asked, why? I said nothing. It was getting dark."*

He then assaulted her and she gave her account of what this man done to her. This was not published in the local papers. However, I located her statement in the National Archives, the young child said as follows:

> "He gave me a penny, he asked me to meet him tomorrow evening. I said 'no that I wouldn't be out.' He then asked me why. I said nothing. He then put his hand round my neck and kissed me. He tried to put his hand under my clothes. I began to cry, and I said let me out. He said, "don't be crying." I said let me go home and I won't cry. He then gave me another penny and let me go and he continued on the road. I went on towards my house; before I reached my house I met my brother Michael. I told him what happened and he went in the direction the soldier had taken. I continued on towards home. I met my mother on the road and told her what the soldier had done to me. We then went home. After a while I heard my mother talking to a man on the road. The voice of this person was the same as the voice of the soldier who assaulted me. I think the soldier who assaulted me was a little smaller than this man. I cannot identify the prisoner now present as the soldier who assaulted me. The soldier did actually put his hand up under my clothes."

The alleged victim's mother deposed that:

> "My daughter lives with me. She will be twelve years of age in December next. On the evening in question I was in my house. I went to get water from a well in our garden near the house; when there, a soldier came down the road from the Mullingar direction. He spoke to her and went on. Afterwards, I went back to the well to get another bucket of water. I heard my daughter scream, I ran back to the house and told my son Michael, who ran out. I met my daughter, she was crying, shivering and frightened. My daughter told me what happened. Sometime after that her son came into the house and asked her out. When I went out I noticed a soldier approaching the house from the direction of Walshestown chapel. I asked him was he the young man that interfered with the young girl on the road? He said he wasn't. Michael, her son then said, "You're the very boy." The soldier replied, "It must be another soldier." My son then caught him by the collar of the coat and called out my daughter. When she came out, the soldier gave a chuck and ran away towards Mullingar. It was dark and she could not see him distinctly. A neighbour, Willie Ryan approached and when he heard what happened, my son and Ryan decided to follow the soldier. They caught up with him and started to beat him on the road. I followed them up the road to see what was going on. I shouted at them not to kill him and to let him go. They let him go and he went in the direction of Mullingar. My son kept his cap and later gave it to the Head Constable. I did not see any other soldier on the road that evening."

The alleged victim's brother Michael deposed that:

"I was taking my tea on the evening in question. As I was looking out through the window towards the road I saw a soldier pass in the direction of Walshestown chapel. He almost stood on the road to look in while passing our house. It was dark at the time. A short time after the soldier had passed, my mother called me and in consequence of what she told me I went out on the road in the direction of Flanagan's house. I met my sister; she was crying and excited and, in consequence of what she told me, I went in the direction of Walshestown chapel. On coming back I met William Ryan and spoke to him. Sometime later, I saw a soldier coming from the direction of Walshestown chapel. I called my mother out. She asked the soldier if he was the man who interfered with the girl on the road, he said he was not. To which I replied, "You're the very boy." When my sister came out he broke away from me. Myself and Ryan followed the soldier, knocked him down and beat him. After letting him up off the road the soldier said that he was not the man; that it was a "Butty" of his and he would get him, I told him to come along and tell us where he is. He tried to get away again but we overtook him and beat him again. While we were beating him the second time my mother came up and saved him. The soldiers cap was knocked off in the scuffle, I picked it up and kept it and gave it to Head Constable Crudden."

Patrick Flanagan stated:

"I was coming home from work that evening when a soldier riding a bicycle passed me at Grogan's. Shortly afterwards I saw the alleged victim walking in the direction of her house. The soldier was riding very quickly. I then had my tea and as I was looking out I saw a soldier coming from the direction of Walshestown chapel. He was going towards Mullingar. He was walking quickly. Both soldiers were dressed in khaki."

Francis Geoghegan, Walshestown, stated:

"I saw a soldier passing my father's house on the evening in question. He was going towards Walshestown chapel. He was not as tall as the prisoner, I think he had a large moustache but I only saw his side face."

Head Constable Crudden stated:

"On the evening of 16 September 1907, in consequence of information I received I proceeded to Walshestown. I received the cap (produced) from the alleged victim's brother. On the 17 September I returned to Walshestown, where the young girl pointed out to me on the road the place at which she alleged she was assaulted. The distance from Flanagan's gate to that spot is 55

yards, and from the place where she pointed out to her mother's gate is 231 yards. The young girl's mother pointed out to me the place she was when she alleged she heard her daughter scream. That spot is 275 yards from the place pointed out by the alleged victim. The prisoner admitted to me the cap was his."

The accused was returned for trial to the Quarter Sessions, bail for his appearance being accepted.

Westmeath Examiner, 19 October 1907

Quarter Sessions

Herbert Lambert, Lance–Corporal of the 4th Battalion, Royal Fusiliers, was charged with having on the 16 September 1907, attempted an indecent assault at Walshestown, on a young girl under 13 years of age. He was also indicted for a common assault on the same occasion.

The prosecutor, Mr Kelly, C S, who handed in a plan of the road from the Military Barracks, Mullingar to the scene of the alleged assault, addressed the jury at some length and a number of witnesses were examined.

The chief points in the case largely turned on the question of identification. The witnesses for the most part said it was a very dark night and they could not see the face of the soldier whom they met.

Mr Woods for the defence asked for a direction from his Honour that the jury discharge the prisoner, his Honour said he could not do that.

Mr Woods, having addressed the jury and his Honour having followed, the jury disagreed and the case was put back to the next Quarter Sessions. The accused was granted bail.

Westmeath Examiner, 18 January 1908

Quarter Sessions

Mr Woods made an application in the case of the Crown verses Lance–Corporal Herbert Lambert of the 4th Battalion, Royal Fusiliers, in regard of which the jury disagreed at the last Quarter Sessions. Lambert was charged with an assault on a little girl under 13 years of age.

The application now is to send the accused, who, is on bail, for trial to the next assizes.

The application was granted and bail was renewed.

Westmeath Examiner, 7 March 1908

Winter Assizes

Lance–Corporal Herbert Lambert, 4th Battalion, Royal Fusiliers surrendered to bail on a charge of having attempted an assault on a little girl at Walshestown on 16 September 1907.

When this case was held at the October Quarter Sessions the jury disagreed and the accused was put back on bail.

The evidence was gone into and, as at the previous hearing the question of identification was largely before the jury.

The jury acquitted the young soldier who was then discharged.

So, what do we have here? After reading the evidence, there is no doubt we had a sex predator serving with the 4th Battalion, Royal Fusiliers. He was stationed in Mullingar at the time Mary Walker was murdered. The Fusiliers moved out of Mullingar two months after Miss Walker was killed. Lance Corporal Herbert Lambert continued to, and was entitled to serve as a soldier in Mullingar. Witnesses failed to identify him as the man who attacked the young child. Two witnesses, while giving evidence, mentioned something that could possibly link this case to Heffernan's. One of these witnesses, the victim, stated, that she thought the soldier who attacked her was smaller than the prisoner. Francis Geoghegan said the soldier he saw on the road was not as tall as the prisoner. Geoghegan also thought the soldier had a large moustache; actually, Heffernan was a small man and had a drooping moustache. The chances are, the perpetrator was roughly the same height as Joe Heffernan. Joe's height was a very important piece of evidence that authorities relied upon to identify him as the killer of Miss Walker.

I am positive Lance Corporal Lambert was totally innocent of the crime; he was just in the wrong place at the wrong time. As nobody else was charged with the attack on the young child, the real predator carried on with life as if nothing happened. He no doubt continued to serve in Mullingar barracks until the murder of Miss Walker. I also believe he was the second man to be arrested on the morning after Miss Walker met her death.

The attack on the child commenced with the perpetrator placing his hand around her throat. Miss Walker's body displayed no bruises, scratches or scrapes, this leads me to believe her killer's Modus Operandi was the very same. The attack on the child took place on the road quite close to a number of houses. The child began to cry and the attacker let her go and moved away. The attack on Mary Walker was a different kettle of fish as far as cover and concealment were concerned. Miss Walker was a strong healthy young lady. She no doubt resisted and fought the attacker in an attempt to break his grip on her throat. He was a strong man; he would not let go until she succumbed and collapsed to the ground. Of course, the attacker's hands, wrists and probably his face displayed scratches and scrapes of the kind the prosecution hoped to find on Heffernan's body.

There is no doubt that a sex offender resided in the local barracks at the time Miss Walker was attacked and killed. We also know that sex predators continue to offend until they are apprehended. We do not know for certain how the killer approached Miss Walker, but we know the sex predator approached the child in 1907 with a question. He asked, "Is this the road to Mullingar?" and of course, as he had just walked from Mullingar he knew the answer. The stranger who approached the Nooney's on the canal line also posed a question, he asked "Was this, the Royal Canal?" This occurred shortly before Miss Walker was killed, and I have no doubt this man knew exactly where he was.

I finally located the *Westmeath Examiner* report on Joe Heffernan's previous convictions for theft. As you already know Heffernan received two jail sentences, one for the theft of two clocks, the other for the theft of a mattress. The reports are as follows:

Westmeath Examiner, 19 January 1907
Alleged Larceny of Clocks
Joseph Heffernan, Mullingar, was charged with the larceny of two clocks, the property of Mrs Galway, Jeweller, Dominick Street, Mullingar.
Mrs Galway stated that on the 8 January at about 7.30pm her attention was attracted to the shop connected with her house. She went out and saw the figure of a man pass through the doorway. She could not identify him at the time. He went out on the street and she called him, but he would not answer. She discovered that two alarm clocks were missing. They were valued at about 8s. Afterwards she received information concerning the prisoner. The following day she stopped him in the street and questioned him about the clocks. He admitted being in the shop but denied stealing the clocks.
Mrs Malynn, Mount Street, Mullingar, stated that Heffernan approached her and sold her the clock produced for 1s 6d. She asked him where he got the clock and he replied that he was a dealer in clocks and lived next door.
A little boy named John Callaghan stated that he saw Heffernan selling a clock in Earl Street to a countryman who was under the influence of drink. Heffernan asked 1s 6d for the clock, but the man would only give him a shilling.
Sgt Salter stated that from information he received he arrested the prisoner and charged him with the larceny of two clocks from Mrs Galway's shop. At first he denied the charge and later he admitted that he took the clocks.
Heffernan was sentenced to three calendar months with hard labour.

Westmeath Examiner, 27 March 1909
Alleged Larceny of a Mattress
Joseph Heffernan, Mullingar, was charged with the larceny of a mattress the property of Mr William Walsh, Dominick Street, Mullingar.
Mr Walsh stated that he had a hair mattress in his yard and he missed it one night during the week. He reported the matter to the police; he then accompanied the police to John Hafford's house. The accused was there, and when asked why he took the mattress he replied, "It was lying in the yard and he did not think it was of any use." He added, "He had a bad way of lying and he brought it to lie down on." He said he intended to bring it back in the morning.
Mr Walsh stated that Heffernan, who was in his employment, was taking some drink and he thought he did not know exactly what he was doing. He might

have brought it back. Heffernan stated he brought the mattress home for the night to lie on.

The Chairman sentenced him to two months in jail with hard labour.

CONCLUSION

You have read the evidence and contradictions enshrined in the Joseph Heffernan case. You have read how the evidence was twisted and turned in order to suit the prosecution's case. Is this the behaviour of an honest police force? Or, is it evidence of a police force that knew that the suspect was nowhere near the crime scene when the murder was committed? The authorities knew, without a shadow of doubt, that Heffernan was on Mount Street in the town centre when the killer was seen leaving the crime scene. If the case for the prosecution was as solid as the locals were led to believe, why did the authorities see the need to groom children in order to convict Heffernan? Why were children (as one child admitted) well drilled, and drilled to such an extent, that their stories fell in line with the police's theory of events? Why was Heffernan charged with murder when arrested, and before being questioned? Why was he brought before the Magistrates' solely because he had been seen on the canal line on the afternoon of the murder? Of course there was an assurance by Constable Moore, the arresting officer, that, "I believe I will be able to produce further evidence against him and I ask for a remand for that purpose." How did he know this?

While researching Heffernan's case, I have attempted to do the detective work that Gleeson failed to do. You do not need to be Sherlock Holmes to realise that the evidence did not add up. Nor do you need a degree in criminology to recognise the lies, contradictions, and the eagerness in the behaviour of the police as they concocted a story in order to murder Heffernan.

What do you think? Was Heffernan the victim of one of the biggest miscarriages of justice in Ireland during the twentieth century? Or was he guilty as charged? In your opinion, did the police act honestly and obtain the evidence in a proper manner? Do you think, if the jury had been privy to all the evidence, the verdict would have been different? Do you think if Mr Gleeson questioned all the contradictory evidence presented by the prosecution, Heffernan's life would have been spared? If the Lord Chief Justice conducted the trial as he should have, would the outcome have been different? Why did Dr Dillon–Kelly feel the need to mislead the jury while giving evidence as to Heffernan's physical condition at the time Miss Walker was murdered? Had Heffernan been acquitted, do you think it would have forced the authorities to re–arrest the initial suspect? If so, would the authorities have taken him back to Ireland to stand trial?

Surely you, the reader, after studying the evidence as presented by the prosecution, have come to a conclusion. I hope the results of my research will be beneficial to you as you weigh up the evidence in order to arrive at an honest decision.

It is now time for you to retire to the jury room and decide for yourself, was Joseph Heffernan innocent or guilty as charged.

AFTERWORD

The crime scene puzzles me. Going by the memorial cross, the murder scene is on the Athlone side of the filter beds. I decided to hire a metre wheel to measure the distance from the Green Bridge. According to the measurements submitted by the police and Mr Joyce, the memorial cross is correctly sited and indicates where Miss Walker was attacked and killed, this being the Athlone side of the filter beds. However, Mr Joyce's map of the crime scene and the evidence of Richard Merlehan and Richard Monaghan puts the crime scene on the Mullingar side of the filter beds, close to the signal pole.

According to witnesses and Mr Joyce's map, the murder scene was in one place, while at the same time, Mr Joyce and the police wanted the courts to believe it was approximately 150 yards away. Why would they do this? What was the advantage to the prosecution? Were the Valley Cottages, which were in the process of being built, blocking Monaghan's view so much that the police decided to move the murder scene 150 yards west? This would clear the building site and leave Monaghan with an unobstructed view of the canal. If this was so, then Monaghan witnessed nothing, and, like Ellen Woods and other witnesses, he just went along for the ride.

On a recent trip to northern California I was introduced to a case very similar to Heffernan's, as far as police behaviour is concerned. The case in question highlighted the activities of police officers as they attempted to solve a 1924 murder case. The victim, the Rev. Hubert Dahme was fatally shot behind the left ear at close range. A vagrant and discharged soldier, Harold Israel, was indicted for the murder. Connecticut State attorney, Prosecutor Homer Cummings conducted a thorough investigation and believed that Israel was innocent of the crime. He asked for a dismissal, the judge concurred and immediately obliged.

Hollywood made a film of this particular case. The movie titled Boomerang! was released in 1947, starring Lee J. Cobb. The film premiered at the Palace Theatre in Stamford on March 5, 1947. The staff at Variety gave the film a positive review and wrote:

> *"Boomerang! is gripping, real–life melodrama, told in semi–documentary style. Lee J. Cobb shows up strongly as a chief detective, harassed by press and politicians alike while trying to carry out his duties. Arthur Kennedy was great as the law's suspect."*

If only Moriarty, the Crown Prosecutor in Heffernan's case was as honest and as interested in law and order as Cummings, Joe Heffernan's case would have been thrown out.

ACKNOWLEDGEMENTS

I am grateful to Gregory O'Connor and Aileen Ireland from the National Archives, Bishop Street, Dublin for their assistance and for permitting the publication of the following documents in relation to Heffernan's criminal activities: the original witness and police statements taken during the investigation into the murder of Mary Walker, the map of the crime scene and the General Register of Prisoners, Kilmainham Gaol, Dublin, 1904, 1907, March 1909 and July 1909. Also, Margaret O'Gorman and the Department of Justice, for permitting the publication of the so–called "missing file."

I am also grateful to the Irish Newspaper Archives, the *Westmeath Examiner* and the Westmeath County Library staff for allowing me access to the inquest report, the Magistrates' reports, the assizes report and the Heffernan photograph. Thanks to Richard Coplan, Mullingar, for giving me permission to publish part of his article on the murder of Mary Walker and to Jim O'Herlihy, Cork for his assistance during my research into the history of the police officers attached to the case. Thanks to Davy Hynes, Ruth Illingworth and Mullingar Showcase for sourcing the photographs of Dr Dillon–Kelly and Fr Magee, and to Eamonn MacRodain for giving me his blessing to use the photograph of Head Constable John Crudden and Sgt Thomas Cooke. I am grateful to Irish Rail for allowing me to photograph the crime scene from the railway side, and Niall Bergin, Kilmainham Gaol, for allowing me to photograph the cell where Heffernan perished.

I would like to thank the people of Mullingar who assisted me as I researched the Joe Heffernan story. Believe it or not, some pointed me in the direction of similar injustices that were inflicted upon the people of Mullingar by the occupying forces. However that is another day's work.

I am grateful to the people of Leighlinbridge, Co. Carlow, for their assistance when I paid a visit to Miss Walker's hometown. A special thanks to her great–grand–nephews and nieces: Joe Brennan, Marie Waldron, Kathleen Delaney, Johnny Brennan and Nicholas Brennan, Charlie Keegan (related to Miss Walker through marriage), local historian Martin Nevin and Fr Lalor.

I am indebted to The Manuscript Publisher, especially Oscar Duggan, for his interest, ideas and energy as he prepared the e–book version for worldwide distribution.

A sincere thanks to my wife June and my children, Jack, Marty, Kenny, Lorraine and Paul and my sister–in–law Kay for putting up with me as I researched and wrote the book. Whenever they conversed with me, whether in person, on the phone or by email, I never shut up about Mary Walker or Joe Heffernan. Finally, a big thank you to my brother Tommy who resides in Leixlip, Tommy burned the midnight oil as he trolled through numerous files at the National Archives.

Thank you all for your assistance.